MEDIÆVAL INDIA UNDER MOHAMMEDAN RULE

FOUR EMPERORS: BABAR, HUMAYUN, AKBAR, AND JAHANGIR.

MEDIÆVAL INDIA

UNDER MOHAMMEDAN RULE

(A.D. 712–1764)

BY

STANLEY LANE-POOLE

AUTHOR OF "TURKEY," "THE MOORS IN SPAIN," ETC., ETC.

HASKELL HOUSE PUBLISHERS LTD.

Publishers of Scarce Scholarly Books

NEW YORK, N. Y. 10012

1970

First Published 1903

HASKELL HOUSE PUBLISHERS Ltd.
Publishers of Scarce Scholarly Books
280 LAFAYETTE STREET
NEW YORK, N. Y. 10012

Library of Congress Catalog Card Number: 70-132442

Standard Book Number 8383-1196-2

Printed in the United States of America

PREFACE

THE Mediæval Period of Indian history, though it does not exactly correspond with the Middle Age of Europe, is not less clearly defined. It begins when the immemorial systems, rule, and customs of Ancient India were invaded, subdued, and modified by a succession of foreign conquerors who imposed a new rule and introduced an exotic creed, strange languages and a foreign art. These conquerors were Muslims, and with the arrival of the Turks under Mahmud the Iconoclast at the beginning of the eleventh century, India entered upon her Middle Age. From that epoch for nearly eight hundred years her history is grouped round the Mohammedan rulers who gradually brought under their control nearly the whole country from the Himalayas to the Krishna river. The Period ends when one of the last of these rulers, oppressed by the revival of Hindu ascendency, placed himself under English protection, and Modern India came into being.

Distinct and clearly marked as the Mediæval or Mohammedan Period is, the transition implies no violent change. History is always continuous ; there

can be no 'fresh start'; and each new period carries
on much of what preceded it. In India, as ever in
the East, change is so gradual as to be almost im-
perceptible. Ancient India was too deeply rooted
in its traditions to wither even under the storm of
Muslim conquest. The old Indian life survived the
shock of the new ideas, which it modified at least as
much as it was modified ; it outlived the Muslim
Period, and still endures, but little altered, in the
Modern Age of English domination. It never
really assimilated the foreigners or their ideas.
Despite the efforts of a few wide-seeing men like
Akbar, no true or permanent union, except occa-
sionally among the official and ruling classes, ever
took place between the Muslims and the Hindus;
and the ascendant races, whether Turks, Persians,
Afghans, or Moghuls, remained essentially an army
of occupation among a hostile or at least repellent
population.

The history of the Mohammedan Period is therefore necessarily more a chronicle of kings and courts
and conquests than of organic or national growth.
The vast mass of the people enjoy the doubtful
happiness of having no history, since they show no
development; apparently they are the same yester-
day, to-day, and forever. Nor was there any such
marked change even in the principles and methods
of government as might be expected from the
diversity of successive rulers of various races.
English Collector-Magistrates follow much the same
system, in essential outline, as that which Akbar
adopted from his Hindu Chancellor, and many

executive details and most of the principles of local administration have their origin in probably prehistoric custom. But in the character and life of the rulers there is infinite variety, and it is round the lives of great men — and a few great women, though such seldom emerge before the public gaze in the East — that the chief interest of the Mediæval Period centres. A history of 'the people' is usually assumed, in the present day, to be more stimulating and instructive than the record of kings and courts; but even if true, this can only be understood of Western peoples, of peoples who strive to go forward — or at least change. In the East the people does not change, and there, far more than among progressive races, the 'simple annals of the poor,' however moving and pathetic, are indescribably trite and monotonous compared with the lives of those more fortunate to whom much has been given in opportunity, wealth, power, and knowledge. Such contrasted characters as those of Ala-ad-din, Mohammad Taghlak, Babar, Akbar, and Aurangzib — it is a pity their names are so outlandish — may rival any portrait gallery that could be collected in Europe in the same four centuries; and in the lives and policies, the wars and studies, the habits and ceremonies of such leaders the imagination finds ample scope for the realization of strangely vivid and dramatic situations.

To realize Mediæval India there is no better way than to dive into the eight volumes of the priceless 'History of India as told by its own Historians' which Sir H. M. Elliot conceived and began and which Professor Dowson edited and completed with infinite labour and learning. It is a revelation of Indian life as seen through the eyes of the Persian court annalists. It is, however, a mine to be worked, not a consecutive history, and its wide leaps in chronology, its repetitions, recurrences, and omissions, render it no easy guide for general readers. As a source it is invaluable, and the present book owes an immense debt to it ; indeed, no modern historian of India can afford to neglect it. The well-known and remarkably accurate and judicious ' History ' by Elphinstone of course had not the advantage of the numerous materials brought together by Elliot and Dowson ; but El-phinstone had good authorities and used them with discrimination, and one still turns to him with profit. Another modern work of the highest au-thority, full of ripe learning, fine judgment, and nervous English, is Erskine's ' History of India under Babar and Humayun ' : it is no light loss that the author's death cut short a work planned on such noble lines. Among recent books I have found my friend Mr. H. G. Keene's ' Sketch of the History of Hindustan,' and his other volumes, the most suggestive ; Thomas's 'Chronicles of the Pathan Kings,' the ' Memoirs of the Archæological Survey of India,' Professor Blochmann and Colonel H. S. Jarrett's notes to their translation of the ' Ain-i-Akbari ' of Abu-l-Fazl, Mr. Sewell's ' Vijay-anagar,' and Mr. E. Denison Ross's translation of Haidar's ' Tarikh-i-Rashidi,' have naturally been of great service; but to enumerate the works that

must be consulted by an historian of India would
be almost to publish a catalogue of an Indian
library. For the chapters on the emperors Babar
and Aurangzib I have naturally drawn largely from
my own two volumes in the 'Rulers of India'
series, with the permission of the Delegates of the
Oxford University Press; and I have also been
allowed to reprint from the 'Quarterly Review'
some pages on mediæval travellers at the court of
the Great Moghul. My thanks are also due to my
friend Mr. Arthur Ransom for his kind assistance
in certain details.

In the matter of the orthography of Indian names
I have attempted a compromise. Nothing can
make these names familiar or pronounceable to the
average reader, and the more they are adorned
with accents and diacritical dots the less beautiful
they appear. I have therefore left the names as
plain and simple as possible. The reader should
remember that the vowels are to be pronounced as
in Italian, not as in English, and that short *a* in
Indian names is sounded obscurely (as in *a*bout).

The Chronological Tables at the end of the volume will supply what is omitted in a necessarily
concise narrative, where general outline is more
important than dynastic or genealogical details.

STANLEY LANE-POOLE.

Note.—As the reader may wish to consult the works of European
travellers in India, to whom frequent reference is made in the later
chapters of this history, the following list of the best English editions
will be useful :

　1608–1611. *The Voyage of François Pyrard of Laval to the East*

Indies, etc. Translated and edited by Albert Gray, assisted by H. C. P. Bell, Ceylon C.S. Two vols. in three. Hakluyt Society, 1887–1890.

1608–1613. *Captain William Hawkins, his Relations of the Occurrents which happened in the time of his residence in India, in the county* [sic] *of the Great Mogoll, etc.* The Hawkins' Voyages, edited by Clements R. Markham. Hakluyt Society. 1878.

1615–1618. *The Embassy of Sir Thomas Roe to the Court of the Great Moghul.* Edited by W. H. Foster, 2 vols. Hakluyt Society, 1899.

1615–1618. *A Voyage to the East Indies.* By the Rev. Edward Terry. London, 1655.

1623–1624. *The Travels of Pietro della Valle in India, from the old English translation of G. Havers.* Edited by Edward Grey, late Beng. C.S. 2 vols. Hakluyt Society. 1892.

1626. *A relation of some yeares travaile begunne anno 1626.* By T. H. Esquier (Thomas Herbert). London, 1634.

1638–1639. *The Voyages and Travels of J. Albert de Mandelslo.* Rendered into English by John Davies of Kidwelly. London, 1662.

1640–1667. *Travels in India by Jean Baptiste Tavernier, Baron of Aubonne.* Translated, etc., by V. Ball, LL.D., F.R S., F.G.S. 2 vols. London, 1889.

1666–1667. *The Travels of M. de Thevenot.* Translated into English by A. Lovell. London, 1687.

1659–1667. *Travels in the Mogul Empire by François Bernier, M.D., of the Faculty of Montpellier.* A revised and improved edition by Archibald Constable. London, 1891.

1673–1681. *A New Account of India and Persia in Eight Letters.* By John Fryer, M.D., F.R.S. London, 1698.

1682–1684. *The Diary of William Hedges.* Edited by Sir H. Yule, K.C.B. 3 vols. Hakluyt Society. 1887–1888.

1689–1692. *A Voyage to Suratt in the Year 1689.* By J. Ovington, M.A., Chaplain to His Majesty. London, 1696.

1695. *A Voyage round the World by Dr. John Francis Gemelli Careri.* Translated into English. (Churchill's Collection of Voyages and Travels, vol. iv. 1745.)

CONTENTS

BOOK I

THE INVASIONS, 712–1206

BOOK II

THE KINGDOM OF DELHI, 1206–1526

BOOK III

THE MOGHUL EMPIRE, 1526–1764

CHRONOLOGICAL SUMMARY

A.D.

1435 ff. King of Malwa takes Kalpi and besieges Delhi.

1440 Malwa defeated by Kumbho, raja of Chitor.

1452 King of Jaunpur lays siege to Delhi.

1477 Bahlol of Delhi conquers Jaunpur.

1477–81 Bahmani conquests in Deccan.

1484–92 Foundation of Deccan kingdoms of Berar, Bijapur, Ahmadnagar, and Bidar.

1498 Vasco da Gama lands at Calicut.

1508 Egyptian naval victory over Portuguese at Chaul.

1509 Almeida defeats Egyptian fleet off Diu.

1512 Kingdom of Golkonda founded.

1513 Portuguese factory established at Diu.

1524 Babar overruns Panjab.

1526 Battle of Panipat : Babar annexes Delhi.

1527 Battle of Kanwaha : Babar defeats Rajputs.

1528 Battle of the Ganges : Babar defeats Afghans.

1529 Battle of the Gogra : Babar defeats Bengalis.

1531 Humayun defeats Afghans near Lucknow.

1535–6 Humayun conquers and loses Malwa and Gujarat.

1538 Humayun in Bengal.

1539 Sher Shah defeats Humayun at Chaunsa.

1540 Battle of Kanauj : flight of Humayun.

1555 Battle of Sirhind : Humayun recovers Delhi.

1556 Battle of Panipat : Akbar king of Delhi.

1560–2 Jaunpur, Malwa, Burhanpur annexed.

1567 Akbar storms Chitor.

1569 Foundation of Fathpur-Sikri.

1572–3 Gujarat annexed.

1574 The Hall of Worship built at Fathpur-Sikri.

1575 Conquest of Bengal.

1582 Todar Mal makes new assessment of lands.

1587 Kashmir. 1592 Sind, 1594 Kandahar annexed.

1599 Conquest of Ahmadnagar in Deccan.

1600 Conquest of Asir in Khandesh.

1600 Incorporation of first East India Company.

1605 Death of Akbar.

1609–11 Hawkins at court of Jahangir : English factory at Surat.

1615–18 Sir Thomas Roe's embassy to Jahangir.

1616 Shah-Jahan's campaign in Deccan.

1622 Kandahar taken by Persia, recovered 1637, lost again 1648.

A.D.

1623	Pietro della Valle in India.
1624	Rebellion of Shah-Jahan against Jahangir and Nur-Jahan.
1627	Death of Jahangir.
1631	Suppression of Portuguese at Hugli.
1635	Shah-Jahan reduces Bijapur to tributary dependence.
1638	Mandelslo at Agra.
1640	Manrique in India.
1646	Death of Nur-Jahan.
1648	Completion of the Taj-Mahall at Agra.
1648	New Delhi, Shahjahanabad, built.
1648	Sivaji raids the Konkan.
1649–52	Aurangzib fails to recover Kandahar from Persians.
1655	Aurangzib viceroy in the Deccan.
1656	Golkonda attacked, Bidar and Kulbarga annexed.
1658	War of succession : battle of Samugarh.
1659	Accession of Aurangzib : death of Shah-Jahan, 1666.
1659–66	Bernier at the court of Aurangzib.
1665	Tavernier in India.
1666	Suppression of Portuguese pirates in Arakan.
1671	Sivaji sacks Surat : Marathas supreme in Deccan.
1672	Satnami rebellion in Mewat.
1676	Reimposition of jizya, poll-tax.
1680	War with Rajputs.
1681	Aurangzib takes command against Marathas.
1686	Fall of Bijapur, and 1687 of Golkonda.
1695	Gemelli Careri at Aurangzib's camp in Deccan.
1707	Death of Aurangzib.
1708	Revolt of the Sikhs.
1738	The Marathas advance to Delhi.
1739	Nadir Shah sacks Delhi.
1748	Afghan invasion under Ahmad Shah routed at Sirhind.
1756	Ahmad Shah sacks Delhi.
1757	Battle of Plassey : Clive defeats Nawab.
1761	Battle of Panipat : defeat of Marathas.
1764	Battle of Buxar : the Great Moghul becomes a pensioner of the East India Company.

ILLUSTRATIONS

PAGE

*** The portraits of Moghul emperors are reproduced from manuscripts in the British Museum, viz. Babar from Add. 5717, four emperors together from Add. 20,734, Shah-Jahan and Aurangzib from Add. 18,801. The illustrations of Bijapur and the Malik-i-Maidan are from Taylor and Fergusson's *Architecture at Beejapoor* (Murray, 1866), and those of Gaur from J. H. Ravenshaw's *Gaur* (Kegan Paul, 1878). All the other views are from photographs taken for the Archæological Survey of India. The coins are from specimens in the British Museum and are fully described in S. Lane-Poole's *Catalogue of Oriental and Indian Coins in the British Museum*.

BOOK I
THE INVASIONS
712–1206

CHAPTER I

INTRODUCTION

THE ARABS IN SIND

712

THE population of India in the present day is over three hundred millions, and every sixth man is a Muslim. Nine hundred years ago there were no Mohammedans east of the Indus; where now there are more than fifty millions, and the king of England rules twice as many Muslim subjects as the sultan of Turkey and the shah of Persia together. For six centuries the Hindus submitted to the sovereignty of Mohammedan kings, and when the great effort was made in 1857 to throw off the British yoke, it was round the Mohammedan emperor of Delhi, though a mere shadow of a famous name, that the mutineers rallied. How the Muslims, foreigners both in creed and race, came to conquer India, and how this small but increasing minority imposed its will upon the greater part of the people of the land, is the subject of this book.

When we speak of the Mohammedans as foreign-

3

ers, we mean of course the original conquerors. The present Muslim population is almost as native as the Hindus themselves. The invaders consisted of armies of men, very few of whom brought their women with them. They married Hindu wives, and the mixed race thus formed intermarried further with the natives, and each generation became more and more Indian. Besides the Muslims descended from the successive armies of invaders and their native wives, a very large proportion of the Indian Muslims were and are native converts from Hinduism. It has been estimated that about fifty thousand Hindus 'turn Turk' annually, and neither the religion nor the rule of the Muslims has proved intolerable to the natives. Islam commended itself to the Indian intellect as a more congenial faith than Christianity, and the disorder and corruption of Mohammedan government were not distasteful to a people who had never known anything better.

We must dismiss at the outset any idea of Arabian influence in India. The Mohammedan conquerors were not Arabs. When the armies of the Saracens spread out over the ancient world in the seventh century, they overcame most human obstacles, but nature itself was sometimes impregnable. They overran North Africa, but the inhospitable desert of the Sahara discouraged any southern expansion; they occupied Spain, but the Atlantic checked their progress west, and being no sailors they left to their European successors the glory of discovering the New World. In the East they trampled over Persia as far as the great rivers of Central Asia; but the icy walls of the Hindu Kush saved India. A famous Arab general subdued Bokhara and Samarkand, but he did not venture to surmount the snows that barred the way into Hindustan. The Arabs never opened that perilous north-west passage which has poured so many foreign hordes into the teeming plains below.

The only Arab attempt upon India came from a different quarter. Little as the Muslims of the desert relished the wonders of the deep, there were seafaring traders on the Arabian coasts to whom the ports of western India had been familiar from the earliest times. Arab merchants sailed from Siraf and Hurmuz in the Persian gulf, coasting along till they came to the mouth of the Indus, and thence on to Sapera and Cambay; or they even struck boldly across from their harbours at Kalhat and Kurayyat in Oman to Calicut and other ports on the Malabar coast. These men brought back tidings of the wealth and luxury of India, of gold and diamonds, jewelled idols, gorgeous religious rites, and a wonderful civilization. The temptation of such wealth was sanctioned by the zeal of the iconoclast, and the spoliation of the idolaters became a means of grace. At a time when the armies of Islam were overrunning the known world, such a field of operations as India could not be overlooked, and accordingly we find a pillaging expedition visiting Tana (near the present Bombay) as early as 637 during the reign of the caliph Omar, the second successor of Mohammad the Prophet. Other forays followed, for the Arabs of the Persian gulf were a venturesome folk and made repeated descents upon the Indian coast.

All these however were mere raids. Plunder, not conquest, was their aim, and they led to nothing more. The only serious invasion of the Arabs went by land from Mekran, the most eastern province of the caliphate on the Persian coast, whose governors frequently came to blows with the Indians across the frontier, where no natural barrier intervened. The invasion was belated, compared with the other campaigns, for the caliphs' hands were full of more pressing affairs. The tremendous successes of the first sweep of Arab conquest are apt to blind us to the tedious and toilsome progress of their arms in all but the earliest campaigns. No doubt their triumph over the degenerate empires of Rome and Persia was comparatively swift. Five years sufficed for the subjugation of Syria, seven more saw Persia at their feet, and two were enough for the conquest of all Egypt. But when the Arabs were opposed by tribes as untamed and warlike as themselves, their advance was slow and difficult, and every mile was obstinately disputed. Carthage, for example, was all but reached within a few years of the conquest of Egypt, but it did not actually fall for nearly half a century, and the vigorous resistance of the Berber tribes delayed the progress of the Muslims in Africa till the close of the seventh century. It was the same in the East. While Persia was speedily overcome as far as the river Oxus, it was not till the first decade of the eighth century that the country beyond its banks was added to the settled provinces of the caliphate. The Arabs were too few for all the work they attempted in widely separated lands, and up

to 700 A.D. they had quite enough to do without
burdening themselves with such an enterprise as the
conquest of India.

The first and only Arab invasion coincided in
date with two other signal successes in distant parts
of the globe. Gothic Spain was shattered at the
battle of the Guadalete in 710; the standards of
Islam were carried from Samarkand to Kashghar in
711–714; and the valley of the Indus was invaded in
712. These three steps mark the apogee of the power
of the Omayyad caliphate, and coincide with the
administration of one of the ablest and most relentless of all Muslim statesmen. Al-Hajjaj, the governor of Chaldæa, sent Kutaiba north to spread Islam
over the borders of Tartary, and at the same time
dispatched his own cousin Mohammad Kasim to
India. The reigning caliph consented unwillingly;
he dreaded the distance, the cost, the loss of life.
Even in those days, to adapt modern phrases, there
were the opposing policies of 'Little Arabians' and
'Imperialists.' Hajjaj was imperialist to the core,
and to him the Arabs owed the impulse which gave
them all they ever won in India.

The story of Mohammad Kasim's adventures is
one of the romances of history. He was but seventeen, and he was venturing into a land scarcely
touched as yet by Saracen spears, a land inhabited
by warlike races, possessed of an ancient and deeply
rooted civilization, there to found a government
which, however successful, would be the loneliest in
the whole vast Mohammedan empire, a province cut
off by sea, by mountains, by desert, from all peoples

of kindred race and faith. Youth and high spirit, however, forbade alike fear and foreboding. The young general had at least six thousand picked horsemen to his back, chosen from the caliph's veterans, with an equal number of camelry, and was supplied with a baggage-train of three thousand Bactrian camels. Marching through Mekran, along the Persian coast, he was joined by the provincial governor with more troops; and five stone-slings for siege-work were sent by sea to meet him at Daibul, the great mediæval port of the Indus valley, the forerunner of Karachi.

There in the spring of 712 Mohammad Kasim set up his catapults and dug his trench. A description of this siege has come down to us from an early historian (al-Baladhuri, writing about 840), from which it appears that the Arab spearmen were drawn up along the trench, each separate company under its own banner, and that five hundred men were stationed to work the heavy catapult named 'the Bride.' A great red flag flaunted on the top of a tall temple, and the order came from Hajjaj, with whom the general was in constant communication, to ' fix the stone-sling and shorten its foot and aim at the flagstaff.' So the gunners lowered the trajectory and brought down the pole with a shrewd shot. The fall of the sacred flag dismayed the garrison; a sortie was repulsed with loss; the Muslims brought ladders and scaled the walls, and the place was carried by assault. The governor fled, the Brahmans were butchered, and after three days of carnage a Mohammedan quarter was laid out, a mosque built,

and a garrison of four thousand men detached to
hold the city.

After the storming of Daibul, the young general
marched up the right bank of the Indus in search of
the main body of the enemy. Discovering their outposts on the other side, he tied a string of boats
together, filled them with archers, made one end fast
to the west bank, and then let the whole floating
bridge drift down and across, like an angler's cast of
flies, till it touched the opposite side, where it was
made fast to stakes under cover of the archers' arrows. The enemy, unable to oppose the landing,
fell back upon Rawar, where the Arabs beheld for
the first time the imposing array of Hindu chiefs,
mounted on armoured war-elephants, and led by
their king Dahir. Naphtha arrows, however, disordered the elephants and set fire to the howdahs; the
king was slain, the Hindus fled, and 'the Muslims
were glutted with slaughter.' The Indian women
showed the desperate courage for which they were
famous. The king's sister called them together, on
seeing the defeat of their men; and, refusing to owe
their lives to the 'vile cow-eaters,' at the price of
dishonour, they set their house ablaze and perished
in the flames. Another victory at Brahmanabad
opened the way to Multan, the chief city of the
upper Indus, which surrendered at discretion, but
not without an exhausting siege. The fighting men
were massacred; the priests, workmen, women, and
children made captives.

The fall of Multan laid the Indus valley at the
feet of the conqueror. The tribes came in, 'ringing

bells and beating drums and dancing,' in token of
welcome. The Hindu rulers had oppressed them
heavily, and the Jats and Meds and other tribes
were on the side of the invaders. The work of conquest, as often happened in India, was thus aided
by the disunion of the inhabitants, and jealousies of
race and creed conspired to help the Muslims. To
such suppliants Mohammad Kasim gave the liberal
terms that the Arabs usually offered to all but inveterate foes. He imposed the customary poll-tax,
took hostages for good conduct, and spared the
people's lands and lives. He even left their shrines
undesecrated: 'The temples,' he proclaimed, 'shall
be inviolate, like the churches of the Christians, the
synagogues of the Jews, and the altars of the
Magians.' There was worldly wisdom in this toleration, for the pilgrims' dues paid to the temples
formed an important source of revenue, and the
puritanical Muslims found it expedient to compound
with idolatry, as a vain thing but lucrative, in the
interests of the public fisc. Occasional desecration
of Hindu fanes took place,—we read of 'a cart-load
of four-armed idols' sent as a suitable gift to the
caliph, who no doubt preferred specie—but such
demonstrations were probably rare sops to the
official conscience, and as a rule the Mohammedan
government of Multan was at once tolerant and
economic. The citizens and villagers were allowed
to furnish the tax-collectors themselves; the Brahmans were protected and entrusted with high offices,
for which their education made them indispensable;
and the conqueror's instructions to all his officers

were wise and conciliatory:—'Deal honestly,' he commanded, 'between the people and the governor; if there be distribution, distribute equitably, and fix the revenue according to the ability to pay. Be in concord among yourselves, and wrangle not, that the country be not vexed.'

The young general's fate was tragic. A new caliph succeeded who was no friend to the conqueror of Sind. Hajjaj was dead, and there was none to oppose factious intrigues at the distant court of Damascus. In spite of his brilliant achievement, Mohammad Kasim was disgraced and put to death. The story runs that he had made too free with the captive daughters of Dahir before presenting them to the caliph's harim, and that he was punished for the presumption by being sewn up alive in a raw cow-hide. 'Three days afterwards the bird of life arose from his body and soared to heaven'; and the hide with its noble burden was sent to Damascus. The young hero had made no protest, never questioned the death-warrant, but submitted to the executioners with the fearless dignity he had shown throughout his short but valiant life. But when the sacrifice was accomplished, the Indian princesses, moved perhaps by the courage of a victim brave as their own devoted race, confessed that their tale was deliberately invented to avenge their father's death upon his conqueror. The caliph in impotent fury had them dragged at horses' tails through the city till they miserably perished, but the second crime was no expiation for the first.

The Arabs had conquered Sind, but the conquest

was only an episode in the history of India and of Islam, a triumph without results. The Indus province, it is true, is as large as England, but it consists chiefly of desert, and the Arabs made no attempt to extend their dominion into the fertile plains beyond. It has been supposed that the crude civilization and austere creed of the Muslims stood paralyzed in face of the rich and ancient culture, the profound philosophy, and the sensual ritual of the Hindus; but these contrasts did not check the later successes of Islam in the same land. The more obvious explanation of the Arabs' failure is found in the as yet unbroken strength of the Rajput kings on the north and east, and in the inadequate forces dispatched by the caliphs for so formidable a project as the conquest of India. After the first expedition under the ill-fated Mohammad Kasim we hear of no reinforcements, and twenty years after his death the Arabs were still so insecure on the Indus that they built a city of refuge as a retreat in times of jeopardy. The province was not only imperfectly subdued but extremely poor, and the caliphs soon abandoned it in all but name as too unremunerative to be worth maintaining. The Arab settlers formed independent dynasties at Multan and at the new city of Mansura which the conqueror's son founded in lower Sind; and when the traveller Mas'udi visited the valley of the Indus in the tenth century he found chiefs of the Prophet's tribe of the Kuraish ruling both the upper and the lower province. A little later another traveller, Ibn-Haukal, explored Sind, where he heard Arabic and Sindi spoken, and observed much friendly toleration between the Muslim and Hindu population. Soon afterwards Multan became a refuge for scattered bands of Karmathians, when the power of these anarchists waned before the rising ascendancy of the Fatimid caliphs of Egypt, and Arabia was delivered from the Karmathian reign of terror. But the meagre annals of this limited and ineffectual occupation of an unimportant province need not detain us. The Arab conquest of Sind led to nothing, and left scarcely a vestige save in the names of certain Arab families and in the ruins of the buildings they destroyed. The Arab cities have perished, but the wrecks of the castles and cities of their predecessors, which formed as usual the quarries for their conquerors' buildings, still bear witness to the civilization which they uprooted.

CHAPTER II

THE IDOL-BREAKER

MAHMUD OF GHAZNI

997–1030

THE Arab invasion was a failure. It attacked from the wrong quarter, entered on the least productive province, and was too feebly supported to spread further. We hear no more of the Arabs as conquerors in India. The rôle devolved upon the Turks, and when we speak of the Mohammedan empire in India we mean the rule of the Turks. Their invasion was no part of the expansion of Islam as a religious movement. It was merely the overflow of the teeming cradle-land of Central Asia, the eastern counterpart of those vast migrations of Huns, Turks, and Mongols, which from time to time swept over Europe like a locust cloud. Huns, Scythians, and Yavanas had poured into India in prehistoric ages through those grim north-western passes which every now and then opened like sluice-gates to let the turbid flood of barbarians down into the deep calm waters of the Indian world. Their descendants still muster in tribes and clans on the borders of Hindustan, and have brought strange customs and beliefs to mingle with that old religion of the Vedas which the Aryan forefathers of the Brahmans and Rajputs bore with them through the same narrow entry. Following in their track Alexander led his armies to meet Porus on the Hydaspes; and after him came Græco-Bactrian legions to inspire new ideas of art and civilization, and to learn perhaps more than they taught. Finally the Muslim Turks discovered the same road, and once familiar with the way, they came again and again until all India, save the very apex of the south, owned their sway.

The southerly migration of the Turks was the master-movement in the Mohammedan empire in the tenth and eleventh centuries. Hitherto the caliphate had remained undisturbed by armed invasion. On the fall of the Omayyad line, the seat of government had been moved from Damascus to the new capital founded by their successors the Abbasid caliphs at Baghdad, and the change had been followed by a large influx of Persian ideas into the Arab system. Persian officials, better educated and shrewder men of affairs, replaced Arabs in many of the chief posts of government, and as the central authority grew weaker and more effeminate, Persian governors acquired almost independent power in the more distant provinces and began to found hereditary dynasties, one of the most powerful and enlightened of which was that of the Samanid princes in the country about the Oxus.

The increase, peaceful as it was, of Persian influence, combined with the constant jealousies and truculence of the Arab tribes settled in Mesopotamia, induced the caliphs to provide themselves with a guard of mercenaries closely attached to the throne, and for this purpose the warlike and handsome young Turks captured on the northern frontier supplied all that was desired in valour and ability. Surrounded by such prætorians the caliphs indulged their love of luxury free from the dread of Persian usurpation or Arab revolt. But it was introducing the wooden horse into the Muslim Troy. The Turkish guard became the masters of the caliphs; Turkish officers gradually acquired the control of provinces; and throughout the Mohammedan empire, from Egypt to Samarkand, the Turks became the dominant race. Their success attracted others of their kind. Like Joseph they soon invited their brethren to come and share their prosperity. Turks overflowed into Persia from their native steppes; the Samanid kingdom, after two centuries of power well employed, fell to a scramble among Turkish adventurers, and this scramble led to the invasion of India.

Among the Turkish condottiere who rose to high office in northern Persia was one Alptagin, who, falling out with his Samanid lord, established himself with a couple of thousand followers in the fortress of Ghazni[1] in the heart of the Afghan mountains (A.D. 962). Here, in a kind of no-man's-land, secure

---

[1] Ghazni, the modern spelling, is written Ghaznin in Persian and Ghazna in Arabic.

from interference, he made his little kingdom, and here after an interval his slave Sabuktagin reigned in his stead (976). The new ruler was not content with the original stronghold of his master. He gathered under his banner the neighbouring Afghan tribes, added whole provinces to his dominions,—Laghman to the east in the Kabul valley, Sistan on the Persian side;—and, when called in to support the tottering Samanid prince of Bukhara against the encroaching Turks, he turned the occasion to his own advantage and placed his son Mahmud in command of the rich province of Khurasan. Sabuktagin was the first Muslim who attempted the invasion of India from the north-west. He went but a little way, it is true; his repeated defeat of Jaipal, the Brahman raja of the Panjab, in the Kabul valley, ended only in the temporary submission of the Indian king and the payment of tribute; but it pointed the way into Hindustan.

Sabuktagin died (997) before he could accomplish any larger scheme, but his son more than realized his most daring dreams. Mahmud had all his father's soldierly energy and spirit of command, joined to a restless activity, a devouring ambition, and the temper of a zealot. Zeal for Islam was the dominant note of the tenth-century Turks, as of most callow converts. The great missionary creed of Mohammad, which to the Arabs and Persians had become a familiar matter of routine, was a source of fiery inspiration to the fresh untutored men of the steppes. To spread the faith by conquest doubled their natural zest for battle and endowed them with

2

the devoted valour of martyrs. Mahmud was a staunch Muslim, and if his campaigns against the idolaters brought him rich store of treasure and captives, it was in his eyes no more than the fit reward of piety; and in the intervals between his forays into heathendom he would sit down and copy Korans for the health of his soul. The caliph of Baghdad, who had probably outgrown such illusions, was not the man to baulk a willing sword. He sent Mahmud his pontifical sanction and the official di-

GOLD COIN OF MAHMUD, STRUCK AT NAISABUR IN KHURASAN,
A.H. 402 (A.D. 1011-12).

ploma of investiture as rightful lord of Ghazni and Khurasan, and in the height of satisfaction Mahmud vowed that every year should see him wage a Holy War against the infidels of Hindustan.

If he did not keep the letter of his vow, he fell little short. Between the years 1000 and 1026 he made at least sixteen distinct campaigns in India, in which he ranged across the plains from the Indus to the Ganges.[1]   His first attack was of course upon

---

[1] Authorities differ as to the number and order of these campaigns. The following is Sir H. M. Elliot's arrangement : 1. Frontier towns, A.D. 1000 ; 2. Peshawar and Waihind, 1001 ; 3. Bhira (Bhatia),

the frontier towns of the Khaibar pass. His father's old enemy Jaipal endeavoured in vain to save Peshawar. Mahmud threw out 15,000 of his best horsemen and utterly routed him, despite his larger forces and his 300 elephants. Jaipal and fifteen of his kindred were brought captives before the conqueror. Their jewelled necklaces, worth, it is said, ninety thousand guineas[1] apiece, were torn off, and half a million of slaves, and booty past counting, according to the florid statements of the oriental historians, fell into the hands of the Muslims. Mahmud was not cruel; he seldom indulged in wanton slaughter; and when a treaty of peace had been concluded, the raja and his friends were set free. With the proud despair of his race Jaipal refused to survive his disgrace. Preferring death to dishonour, he cast himself upon a funeral pyre.

There were many other kings besides Jaipal, however, and when—after a successful raid upon Bhira, where 'the Hindus rubbed their noses in the dust of disgrace,' and another to Multan, whose Mohammedan (or rather Karmathian) ruler fled aghast— Mahmud appeared again at the mouth of the Khaibar in 1008, he found all the rajas of the Panjab,

---

1004 ; 4. Multan, 1006 ; 5. Against Nawasa, 1007 , 6. Nagarkot, 1008 ; 7. Narain, 1009 ; 8. Multan, 1010 ; 9. Ninduna. 1013 ; 10. Thanesar, 1014 ; 11. Lohkot (perhaps = 14), 1015 ; 12. Mathura, Kanauj, 1018 ; 13. The Rahib, 1021 ; 14. Kirat. Lohkot, Lahore, 1022 ; 15. Gwaliar, Kalinjar, 1023 ; 16. Somnath, 1025-6 ; 17. The Jats, 1026.

[1] 180,000 dinars. The Arab gold dinar of this time was almost exactly the weight of a half-guinea, and it is therefore convenient to state values in guineas.

backed by allies from other parts of Hindustan, 'a
measureless multitude,' mustered to resist him, with
Anandpal the son of Jaipal at their head. Mahmud
had never yet encountered such an army, and he
hastily intrenched his camp and waited forty days
facing the constantly swelling forces of the enemy.
His first move, probably a mere reconnaissance, was
disastrous. The thousand archers he sent forward
were chased back into the camp followed by a charging mob of wild Gakkars—a fierce Scythian tribe
whose outbreaks troubled the peace of the north-
west frontier as late as 1857, and whose savage aspect,
bareheaded and barefoot, and barbarous habits of
infanticide and polyandry, struck terror and disgust
among the Muslims. These frantic hillmen rushed
the trenches and slashed right and left; man and
horse fell before their onslaught, and it almost came
to a panic among the Turks. The Rajputs were already advancing under cover of the Gakkars' charge,
and Mahmud was about to sound the retreat, when
one of those lucky accidents happened which have
often turned the fortune of a day. Anandpal's
elephant took fright; the rumour ran that the raja
was flying from the field; vague suspicions and distrust spread about, and a general stampede ensued.
Instead of retreating before a victorious army, in the
turn of an instant Mahmud found himself pursuing
a panic-stricken crowd. For two days the Muslims
slew, captured, and despoiled to their hearts' content. 'They had come through fire and through
water, but their Lord had brought them into a
wealthy place.'

On a spur of the snow mountains, surrounded by a moat, stood the fortress of Kangra (Nagarkot), deemed impregnable by mortal power. Here the rajas and wealthy men of India were wont to store their treasure, and hither the triumphing Muslims came, hot with pursuit and victory. The panic that had dissolved the hosts of the Panjab seized also upon the garrison of the fortress, weakened as it must have been by the general levy to oppose the invaders. At Mahmud's blockade the defenders 'fell to the earth like sparrows before the hawk.' Immense stores of treasure and jewels, money and silver ingots, were laden upon camels, and a pavilion of silver and a canopy of Byzantine linen reared upon pillars of silver and gold were among the prizes of the Holy War. The booty was displayed in the court of the palace at Ghazni, 'jewels and unbored pearls and rubies, shining like sparks or iced wine, emeralds as it were sprigs of young myrtle, diamonds as big as pomegranates.' The eastern chroniclers tell of seventy million silver dirhams, and hundreds of thousands of pounds' weight of silver cups and vessels; and, with every allowance for exaggeration, the spoils must have been colossal. All the world flocked to Ghazni to gaze upon the incredible wealth of India.

Such rewards were incentives enough to carry on the pious work. Year after year Mahmud swept over the plains of Hindustan, capturing cities and castles, throwing down temples and idols, and earning his titles of 'Victor' and 'Idol-breaker,' *Ghazi* and *Batshikan*. Little is known of the political condition of India at the time of these raids, but it is evident that after the great rout in the Panjab there was no concerted resistance. The country was split up into numerous kingdoms, many of which were at feud with one another. There were the Brahman kings of Gandhara on the Indus, the Tomaras at Delhi and Kanauj, the Buddhist Palas of Magadha on the lower Ganges, the survivors of the Guptas in Malwa, the Kalachuris on the Narbada, the Chandillas of Mahoba, and many more, who united might have stemmed any invasion, but whose jealousies brought their ruin. Internal division has proved the undoing of India again and again, and has sapped the power of mere numbers which alone could enable the men of the warm plains to stand against the hardy mountain tribes and the relentless horsemen of the Central Asian steppes. To the contrasts of union and disunion, north and south, race and climate, was added the zeal of the Muslim and the greed of the robber. The mountaineers were as poor as they were brave, and covetous as they were devout. The treasures of India, heaped up round the colossal figures of obscene idols, appealed irresistibly to these hungry fanatics. It was no wonder that they carried all before them, devoured the rich lands like a cloud of locusts, and returned to their frozen homes with a welcome such as meets the mooring of an argosy. Each campaign made them stronger and more terrible. They brought home not treasure only but recruits, and to the volunteers who flocked to the spoil from the Oxus and Iaxartes, and to the unrivalled cavalry of

their native steppes, they gradually added a powerful
force of elephantry fit to confront the heavy arm
that formed the first line in an Indian battle.

Mahmud's success, however, was not won without
hard fighting and sore privations. Man was more
easily overcome than nature, and the endurance of
the hardy and vigorous northmen was often tested
almost to the breaking-point. When they set out in
1013 to invade 'the capital of India,' whose king
had failed to pay his annual tribute of fifty laden
elephants and two thousand slaves, they were checked
at the frontier by deep snow; the mountains and
valleys appeared almost level under the treacherous
white mantle, and the army was forced to protect
itself in winter quarters. Moving onwards in the
warmer weather, they wandered for months 'among
broad deep rivers and dense jungles where even
wild beasts might get lost.' At last they found 'the
king of India'—probably one of the Sahi dynasty of
Gandhara—posted in a narrow pass with his vassals
at his back. The veterans from the Oxus and those
'devilish Afghan spearmen bored into the gorge like
a gimlet into wood,' but it took several days of hard
fighting before the place was carried. Then followed
a weary march across the stern desert of Rajputana
to Thanesar, a day's journey from Delhi, and here
again a local raja had to be dislodged from a steep
pass where he waited with his splendid troop of Ceylon elephants behind a rapid river. But Mahmud was
no novice in tactics. He forded the river and
crowned the heights on either side, and while two
detachments fell upon the enemy's flanks the sultan's

main battle flung itself into the ravine and the position was stormed. The river ran blood, the pass was a shambles; but the Hindus fled, their famous elephants were captured, and their town gave up its spoil.

There was no lack of volunteers to aid in the Holy War. Mahmud's victories were known all over the East, and twenty thousand warriors came to him from the country beyond the Oxus, praying to be granted the privilege of fighting for the faith and so perchance attaining the crown of martyrdom. With a large army, stiffened by these zealots, the sultan fought his greatest campaign in 1018, and pushed further east than ever before. He marched upon Kanauj, the capital of the Tomara rajas and then reputed the chief city of Hindustan. The march was an orgy and an ovation. Everywhere envoys waited on the conqueror bearing proffers of homage and welcome. The chief who held the passes of Kashmir, which immemorial jealousy had guarded with infinite precaution from foreign footsteps, tendered his fealty and his service as a guide. One after the other the rivers of India were crossed, Indus, Jehlam, Chenab, Ravi, Sutlej, with scarcely a check. Forts and cities surrendered as the great sultan passed by; abject chiefs placed their followers at his disposal; through the thick jungle he penetrated 'like a comb through a poll of hair,' fighting when necessary, but more often triumphing by mere prestige. Early in December he reached the Jumna and stood before the walls of Mathura, an ancient home of Hindu worship, filled with temples 'not

built by man but by the Jinn,' where colossal golden
idols flashed with jewels, and silver gods of loathly
aspect stood so huge that they had to be broken up
before they could be weighed.

Pressing eastwards, Kanauj was reached before
Christmas. The raja had already fled at the mere
bruit of the sultan's coming, and the seven forts
of the great city on the Ganges fell in one day.
Of all its gorgeous shrines not a temple was spared.
Nor were the neighbouring princes more fortunate.
Deep jungles and broad moats could not protect
Chandal Bhor of Asi; and even Chand Rai, the
great lord of Sharwa, when he heard the ominous
tramp of the Turkish horsemen, gathered up his
treasures and made for the hills: for it was told him
that 'Sultan Mahmud was not like the rulers of
Hind, and those who followed him were *not black
men.*' Flight did not save Chand Rai; the enemy
tracked him through the forest, and coming up with
him at midnight attacked in the dark, routed, plundered, and revelled for three days, and carried home
such booty and mobs of prisoners that the slave
markets of Persia were glutted and a servant could
be bought for a couple of shillings.

Two years later the sultan met the evasive raja of
Kanauj. It was at the 'Rahib,' — probably the
Ramaganga, — a deep river with a black bituminous
bottom, 'fit to scald a scabby sheep.' Fording was
out of the question, and Mahmud ordered his ad-
vance-guard to swim the river on air-skins, plying
their bows as they swam. The men plunged in,
the Hindus scurried away, and once more victory

declared for the men of the north. In the next two campaigns Lahore, Gwaliar, and Kalinjar surrendered to a conqueror who would take no denial, and in the winter of 1025–6 the sultan made his final march into Gujarat, crowned with the capture of Somnath, its costly temple and its wondrous god. There a hundred thousand pilgrims were wont to assemble, a thousand Brahmans served the temple and guarded its treasures, and hundreds of dancers and singers played before its gates. Within stood the famous linga,[1] a rude pillar-stone adorned with gems and lighted by jewelled candelabra which were reflected in the rich hangings, embroidered with precious stones like stars, that decked the shrine.

So long as this worshipful emblem stood inviolate, Mahmud could not rest from his idol-breaking, nor his treasury boast the finest gems in India. Hence his arduous march across the desert from Multan to Anhalwara, and on to the coast, fighting as he went, until he saw at last the famous fortress washed by the waves of the Arabian sea. Its ramparts swarmed with incredulous Brahmans, mocking the vain arrogance of the foreign infidels whom the god of Somnath would assuredly consume. The foreigners,

---

[1] As has often been pointed out, the legend in Firishta's history that the priests tried to bribe Mahmud to spare the idol, and that he clove it in two with his sword, whereupon a vast hoard of jewels poured from its vitals, is manifestly absurd. The idol, as Sir W. W. Hunter observed, ' was merely one of the twelve lingas or phallic emblems erected in various parts of India,' and could not be cut by a sword ; though it is possible that a hiding-place was excavated in it.

nothing daunted, scaled the walls; the god remained dumb to the urgent appeals of his servants; fifty thousand Hindus suffered for their faith, and the sacred shrine was sacked to the joy of the true be-

INDIAN BILLON CURRENCY OF MAHMUD, STRUCK AT MAHMUDPUR,
A.H. 418 (A.D. 1027).

lievers. The great stone was cast down, and its fragments carried off to grace the conqueror's palace. The temple gates were set up at Ghazni,[1] and a million pounds' worth of treasure rewarded the iconoclast.

The sack of Somnath has made Mahmud of Ghazni a champion of the faith in the eyes of every Muslim for nearly nine centuries, and the feat, signal enough in itself, has been embellished with fantastic legends. The difficulties of the outward march were renewed on the return; the army was led astray by treacherous guides and almost perished in the waterless desert, from which it escaped only to fall into the hands of the predatory Jats of the Salt Range, who harrassed the exhausted troops as they toiled home-

---

[1] The deodar gates at Agra, which were brought by Lord Ellenborough from the tomb of Mahmud in 1842 and were paraded as the gates of Somnath, are obviously later, and bear an epitaph of the sultan.

wards laden with spoils. It was to punish their temerity that before the year was over Mahmud led his army for the last time into India. He is said to have built a fleet at Multan, armed it with spikes and rams, and placed twenty archers with naphtha bombs on each of his fourteen hundred boats, which engaged the vessels of the Jats, four thousand in number, and by rams and naphtha sank or burned their craft. Whatever really happened, we may be sure that there were never five thousand boats on the upper Indus, and that mountain tribes do not usually fight naval battles. Having chastised the Jats, whether by land or water matters little, Mahmud retired to Ghazni, where he died four years later (30 April, 1030).

In all these laborious though triumphant campaigns the thought of their home-coming must have been uppermost in every man's mind, from sultan to bhisti. There was no dream of occupying India. The very disunion and jealousy of the Hindu rajas, which smoothed the way to wide and successful forays, offered obvious obstacles to permanent annexation. Each victory meant no more than the conquest of one or more princes; the rest were unaffected, and, since there was no single supreme head to treat with, the most complete success in the field did not imply the submission of the country. The mass of the people, no doubt, did submit, just as they have patiently submitted to a series of foreign rulers with immovable indifference; but so long as there were chiefs in arms, followed by bands of desperate Rajputs, an occupation of India was beyond the means of the forces of Ghazni. But Mahmud did not aim at permanent conquest. The time had not yet come when the Turks could think seriously of living in India. Their home was still beyond the passes, and in the latter years of his reign Mahmud had extended his rule over the greater part of Persia, as far as the mountains of Kurdistan,—a land of Muslims and in every way, save wealth, infinitely preferable in Turkish eyes to sultry Hindustan, though not perhaps to the climbing terraced villages among the sweet green valleys and familiar crags of the Afghan hills.

Mahmud had overrun northern India from the Indus to the Ganges, but his home was still Ghazni, his *patria* was among the mountains. Here he stored his immense treasure, and here he presided over a stately and cultivated court. Like many a great soldier he loved the society of educated men. The man of action is every whit as inapt to 'suffer fools gladly' as the man of culture; and this restless adventurer, after sweeping like a pestilence for hundreds of miles across India, or pouncing like a hawk upon Khwarizm beside the sea of Aral, and then coursing south to Hamadhan almost within call of Baghdad itself, would settle down to listen to the songs of poets and the wise conversation of divines. If Mahmud is to Muslims for all time a model of a god-fearing king, zealous for the faith, his court has not less been held a pattern of humane culture, and it deserved its reputation. Napoleon imported the choicest works of art from the countries he subdued to adorn his Paris; Mahmud did better, he brought the artists and the poets themselves to

illuminate his court. From the cities of the Oxus
and the shores of the Caspian, from Persia and
Khurasan, he pressed into his service the lights of
oriental letters, and compelled them, not unwillingly,
to revolve round his sun like planets in his firmament
of glory. The ruin of the Samanid dynasty, who
had been noble fosterers of Persian literature, left
many scholars and poets unprovided, and these came
eagerly to the new home of learning.

The names of the many luminaries who shone at
the court of Ghazni may not convey very definite
ideas to Western readers, but they are among the
leaders of Eastern literature and science, and some
have a reputation outside the circle of orientalists.
Biruni, the astronomer, chronologist, and even student of Sanskrit; Farabi, the philosopher, whom
Mahmud prized the more since Avicenna himself
refused to be lured to Ghazni; Utbi, the historian
and secretary to the sultan; Baihᵃki, whose gossiping memoirs have earned him the title of 'the
oriental Mr. Pepys'; Unsuri and Farrukhi and As-
judi, among the earliest poets of the Persian revival,
and above all Firdausi, the Persian Homer, in whose
'Shah Nama' the heroes of old Persian legend live
for ever—these were among the men to whom Mahmud was gracious and who in return made Ghazni
and its master renowned beyond the fame of glorious
war. There is no need to repeat here the oft-told
story of Firdausi's wrath at the silver guerdon with
which the sultan crowned the famous epic. Sixty
thousand pieces of silver—even though the poet
had been promised gold—represent something like

£2500, and would be a welcome remuneration for a library of epics in the present day. Milton had to be content with the two hundred and fiftieth part of such a sum for 'Paradise Lost.' The notable part of the story is, not that the poet indignantly spurned the gift, threw it loftily among the menials, and then rewarded Mahmud's kindness and support by a scathing satire—such outbreaks belong to the *genus irritabile*—but that the great sultan at last forgave the insult and sent a second lavish gift, of 50,000 guineas, to appease the offended poet in his exile. It was the usual irony of fate that the reward reached Firdausi's home in Khurasan just at the moment when his body was being borne to the grave.

Though one must acquit the sultan of any want of appreciation of Firdausi's great work, or indeed of literary and scientific achievement in general, tradition will have it that he was avaricious; and there is a quaint anecdote in Sa'di's ' Rose Garden ' —a tedious but renowned Persian classic—in which it is related how a certain king of Khurasan dreamed that he saw Mahmud a hundred years after his death, and perceived that, whilst his body had crumbled to dust, the eyes still rolled in their sockets, as if seeking the wealth that had vanished from their sight. Yet it is hard to reconcile this reputation for avarice with what is recorded of the sultan's gifts; with his annual grant of two hundred thousand guineas to men of letters; his foundation of a university at Ghazni, endowed with a great library, a museum, salaried professors, and pensions for scholars; his sumptuous mosque of marble and granite, furnished with gold and silver lamps and ornaments and spread with costly carpets; or the aqueducts, fountains, cisterns, and other improvements with which he enriched his capital. If Mahmud was fond of money, assuredly he knew how to spend it wisely ·and munificently; and the splendour of his courtiers' palaces, vying with his own, testified to the liberal encouragement of the arts which raised Ghazni, under the rule of the Idol-breaker, from a barrack of outlaws to the first rank among the many stately cities of the caliphate.

The man who could so create and develop a centre of civilization was no barbarian. Like some other ugly men, Mahmud is said to have devoted himself to the cultivation of his mind in order to efface the impression of his physical defects; but it was no ordinary mind that he had to work upon, and no mean genius that could expand a little mountain principality into an empire that stretched to the Caspian and Aral seas and almost to the Tigris, and that covered, at least for the time, half the vast plains and teeming population of Hindustan. Brief as was the occupation of most of this immense territory, it was a stupendous feat of acquisition. He was aided, no doubt, by the dissensions of his neighbours; the break-up of the Samanid kingdom and the divisions of the Buwaihid princes in Persia opened the road to annexation in the west, just as the jealousies of the Indian rajas favoured aggression in the east. But it must not be forgotten that Persia was full of Turkish chiefs of the same warlike temper as Mahmud's forefathers, and that his northern frontier was perpetually menaced by the vigorous and aggressive tribes of Central Asia, against whom, nevertheless, he was always able to hold his own. When Ilak Khan, the chief of the Turks on the Iaxartes, came south to invade Khurasan in 1006 with a great host of his dreaded horsemen, Mahmud did not evade the shock. He led his army in person against the troopers of the steppes, and after bowing to the earth in prayer, reciting his Muslim ' *Vater, ich rufe Dich*,' which he never forgot before a battle, he mounted his elephant and smote the enemy hip and thigh back to their own land.

A great soldier, a man of infinite courage and indefatigable energy of mind and body, Mahmud was no constructive or far-seeing statesman. We hear of no laws or institutions or methods of government that sprang from his initiative. Outward order and security was all he attempted to attain in his unwieldy empire; to organize and consolidate was not in his scheme. He left his dominions so ill knitted together that they began to fall asunder as soon as he was no longer alive to guard them by his vigilant activity. But so long as he lived he strove to govern every part with even justice. The most sagacious and high-minded Asiatic statesman of the Middle Ages, the famous Seljuk vezir Nizam-al-mulk, in his treatise on the art of government, cites many anecdotes of Mahmud's conscientious exercise of justice and the pains he took to protect his widely scattered subjects. ' Mahmud,' wrote the great vezir, ' was a just sovereign, a lover of learning, a man of generous nature and of pure faith.'

3

CHAPTER III

THE MEN OF THE MOUNTAIN

GHAZNI AND GHOR

1030–1206

GIBBON sums up the history of Asiatic dynasties as 'one unceasing round of valour, greatness, discord, degeneracy, and decay.' We have seen the valour and the greatness of Mahmud: the rest was soon to follow. The kingdom he founded endured indeed for a century and a half after his death, but it diminished with every decade. It was not so much the result of the 'discord and degeneracy' of his successors, though discord began at once in the rivalry between his sons, and degeneracy was shown in the luxury and effeminacy of the court. It was rather the inevitable consequence of the increasing pressure of the western Turks, the Ghuzz and other Turkman clans who were pouring into the pastures of Khurasan. What the adventurers of Ghazni had done, others of the same bold and capable race might also achieve, and the pastoral Seljuks who now flocked from the Oxus lands southward

34 .

into Persia were led by chiefs who proved themselves Mahmud's equals in generalship and his superiors in power of organization. Their history, which carried them from Samarkand to the shores of the Ægean, has nothing to say to the present subject, except in so far as their brilliant career of conquest cut off all Mahmud's Persian possessions in less than ten years after the Idol-breaker had passed away from the scene of his triumphs. By 1038 Tughril Beg the Seljuk was proclaimed king of Khurasan, and when Mahmud's son, Mas'ud, at last awakened to the danger of the shepherd clans whose presence he had tolerated within his borders, marched in 1040 to subdue the rebels, he was utterly defeated at Dandanakan near Merv, and thenceforward Persia was lost to the house of Ghazni.

The barrier thus set up on the west, whilst it bounded the ambitions of Mahmud's successors, did not immediately throw them into the far more valuable provinces of India. They continued to hold the Panjab, the only part of his Indian conquests that was permanently annexed, but even here their authority was uncertain, and when it was strongest under a firm governor there was most risk of separation. A capable Turkish amir who had witnessed the successful rise of other Turks in Asia was likely to be tempted to convert his distant Indian province into a kingdom. Troubles of this kind began very soon. Mahmud had left Ali Ariyaruk as governor and commander-in-chief in India. Under Mas'ud, this viceroy's power became dangerous, and he was allured to Ghazni, where his numerous following of

truculent retainers confirmed the fears of the court.
Like many Turks, Ariyaruk had a weakness for
drink, which proved his undoing. The wise vezir,
Khwaja Ahmad Hasan Maimandi, who was in oriental phrase 'a great cucumber' or man of guile, led
the unlucky general on; the king sent him fifty
flagons of wine when he was already excited; the
poor wretch staggered into the court, lured on by
the conspirators, and there was an end of him.

The whole miserable tragedy is described by the
garrulous Baihaki, the chronicler of Mas'ud's court,
with the vivid touch of an eyewitness. Such scenes
were not uncommon at Ghazni, where zeal for the
faith was often combined with a reckless disregard of
the law of Islam which forbids the use of fermented
liquor. It was not merely that the soldiery and
their officers indulged in drunken brawls; the sultan
Mas'ud himself used to enjoy regular bouts in which
he triumphantly saw all his fellow topers 'under the
table.' We read in Baihaki's gossiping memoirs how
'the amir' — the Ghazni king adopted this title like
his modern representative the amir of Afghanistan—
went into the Firozi Garden and sat in the Green
Pavilion on the Golden Plain, where, after a sumptuous feast, the army passed before him in review:
first the star of the crown prince Maudud, next the
canopy and standards borne by two hundred slaves
of the household, with jerkins of mail and long
spears; then many led horses and camels; after
which the infantry in their order, with banners and
stars, and so forth.

When they had all passed by, the serious business

of the day began: 'let us to it without ceremony,' cried the amir: 'we are come into the country, and we will drink.' Fifty goblets and flagons of wine were brought from the pavilion into the garden, and the cups began to go round. 'Fair measure,' said the amir, 'and equal cups—let us drink fair.' They grew merry and the minstrels sang. One of the courtiers had finished five tankards — each held nearly a pint of wine — but the sixth confused him, the seventh bereft him of his senses, and at the eighth he was consigned to his servants. The doctor was carried off at his fifth cup; Khalil Dawud managed ten, Siyabiruz nine, and then they were taken home; everybody rolled or was rolled away, till only the sultan and the Khwaja Abd-ar-Razzak remained. The khwaja finished eighteen goblets and then rose, saying, 'If your slave has any more he will lose both his wits and his respect for your Majesty.' Mas'ud went on alone, and after he had drunk twenty-seven full cups, he too arose, called for water and prayer-carpet, washed, and recited the belated noon and sunset prayers together as soberly as if he had not tasted a drop; then mounted his elephant and rode to the palace. 'I witnessed the whole of this scene with mine own eyes, I, Abu-l-Fazl,' says Baihaki.

Such orgies were characteristic of the Turkish rulers of Ghazni. Even the great Mahmud had his drinking fits, which he excused on the ground that they afforded a rest to his people; but his son Mas'ud carried them to far greater excess. Fortunately he had a remarkably able prime minister in

Maimandi, who had served the father till he fell under
his displeasure, and whom the son released from
prison and restored to office with extraordinary
marks of respect.   The khwaja (to use the title
given to the vezirs of Ghazni, though the word
properly means a holy man, and has now degenerated to nothing more respectable than ' Mr.') made
his formal re-entrance at the levee at noon, after
careful consultation with the astrologers, who determined the auspicious hour.   He was dressed in scar-
let cloth of Baghdad embroidered with delicate
flowers, and wore a large turban of the finest muslin
bordered with lace, a heavy chain, and a girdle weighing a thousand gold pieces, studded with turquoises.
The captain of the guard, sitting at the door of the
robing-room, presented him according to custom
with a piece of gold, a turban, and two immense
turquoises set in a ring.   On entering the presence,
he was congratulated by the amir, and kissing the
ground offered his sovereign a valuable pendent of
pearls.   Then Mas'ud gave him the signet of state,
engraved with the royal seal, ' that the people may
know,' he said, ' that the khwaja's authority is next
to my own.'   The minister kissed hands, bowed
to the earth, and retired, escorted by a splendid reti-
nue, and all the world hastened to congratulate him
and make him presents.   Two days later he took his
seat in his office.   A fine cloth of brocade set with
turquoises was spread for him, and on it he knelt
and went through two bowings of prayer ; then calling for ink, paper, and sand, he wrote in Arabic a
sentence of thanksgiving.   All that day till nightfall

gifts were pouring in; gold and silver, rich cloths, slaves of high price, pedigree horses and camels—and all were dutifully sent on to the amir, who marvelled why the khwaja would not keep them, and rewarded him with 10,000 gold pieces, half a million of silver from the treasury, ten Turkish slaves, four horses from the royal stable, and ten camels.

Meanwhile the minister whom he had superseded presented the reverse of the glittering shield. Not only disgraced, Hasanak was accused of heresy, and sent to the scaffold. Clad in nothing but his turban and trousers, his hands clasped together, 'his body like shining silver, his face a picture,' he calmly faced his doom. All men wept for him and none would cast the fatal stones. The executioner spared him the indignity of lapidation by a friendly noose. The fallen vezir's head was served up in a dish at a feast, to the horror of the guests; his body hung seven years on the gibbet; but his mother, weeping beneath, cried aloud in bitter irony, 'What good fortune was my son's! Such a king as Mahmud gave him this world, and *such a one* as Mas'ud the next!'

Such pictures of life at Ghazni are valuable for the history of India, since it was on the model of Mahmud and his successors that the later courts of Lahore, Agra, and Delhi were formed. It would be a mistake, however, to measure Mas'ud by his luxury and revels. He was no fainéant son of his great father. His generosity won him the name of 'the second Ali,' and he was so brave that they called him 'another Rustam,' after the famous hero of the 'Shah Nama.' His father envied his strength, and

it was said that he could fell an elephant at a blow.
No other man could wield his battle-axe. He ex-
celled, moreover, as a patron of letters, and was
himself an architect of skill, who adorned his country
with noble buildings. He also took a prudent interest in his Indian possessions, and personally
interfered in the management of the Panjab. The
viceroy who succeeded Ariyaruk proved even more
ambitious. This Ahmad Niyaltagin had been Mahmud's treasurer and had accompanied him on all his
journeys and knew the ways and plans of the late
king. They called him Mahmud's ' sneeze ' or *alter
ego*. On his appointment as governor of Hindustan
he was instructed by the vezir Maimandi not to med-
dle with political or revenue matters, which belonged
to the function of Kazi Shiraz, the civil administrator,
but to keep to the duties of commander-in-chief.
Besides these military and civil governors, there
was the head of the intelligence department to
whom all orders from the sultan and ministers were
sent and who reported everything that occurred to
his master. 'You two must not give trouble to the
court,' continued the khwaja, 'what you have to
write to me must be stated in detail in order to
receive a distinct reply. His Majesty thinks it ad-
visable to send with you some of the Dailami chiefs,
to remove them to a distance from the court, since
they are foreigners ; and also some suspected persons
and refractory slaves. Whenever you go on a campaign you must take them with you, but be careful
that they do not mingle with the army of Lahore,
and let them not drink wine or play polo. Keep

spies and informers to watch them, and never neglect this duty. These be the king's secret orders, not to be divulged.' To retain a hold on the new viceroy, his son was detained as a hostage.

In spite of all these counsels, Niyaltagin quickly fell out with his civil colleague, and complaints reached Ghazni. Full of the example of his old master, he was not content with managing a mere province, but copied the Idol-breaker's daring raids, and actually surprised Benares. No Mohammedan army had ever before pushed so far east, and the great city on the Ganges with its forest of temples was a splendid prize. The invaders did not dare to hold it more than a few hours, lest they should be overwhelmed by the Hindus, and before midday they had plundered the markets and got off scot free with an immense booty. Niyaltagin was sus-pected of still more daring schemes; he was said to be buying Turkish slaves secretly, and gave himself out as a son of sultan Mahmud. Not only was the army of Lahore devoted to him, but the Turkmans and adventurers of all sorts were flocking to his standard. The policy of sending suspected and dis-orderly persons to India was bearing fruit. In short everything was ripe for rebellion, and in the summer of 1033 news came that the viceroy was in open revolt, the kazi shut up in a fort, and all was turmoil and bloodshed.

To restore order Mas'ud appointed Tilak the Hindu to take over the command in the Panjab. The other generals showed themselves backward in volunteering for the dangerous task, and Tilak's

eager bid for the command pleased the sultan. The
fact that a Hindu should have attained such a position shows how far the process of assimilation between the Turks and the Indians had already gone.
Tilak was the son of a barber, a good-looking, plausi-
ble fellow, eloquent of speech, a fluent writer both
in Hindi and Persian, and a master of dissimulation,
which he had studied under the best professors in
Kashmir, the home of lies. He is also described as
'proficient in amours and witchcraft,' and everyone
was in love with him. He gained a great influence
over Mas'ud, who set him over the Indian troops,
and he was equally intimate with the khwaja, who
made him his confidential secretary and interpreter.
He was granted the distinction of a state tent and
parasol, kettledrums were beaten at his quarters,
after the Hindu fashion, and his banners had gilt
cusps.

This Hindu paragon set out to chastise Niyaltagin.
Matters were going badly and there was anxiety at
Ghazni. The Seljuks were beginning to cause serious
alarm in the west, and a battle had been lost at Karman in the eastern hills, where the sultan's Hindu
troops, who formed half the cavalry, had behaved like
poltroons and fled the field. When they came back,
Mas'ud shut their officers up in the chancery, where
six of them committed suicide with their daggers.
'They should have used those daggers at Karman,'
said the sultan. At last the news came that the barber's son had routed Niyaltagin, and that the Jats had
caught the fugitive viceroy and cut off his head, which
they sold to Tilak for a hundred thousand pieces of

silver. The elated sultan vowed that he would himself go to India and take the fort of Hansi, which he
had once before attacked. The ministers in vain tried
to dissuade him, urging the troubles in other parts
of his empire. If the Seljuks should conquer Khurasan, or take even a village there, they argued, 'ten
Holy Wars at Hansi would not compensate.' But
he was immovable. 'The vow is upon my back,' he
said, 'and accomplish it I will.'

Leaving the khwaja as his deputy, and appointing
Prince Maudud viceroy at Balkh, the sultan set out
for India by way of Kabul in November, 1034.
Falling ill on the road, he determined to renounce
wine, threw all the liquor he had into the Jehlam,
and broke his flagons. No drinking was allowed
throughout the army. How slight was the hold of
the Muslims on Hindustan may be realized from the
fact that the march to Hansi (about two thirds of
the distance from Lahore to Delhi) was regarded as
a dangerous adventure. The fortress made a desperate resistance, but was mined in five places, and
stormed at the sword's point at the beginning of
February. The priests and officers were killed, and
the women, children, and treasure carried to Ghazni.
Returning through deep snow, Mas'ud kept the
New Year's spring festival at home, and amply repaid himself for his abstinence on the march.

The state of affairs on his return showed that the
campaign with its insignificant result had been a
mistake. The ministers had been right in urging
him to go west instead of east. Khurasan was rapidly falling into the hands of the Seljuks; western

Persia was throwing off the yoke of Ghazni; the empire was breaking up. Mas'ud attempted too late to stem the tide. His generals were defeated, and his own last despairing effort near Merv in 1040, as has been related, ended in utter rout. In a panic he prepared to fly to India before the terror of a Seljuk invasion. The treasures were packed up, the court and the harim were equipped for the journey, and the whole army left Ghazni. As he crossed the Indus, the dishonoured prince was seized by mutineers, who set his brother on the throne — the brother he had blinded on his own accession,— and after a brief captivity in the fort of Kiri, Mas'ud was done to death in 1040. 'Let wise men reflect upon this,' concludes Baihaki, 'and be well assured that man by mere labour and effort, notwithstanding all the wealth and arms and warlike stores he may possess, can in no wise succeed without the help of God Most High. . . . "Man cannot strive against fate." This prince spared no effort, and gathered vast armies. Though he was one who thought for himself and spent sleepless nights in devising plans, his affairs came to nought by the decree of the Almighty. God knoweth best.'

The hasty flight to India was premature. The Seljuks were busy in subduing Persia, and left Ghazni undisturbed; thither, after a while, Mas'ud's son returned with the army, and for more than a century the Ghaznawids, as his descendants are called, dwelt in their mountain city with gradually decaying power. Their names and dates are given in the table at the end of this volume, but their in-

dividual reigns are of little importance for the history
of India. They are described as men of benevolent
character and signal piety; and some of them, such
as Ibrahim, devoted themselves to the improvement
and good government of their subjects. The fact
that Ibrahim and Bahram sat on the throne, the
one for over forty, the other for thirty-five years,
shows that there was peace and stability, at least
in the central government.

But peace was purchased at the cost of power.
The later kings of Ghazni, learning by a series of defeats that their western neighbours were not to be
trifled with, made terms with the Seljuks and allied
the two dynasties by politic marriages; thus Ghazni
fell from the proud position of the capital of a kingdom to little more than a dependency of the empire
of Malik Shah. The fratricidal struggles, which
were a common feature of Ghaznawid successions,
even brought these dangerous neighbours into the
mountains, and in 1116 we find the Seljuk Sanjar in
temporary possession of Ghazni as the protector of
Bahram against his brother Arslan Shah.

There was little danger, however, of the enemy
settling permanently in the Afghan country. There
was more attractive land to the west, and a dynasty
that had spread its dividing branches to the Mediterranean and Damascus was not likely to be enam-
oured of the crags and glades beneath the Hindu
Kush. So long as the kings of Ghazni preserved an
attitude of decorous deference, there was little fear
of Seljuk aggression. Nor was there much danger
of reprisals from the side of India. An army of

80,000 Hindus did indeed seize Lahore in 1043; but
the enemy hastily withdrew on the approach of the
forces of Ghazni. The terror of Mahmud's campaigns had left too crushing an impression to permit
the Indians to dream of serious retaliation. The
Panjab remained a Muslim province, and a century
later became the last refuge of Mahmud's descendants.

The force that uprooted the Ghaznawids came
neither from the east nor from the west. It grew
up in their midst. In the rugged hills of Ghor, between Ghazni and Herat, stood the castle of Firoz-
koh, the 'Hill of Victory,' where a bold race of
Afghan highlanders followed the banner of the chief
of Sur. The castle had submitted to Mahmud in
1010, but the conqueror left the native chief in tribu-
tory possession, and the Suri horsemen eagerly took
the sultan's pay and fought in his campaigns against
the infidels. These fiery hillmen respected the great
soldier, but for his weak successors they cared little,
and feared them less. A conflict was brought about
by the death of one of the Suri chiefs at the hands
of Bahram Shah. The highlanders of Ghor marched
to avenge his murder, and their rude vigour so over-
mastered the troops of Ghazni, enfeebled by a century of inglorious ease, that Bahram and his army
were driven pell-mell into India (1148). It is true he
returned with fresh forces in the winter, when snow
cut off the usurpers from their headquarters in Ghor,
but the vengeance he took upon the intruders and
the execution of their leader only heated the fury of
the chief of Firoz-koh.

Two brothers of the princely race of Sur had now successively been slain by the king of Ghazni: a third brother avenged them. In 1155 Ala-ad-din Husain, reprobated for all time by the title of 'World-burner' (Jahan-soz), burst into Ghazni on a wave of slaughter and destruction, slew the men without mercy, enslaved the women and children, and carried fire and sword throughout the land. Of all the noble buildings with which the kings had enriched their stately capital hardly a stone was left to tell of its grandeur. The very graves of the hated dynasty were dug up and the royal bones scattered to the curs — but even Afghan vengeance spared the tomb of Mahmud, the idol of Muslim soldiers. That tomb and two lofty minarets, at a little distance from the modern town, alone stand to show that Ghazni was. On one of the minarets one may still read the resonant titles of the Idol-breaker, and on the marble tombstone an inscription entreats 'God's mercy for the great Amir Mahmud.'

India was now to witness something very like a repetition of his swift irresistible raids. For more than a century there had been, if not peace, at least little war. The later kings of Ghazni had been mild unambitious rulers, and had left the Panjab very much to itself. Probably their Hindu troops and Hindu officials had to some extent Indianated them, and the last descendants of Mahmud made their home at Lahore without difficulty. The attempt of Bahram's son, Khusru Shah, to recover the command in Afghanistan utterly failed; he found Ghazni and the other towns in ruins, the tribes disloyal, and the

Ghuzz Turkmans overrunning the land.   The comparatively orderly rule of the kings of Ghazni had given place to anarchy, and so it remained for many years.   Ala-ad-din the 'World-burner' was content to rule his clan at Firoz-koh ; but after his death in 1161, and that of his son two years later, his nephew Ghiyas-ad-din son of Sam became chief of Ghor, and

COIN OF GHIYAS-AD-DIN, SHOWING SPEARMAN ON ELEPHANT.

with his accession the Afghan highlanders entered upon a new phase of activity.   Ghiyas-ad-din recovered Ghazni from the mob of Ghuzz in 1173–4, and established his brother Mu'izz-ad-din on the ruined throne of Mahmud.   The two brothers exercised a joint sovereignty, but whilst the elder maintained his hereditary chiefdom in his forefathers' castle of the 'Hill of Victory,' Mu'izz-ad-din, commonly known as Mohammad Ghori, led a series of campaigns in India which recalled the glorious days of the Idol-breaker nearly two centuries before. Thirty years had Mahmud ravaged Hindustan from the Indus to the Ganges; and for thirty years Mohammad Ghori harried the same country in the same way.

His first object was to gather the Mohammedan

provinces of India under his control. He began with the old Arab colony on the Indus, took Multan in 1175 from the heretical Karmathians, whom Mahmud had but temporarily dislodged, marched thence to Anhalwara in 1178, and by 1182 he had subdued the whole of Sind down to Daibul and the sea-coast. Meanwhile his armies had not left the exiled king of Ghazni undisturbed. Peshawar was taken in 1179, and Khusru Malik, the last of the Ghaznawids, a feeble gentle soul, utterly unequal to the task of mastering the anarchy which was ruining the remnant of his fathers' kingdom, hastened to give his son as a hostage and to offer deprecatory presents to the invader. The final catastrophe was thus delayed for a few years. In 1184, however, Mohammad Ghori ravaged the territory of Lahore and fortified Sialkot. This was coming to close quarters, and the king in desperation called in the help of the Gakkars and laid siege to the fortress. The Ghorian outmanœuvred him by a trick, and getting between Khusru and his capital compelled him to surrender (1185 or 1186). The prisoner and his son were taken to Firoz-koh, and confined in a fort, where after five years the last of the Ghaznawids were put to death.

Mohammad Ghori had thus rid himself of all Muslim rivals in India: he could now turn to the Hindus. From the accounts of the Persian historians it is clear that the process of assimilation which had been going on between the Turkish conquerors and the subject Hindus was now checked. The policy of employing native Indian regiments was

4

abandoned, and the new invaders, Afghan Muslims, numerously supported by Turks, were full of religious zeal and eager to send the 'grovelling crow-faced Hindus to the fire of hell.' Mohammad's first step was to seize and garrison Sirhind. This brought upon him the whole force of the Rajputs, led by Prithwi Raja, the chief of the Chohan dynasty that had succeeded the Tomaras in Delhi and Ajmir. This was a different kind of enemy from those the Afghans had been accustomed to meet. They were well acquainted with the modes of fighting of the Seljuks and other Turks of the Oxus land, but in the Rajputs they encountered a soldiery second to none in the world, a race of born fighters who fought to the death, many of whose principalities never submitted in more than name to Muslim rule. They formed the military caste of the ancient Hindu system, and preserved their old feudal system.

'Each division,' as Elphinstone remarks, 'had its hereditary leader, and each formed a separate community, like clans in other countries, the members of which were bound by many ties to their chief and to each other. As the chiefs of those clans stood in the same relation to the raja as their own retainers did to them, the king, nobility, and soldiery all made one body, united by the strongest feelings of kindred and military devotion. The sort of feudal system that prevailed among the Rajputs gave additional stability to this attachment, and all together produced the pride of birth, the high spirit, and the romantic notions so striking in the military class of that period. Their enthusiasm was kept up by the

songs of their bards, and inflamed by frequent contests for glory or for love. They treated women
with a respect unusual in the East, and were guided,
even towards their enemies, by rules of honour
which it was disgraceful to violate.' With much of
the chivalry, they had not the artificial sentiment of
the knights of the 'Faerie Queene,' and, save for
their native indolence, they resembled rather the
heroes of the Homeric poems, or of their own 'Mahab-
harata,' than those of the Round Table. No doubt
they had degenerated in a long period of inglorious
obscurity, but what the Rajputs are in the present day
may teach us that in the twelfth century they were
a brilliant and formidable array.

Mohammad Ghori's first encounter with the Rajputs was like to have been his last. The two armies
met in 1191 at Narain, ten miles north of Karnal, on
another part of the great plain which includes the
historic field of Panipat, and on which the fate of
India has been decided again and again. All the
dash of the Muslim cavalry was powerless against
the Hindus. The Afghan charges were met by skilful flanking movements, and the sultan found himself cut off from his shattered wings and hemmed in
by Rajput squadrons. He tried to save the day by
personal gallantry, charged up to the standard of the
raja's brother, the viceroy of Delhi, and with his
spear drove his teeth down his throat; but his
rash exposure nearly cost him his life, and he was
only saved by the devotion of a Khalji retainer
who mounted behind him and carried him off the
field. The sultan's retirement led to a panic. The

Muslims were soon in full retreat, pursued for forty miles by the enemy, and Mohammad did not even stop at Lahore, but hastened to cross the Indus into his own country.   Never had the armies of Islam been so worsted by the infidels.

FORT OF AJMIR.

The sultan could not forget the disaster.   At Ghazni, he confessed, 'he never slumbered in ease nor waked but in sorrow and anxiety.'   The next year saw him again in India, at the head of 120,000 men, Afghans, Turks, and Persians.   Prithwi Raja had taken Sirhind, after a year's siege, and awaited his enemy on the same field of Narain.   The sultan had profited by his former lesson. His cavalry in four divisions of ten thousand each harassed the Rajputs on all sides, and when he found their famous soldiery still unbroken he lured them to disorder by a feigned retreat. Then, taking them at a disadvantage, he charged at the head of twelve thousand picked horsemen in steel armour, and 'this prodigious army once shaken, like a great building, tottered to its fall and was lost in its own ruins.' Many of the Rajput chiefs were killed in the battle. Prithwi Raja himself mounted a horse and fled, but was captured near Sirsuti and 'sent to hell.'

The result of this victory was the annexation of Ajmir, Hansi, and Sirsuti, ruthless slaughter and a general destruction of temples and idols and building of mosques (1192). Ajmir was left in charge of a son of the late raja, as a vassal of the sultan, and Kutb-ad-din Aybek, a slave of Mohammad Ghori, was appointed viceroy of India, where after his master's death he founded the Kingdom of Delhi. There was much, however, to be done before there could be any talk of kingship. Delhi and Koil indeed fell before the attacks of Kutb-ad-din the same year, but beyond them lay the dominions of the powerful Rathors, who had become rajas of Kanauj on the downfall of the Tomaras. Mohammad, returning from Ghazni, himself led the campaign against them in the following year, and, after a crushing defeat on the Jumna between Chandwar and Etawa, the Rathors fled south to found a new principality at Marwar, and Kanauj and Benares became part of the empire of Ghor. The Muslims were now in Bihar, and it was not long before they found their way into Bengal. Whilst Kutb-ad-din was reducing the cities further west, another general, Mohammad Bakhtiyar, pushed his way to Oudh and on to Lakhnauti, then the capital of Bengal, and thus brought the extreme east of Hindustan under Muslim rule.

Meanwhile the sultan or his viceroy had conquered, if they had not subdued, the greater part of northern India. Gwaliar, Badaun, Kalpi, Kalinjar, Anhalwara, had fallen, and if Mohammad had been content with an Indian empire he might have enjoyed his wish. But the kings of Ghazni were ever looking backward towards the west, where Mahmud had held so vast a sway. Tradition led them to long for the orchards and fat pastures of the Oxus and the rich cities and luxury of Persia. The wealth of India could not satisfy these hungry hillmen. Mohammad Ghori must needs invade Khwarizm, the modern Khiva, where his momentary success was followed by such disastrous defeat that he burned his baggage, purchased his bare life, and fled (1203). Such an overthrow means anarchy in an oriental state. Everywhere the tribes and governors rose in revolt. Ghazni shut its gates in its sultan's face, Multan proclaimed a new king, the Gakkars seized Lahore and laid waste the Panjab; the wide dominion of the house of Ghor broke asunder. The recovery of his shattered kingdom was Mohammad's greatest feat. Kutb-ad-din remained true to him, and so did several cities held by the sultan's kindred. Mohammad swept down upon

Multan and regained it ; Ghazni repented ; the Gakkars were subdued and even nominally converted. But conversion did not wipe out the blood-feud, and when the sultan set out once more to gather forces for another effort to realize his useless dream of western empire, he was murdered in his tent beside

SILVER COIN OF MOHAMMAD GHORI, STRUCK AT GHAZNI,
A.H. 596 (A.D. 1199).

the Indus by a band of Gakkars who had the deaths of their kinsfolk to avenge (1206).

Compared with Mahmud, the name of Mohammad Ghori has remained almost obscure. He was no patron of letters, and no poets or historians vied with one another to praise his munificence and power. Yet his conquests in Hindustan were wider and far more permanent than Mahmud's. A large part of these conquests were of course partial, and there were still revolts to be crushed and chiefs to be subdued : India was not to be subjugated in a generation. But the conquest was real and permanent, and though Mohammad was no Indian sovereign, but still king of Ghazni with eyes turned towards Persia and the Oxus, he left a viceroy in Hindustan who began the famous Slave dynasty,

the first of the many Muslim kings that have ruled
India.

Of the two tides of Mohammedan invasion that
surged into India, Mahmud's had left little trace.
It had been but a series of triumphant raids, and
when its violence was spent scarcely enough
strength remained to hold a single province. That
province however had been held, not without a
struggle, and in the Panjab Mohammad Ghori found
the ποῦ στῶ, the necessary leverage, whence to
bear upon a wider territory than his precursor. He
rose from even smaller beginnings than Mahmud,
but his followers possessed the same hardihood and
power of endurance as the earlier invaders from the
same mountain valleys, and they carried their arms
further and left surer footprints. The dynasty of
Ghor relapsed into the insignificance of a highland
chiefdom after its great sultan's death; but the
dominion it had conquered in India was not lost to
Islam. It was consolidated under other rulers, and
from the days of Mohammad Ghori to the catas-
trophy of the Indian mutiny there was always a
Mohammedan king upon the throne of Delhi.

BOOK II

THE KINGDOM OF DELHI

1206–1526

CHAPTER IV

THE SLAVE KINGS

THE TURKS IN DELHI

1206–1290

AT length in 1206 India had a Mohammedan king of its own, ruling not from an outside capital but in India itself. Mohammad Ghori's viceroy Aybek was the first of the thirty-four Muslim kings who ruled at Delhi from the beginning of the thirteenth century to the invasion of Babar in 1526. These thirty-four kings fall into five successive dynasties. First came the Slave Kings, descended from Aybek the slave of Ghori, or from Aybek's slaves: these were all Turks. Next followed the Khaljis, probably Turks in origin but essentially Afghans in association and character. The third was the Turkish house of Taghlak. The irruption of Timur, who burst into India in 1398, put an end to the domination of the Taghlak princes, and broke up the Kingdom of Delhi; but the dynasty of the Sayyids or 'nobles'—so called because, though natives of India, they claimed Arabian descent from the family of the

Prophet Mohammad — assumed authority at the capital. The fifth dynasty was that of the Afghan Lodis, who held what remained of the kingdom until defeated by the Emperor Babar on the fatal field of Panipat.

In tracing the history of these three centuries of predominant Turkish rule in India we shall have little to say about anything but a few conspicuous men. History in the East does not mean the growth of constitutions, the development of civic 'rights,' the vindication of individual liberty, or the evolution of self-government. These are Western ideas which have no meaning in India. If translated into Hindustani they represent nothing that the natural Hindu comprehends or desires. The European assumption that every man is more or less competent to carry on the work of government is flatly denied in the East. The Western panacea of self-government possesses no attraction to the unsophisticated oriental. To the Indian, power is a divine gift, to be exercised absolutely by God's anointed, and obeyed unquestioned by everyone else. A king who is not absolute loses in the oriental mind the essential quality of kingship. Every Eastern people, if left to itself, sets up a despot, to whose decrees of life and death it submits with the same resignation and assent that it shows towards the *fiat* of destiny. In the East *l'état c'est moi*, the King is the State, its ministers are his instruments, its people are his slaves. His worst excesses and most savage cruelties are endured in the same way as plague and famine: all belong to the irresistible and inscrutable manifesta-

tions of the divine order of the universe. The only
kind of king that the. East tolerates with difficulty is
the fainéant. Let him be strong and masterful, and
he may do as he pleases; but the weak sovereign
rarely keeps his throne long, and keeps it only by
force of traditional loyalty or dread of the unknown
risks of revolution.

In the history of Mohammedan India, then, we
have to do with kings and their works. They are
surrounded by a court of officers and functionaries,
who are raised or displaced at the royal pleasure.
Beneath them toil incessantly the millions of pa-
tient peasants and industrious townsfolk. These
people have not changed in any essential characteristic since the dawn of history. They have witnessed the successive inroads of horde after horde of
invading foreigners, and have incorporated some
part of each new element into their ancient system.
They have obeyed the king, whether Aryan, Hun,
Greek, Persian, Rajput, Turk, Afghan, Mongol, or
English, with the same inveterate resignation, contented or at least not very discontented with their
immemorial village system and district government,
which corrected to some extent the contrasts of successive foreign innovators. Whatever king may
rule,—so the Indian would resignedly argue—there
will still be plague and famine and constant but not
energetic labour, and so long as the rice and millet
grow and salt is not too dear, life is much the same
and the gods may be propitiated. The difference
caused in the rayat's life by a good or a bad king is
too slight to be worth discussing. The good and the

ill are alike things of a day; they pass away as the life passes when the king decrees a death or massacres a village; but others follow and the world goes on, and the will of God is eternal.

The kings whose deeds are to be described were foreigners in origin, but this made little if any difference in the respect which their authority implied. There is of course as great a contrast between a Muslim Turk and a Hindu Rajput as between a Scottish Presbyterian and a Spanish Catholic; but the reverence paid to power overbore all distinctions of race. The caste system had accustomed Indians to immovable barriers between classes, and though the Muslim kings had no claim of pedigree and not much distinction of ceremonial purity, they formed in a way a caste, the caste of Islam, a fellowship of equal brotherhood unsurpassed in coherence and strength in all the world. The great power of Islam as a missionary influence in India has been due to the benefits of this caste. The moment an Indian accepts Islam he enters a brotherhood which admits no distinctions of class in the sight of God, and every advancement in office and rank and marriage is open to him. To those outside Islam the yoke of the alien ruler was no worse than that of the native raja. Both represented a separate caste, and both belonged to the inscrutable workings of providence.[1]

The essential union of the Muslims as a conquering caste was indeed the chief cause of their successful hold of the vastly preponderating multitudes

[1] Compare the suggestive thoughts on this subject in Mr. MEREDITH TOWNSEND'S *Asia and Europe* (1901).

they governed. Their power in India was always
that of an armed camp, but it was a camp in which
all the soldiers fought shoulder to shoulder for the
same cause, in which all were equal brothers; and it
had the immense resource of being able to draw continually and in unlimited numbers upon the recruiting grounds of the Mohammedan countries behind
it, which were always reinforcing their co-religionists
by fresh bodies of hardy adventurers, free from the
lethargy of self-indulgence that too often etiolates the
exotic in the Indian forcing-house. The very bigotry
of their creed was an instrument of self-preservation;
in mere self-defence they must hold together as God's
elect in the face of the heathen, and they must win
over proselytes from the Hindus, whether by per-
suasion or by the sword, to swell their isolated minority. Hence the solidarity and the zeal which,
added to their greater energy and versatility, gave
the Muslims their superiority over natives who were
sometimes their equals in courage, though never in
unity, in enthusiasm, or in persistence. The clan-
nishness of the Hindus, their devotion to local chiefs,
and their ineradicable jealousies of each other, prevented anything approaching national patriotism;
and their religious system, which rested upon birth
and race and class, whilst precluding the very idea
of proselytism, deprived them of the fanatical zeal of
the missionary. Moreover they were always on the
defensive, and except behind ramparts the defensive
position is the weaker part. The Muslims, inspired
by the spirit of adventure, of militant propaganda,
of spreading the Kingdom of God upon earth, as well

as seizing the goods of this world, had every advantage over the native Hindus, and when the invaders were led by kings who embodied these masterful qualities their triumph was assured.

The example of the warrior king, like Mohammad Ghori, bred heroic followers. Whatever may be said against the slave system, in the East it tends to the production of great men. While a brilliant ruler's son is apt to be a failure, the slaves of a real leader of men have often proved the equals of their master. The reason of course is that the son is a mere speculation. He may or may not inherit his father's talents; even if he does, the very success and power of the father create an atmosphere of luxury that does not encourage effort; and, good or bad, the son is an immovable fixture: only a father with an exceptional sense of public duty would execute an incompetent son to make room for a talented slave. On the other hand the slave is the 'survival of the fittest'; he is chosen for physical and mental abilities, and he can hope to retain his position in his master's favour only by vigilant effort and hard service. Should he be found wanting, his fate is sealed.

The famous Seljuk empire furnished a notable example of the influence of a great man upon his slaves. The mamluk guard of the emperor Malik Shah formed a school of capable rulers. 'However servile in origin, the pedigree carried with it no sense of ignominy. In the East a slave is often held to be better than a son, and to have been the slave of Malik Shah constituted a special title of respect.

The great slave vassals of the Seljuks were as proud
and honourable as any Bastards of mediæval aristocracy; and when they in turn assumed kingly powers, they inherited and transmitted to their lineage
the high traditions of their former lords.'[1]   The
same process was seen in the great slave leaders who
were among the earliest Mamluk Sultans of Egypt
in the thirteenth century; and an equally conspicu-

BILLON COIN OF YILDIZ, SHOWING CHOHAN HORSEMAN.

ous example is found in India in the slaves of Mohammad Ghori.   When someone condoled with
him on his lack of male offspring to carry on his line,
he replied ' Have I not thousands of children in my
Turki slaves?'   Four of his mamluks rose to high
command: Yildiz in the Afghan mountains, Kubacha on the Indus, Bakhtiyar in Bengal, Aybek at
Delhi.   Of these Kutb-ad-din Aybek[2] was the chief.
Brought as a child, like so many slaves of the period,
from Turkistan to Khurasan he was well-educated

---

[1] LANE-POOLE, *Saladin*, 22, 23.

[2] Aybek means ' Moon-lord,' probably with reference to personal
beauty.   The common statement that it signified ' maimed,' on account of his loss of a finger, is due to a misreading of a passage in
the *Tabakat-i-Nasiri.*

5

by his owner, the chief kazi of Naishapur, and when
grown up he was sent in a merchant's caravan to
Ghazni, where he was purchased by Mohammad
Ghori.   His brave and generous character soon won
him favour, and rising step by step to be master of
the horse, he accompanied the sultan in his campaigns, was taken prisoner in Khwarizm and fortunately recaptured ; and after the defeat of Prithwi
Raja of Ajmir the government of India was confided
to the successful slave.

Aybek's chief exploits were achieved during his
viceroyalty.   Hansi, Mirat, Delhi (1191), Rantambhor, Koil fell before his assault, and he led the van-
guard of the Ghorian army in 1194 when it conquered
Benares.   When the sultan returned to Ghazni after
this crowning triumph, it was Aybek who subdued
the ill-timed revolt of the vassal raja of Ajmir.
Master and slave humbled the pride of Gwaliar, that
' pearl of the necklace of the castles of Hind,' and
compelled the raja Solankhpal to render tribute in
1196; and in the following year Aybek won a signal
victory over the vast array of the prince of Anhalwara, who left fifty thousand dead on the field, while
twenty thousand prisoners and immense booty fell
into the Muslims' hands.   Thus the kingdom of Gujarat came under the power of Ghor.   Kalinjar, the
seat of the Chandel rajas, after a desperate resistance,
fell before Aybek's attack in 1202 ; its temples were
turned into mosques and fifty thousand men put on
the ' collar of slavery.'   At the same time Mohammad Bakhtiyar, a fellow marshal (Sipahsalar), who for
the first time had carried the Muslim arms across

THE KUTB MINAR AT DELHI.

Bihar into Bengal, and made Lakhnauti his capital, brought his spoils and his homage to the great viceroy. The energy of Aybek and Bakhtiyar had completed the successes of Mohammad Ghori, and nearly all Hindustan north of the Vindhya range was under Muslim sway.

What that sway meant we know only from the chroniclers of the conquering races. According to Hasan Nizami, who wrote at Delhi in the midst of these campaigns and knew Aybek well, the viceroy administered his wide provinces ' in the ways of justice ' and 'the people were happy.' Tribute and military service were exacted as the price of toleration, and Aybek's impartiality is extolled in the metaphorical phrase that ' the wolf and the sheep drank water out of the same pond.' ' The roads were freed from robbers,' and the Hindus both ' high and low were treated with royal benignity,' which however did not prevent the viceroy from making an immense number of slaves in his wars. So munificent was he that he was called ' Lakhbakhsh ' or ' Giver of lacs.' At Delhi he busied himself in building the great mosque or Jami' Masjid and the famous minaret known after his surname as the Kutb Minar, which stood originally 250 feet high and is the tallest minaret in the world. Its boldly jutting balconies, alternate angular and rounded fluting, and fine Arabic inscriptions set off the natural contrasts of white marble and red sandstone of which it is built. The mosque, like Aybek's other mosque at Ajmir, was constructed of the materials of demolished temples, and the ornament was supplied from

the idols of the Hindus. Aybek was a staunch
Muslim, and though policy dictated toleration in the

THE GREAT MOSQUE OF AJMIR, WITH INSCRIPTION OF ALTAMISH.

case of powerful Hindu vassals, he was a mighty
'fighter in the way of God.' 'The realm was filled
with friends and cleared of foes,' says a contemporary

chronicler, 'his bounty was continuous, and so was his slaughter.'

Aybek survived his master only a few years, and his own full sovereignty as the first Slave sultan of Delhi ended in 1210, when he died from a fall from his horse whilst playing mall or polo, an ancient and favourite sport in Persia and India. A time of confusion followed. An incompetent son opened the way to rivals. Kubacha held Multan and Sind to the mouth of the Indus and strove with Yildiz for the possession of Lahore; Bakhtiyar's successor was supreme in Bihar and Bengal; and Shams-ad-din Altamish,[1] a slave of Aybek, deposing his master's son, took the throne of Delhi for himself. Altamish is the true founder of the dynasty of the Slave Kings, which Aybek did not live long enough to consolidate. The new leader was a Turk of Albari, unequalled (says his contemporary, Minhaj-as-siraj) 'in beauty, virtue, intelligence, and nobleness' of character. 'No king so benevolent, sympathetic, reverent to the learned and the old, ever rose by his own efforts to the cradle of empire.' Taken to Ghazni in his youth, he was purchased by Aybek, who carried him to Delhi, made him captain of his guard, and eventually governor of Gwaliar (1196). What Aybek had been to Mohammad Ghori, Altamish was to Aybek, who used him like a son. When Aybek's real son proved unfit to rule, the chiefs of the army begged Altamish to take the throne.

[1] Altamish or Altamsh is the Persian spelling, but the original Turki name, as written on coins and inscriptions and transliterated into Nagari, was probably Il-tutmish, 'Hand-grasper.'

It was a stormy advent. Yildiz indeed, ruling at Ghazni, saw the wisdom of conciliation, and sent him the sceptre and umbrella of state; but Kubacha refused to surrender Lahore, and it was not till 1217 that Altamish obtained possession of the northern Panjab by the defeat of his rival. These contests were as nothing compared with the tumult to come. A new and incalculable danger threatened all Asia. The hordes of the *flagellum Dei*, Chingiz Kaan, had begun to overflow their steppes; and the first sign of the Mongols' approach was the flight of Yildiz into India, driven by the broken armies of the Khwarizm Shah, themselves flying panic-stricken before the victorious savages. One after the other they came down from the mountain passes: first the Turkish governors, then the Khwarizmian fugitives, and hard on their heels the dreaded Mongols. Jalal-ad-din, the last shah of Khwarizm and heir of an empire which once spread from Otrar and Khiva, Samarkand and Bukhara, to Herat and Isfahan, retreated fighting his way to the Indus, whither Chingiz pursued him, beat him (1221), and drove him still dauntless into Sind. The adventures of this heroic prince, who battled his way back through Persia only to succumb at last after a decade of daring energy, form a stirring page of romantic history.

The tumult was tremendous, but the storm passed away as quickly as it came. The Mongols wintered and then retired: fortunately for India their eyes were set westward. Out of this turmoil Altamish emerged stronger than before. Yildiz and Kubacha disappeared from history: the one died in prison;

the other, after many a struggle with the forces, Mongol and Khwarizmian,[1] that in turn ravaged his border-provinces, at last saw his chief cities falling before the siege of Altamish, and in his desperation drowned himself in the Indus (1230). Before this the king of Delhi had marched into Bengal (1225) and received the homage of the governor, who had not only attained independent power but proclaimed it by his coinage.[2] The whole of the dominions of Aybek were now in the hands of his slave, and in 1234 expeditions into Malwa as far as Ujjayn completed the submission of all India north of the Vindhyas.

The seal was set on a career of unvaried success when the caliph of Baghdad (in 1229) sent an embassy of state to invest Altamish with the robe of office as recognized sovereign of India. Thenceforth the king inscribed upon his coins not only the proud legend 'The Mighty Sultan, Sun of the Empire and the Faith, Conquest-laden, Il-tutmish,' but also 'Aid of the Commander of the Faithful,' Nasir-Amir-al-Muminin. The broad silver pieces on which these titles appeared were new to the currency of India. Hitherto the invaders had issued small billon coins of the native form, inscribed with their names in the Nagari and sometimes in Arabic character, and bearing symbols familiar to the Hin-

---

[1] The Khwarizm troops under their general Hasan Karlagh and his son Mohammad held Sind until at least 1260.

[2] See the coins of Ghyas-ad-din Iwaz of 1223 in LANE-POOLE, *Catalogue of Indian Coins in the British Museum : Mohammedan States*, p. 9, and Introd., p. x.

dus, such as the bull of Siva and the Chohan
horseman. Altamish was the first to introduce a
purely Arabic coinage, such as had long been in use
in countries further west, and to adopt as his standard coin the silver tanka, the ancestor of the rupee,
weighing 175 grains, and thus exactly corresponding
to our florin. Gold tankas of the same weight were
introduced somewhat later by Balban.

For ten years after the death of Altamish in 1236
his kingdom suffered from the weakness and de-

SILVER COIN OF ALTAMISH.

pravity of his sons. The first, Firoz Shah, was a
handsome, generous, soft-hearted, convivial, young
fool, who spent his money upon singers and buffoons
and worse, and swaying drunk upon his elephant
through the bazars showered red gold upon the
admiring crowd. 'God forgive him,' says the chronicler of his time, 'sensuality, frivolity, and the company of the lewd and base bring an empire to ruin.'
His mother, a Turkish slave, managed the government, whilst her son wantoned, till her savage
cruelty caused a general revolt. The pair were
imprisoned, and Firoz died after a nominal reign of
not quite seven months. His sister Raziyat-ad-din

('Devoted to the Faith') was chosen in his place. She was the only child after her father's heart. 'Sultan Raziya,' says the same chronicler, who knew her, 'was a great monarch: wise, just, generous, a benefactor to her realm, a dispenser of equity, the protector of her people, and leader of her armies; she had all kingly qualities except sex, and this exception made all her virtues of no effect in the eyes of men, may God have mercy upon her!' Altamish had perceived her great qualities, trusted her with power, and named her his heir. When the astonished ministers remonstrated on the unprecedented idea of setting a woman on a Muslim throne, he said, 'My sons are given over to the follies of youth: none of them is fit to be king and rule this country, and you will find there is no one better able to do so than my daughter.'

By a curious coincidence three Muslim queens, the only three women who were ever elected to the throne in the Mohammedan East, reigned in the thirteenth century. Shajar-ad-durr, the high-spirited slave-wife of Saladin's grand-nephew, the woman who defeated the crusade of Louis IX and afterwards spared the saintly hero's life, was queen of the Mamluks in Egypt in 1250. Abish, the last of the princely line of Salghar, patrons of Sa'di, ruled the great province of Fars for nearly a quarter of a century during the troubled period of Mongol supremacy. Raziya, daughter of Altamish, less fortunate, sat on the throne of Delhi for only three years and a half (1236–40). She did her best to prove herself a man, wore manly dress, and showed her face fearlessly as she rode her elephant at the head of her troops. But nothing could convince the Turkish chiefs that a woman could or should lead them.

TOMB OF ALTAMISH AT DELHI.

The Arabian Prophet had said truly that 'the most precious thing in the world is a virtuous woman,' but he had also said that 'the people that makes a woman its ruler will not find salvation.' Raziya was clearly impossible, and her preference for the Abyssinian Yakut, though perfectly innocent so far as any evidence goes, roused the jealousy of the dominant Turks.

The slave system had grown stronger by the successful careers of Aybek and Altamish. The latter had formed a corps of Turkish mamluks known as 'the Forty,' and these men, profiting by the removal of the master's hand, shared among themselves the wealth and power of the kingdom. The free-born men who had served Altamish with great ability in various offices were removed, and all control was in the hands of 'the Forty.' These khans[1] were not likely to endure the insult of seeing an Abyssinian set over them by a partial woman. They rose in rebellion, and though at first the gallant queen made head against them, she was finally taken prisoner by the rebel governor Altuniya (1240). Even then she subdued her captor and became his queen, and the two set forth to regain her throne. But her brother was already proclaimed in her stead; her army was beaten; and Raziya and her husband, deserted by their troops, fled into the jungles and were killed.

There is no need to dwell upon the brief and inglorious reigns of Bahram and Mas'ud, the one a brother, the other a nephew of Raziya. The former is described as 'a fearless, intrepid, and sanguinary man: still he had some virtues — he was shy and unceremonious, and had no taste for gorgeous attire.' His two years of power were spent in plots and counterplots, treacherous executions, and cruel murders, and he was killed after a siege of Delhi by the exasperated army. The next, Mas'ud, 'acquired

---

[1] 'Khan' is a Persian term for 'lord,' answering to the Arabic 'amir.' In India it was specially applied to Turkish and Afghan nobles or officers, and still implies Afghan race though not rank.

the habit of seizing and killing his nobles,' and spent his time in abandoned pleasures. It was no time

SILVER COIN OF QUEEN RAZIYA, STRUCK AT LAKHNAUTI.

for weak rulers. The Mongols were again on the march; they had massacred the inhabitants of La- hore in December, 1241, and established themselves on the Indus with every appearance of permanent conquest.[1]

At this juncture another remarkable slave came to the rescue of the state. The nominal king was Nasir-ad-din, a third son of Altamish; but the reins of power were in the strong hands of Balban. He was a Turk of the same district as Altamish and boasted his descent from the Khakans of Albari; his father ruled ten thousand kibitkas, and his kins- men still governed their ancestral tribes in Turkistan. But Balban was not to enjoy such obscure distinc- tion. 'The Almighty desired to grant a support to the power of Islam and to the strength of the Mo- hammedan faith, to extend His glorious shadow over

---

[1] E. THOMAS, *Chronicles of the Pathan Kings*, 121, has conclu- sively shown that the statement that the Mongols reached Lakhnauti in Bengal is due to a misreading of the Persian text of the *Tabakat- i-Nasiri.*

it, and to preserve Hindustan within the range of His favour and protection. He therefore removed Balban in his youth from Turkistan, and separated him from his race and kindred, from his tribe and relations, and conveyed him to this country for the purpose of curbing the Mongols.' In short Balban was kidnapped or taken prisoner as a child and brought to India, where he was purchased by Altamish. The story runs that the sultan refused at first to buy him, because of his shortness and ugliness. ' Master of the world,' cried the slave, ' for whose sake have you bought these other servants?' ' For mine own,' said Altamish, laughing. ' Then buy me for the sake of God,' begged Balban. ' So be it,' said the sultan, and the ugly slave was set among the bhistis or water-bearers. He soon showed that he was fitted for better things, rose to distinguished offices, and was enrolled in the famous corps of ' the Forty ' slaves.

' The hawk of fortune ' was thus set upon his wrist. He served Raziya as chief huntsman, and retained his post under Bahram. ' The steed of rule came under his bridle.' He was given a fief (*jagir*) or grant of lands. When the sultan was besieged in Delhi, Balban was among the leading rebels, and the success of the conspiracy brought him, in reward for his help, the government of Hansi, where he showed himself an improving and benevolent ruler, at once just and generous. In 1243 as lord chamberlain he subdued rebellion and pacified the country, and when the Mongols under Mangu Kaan pushed their way across the Indus, it was mainly due to the urgent advice and strenuous efforts of Balban — who received the title of Ulugh Khan, ' Puissant lord,' — that the army of Delhi accomplished their defeat. It was he who compelled the Mongols to raise the siege of Uchh (1245) and retire to the hills, where he pursued them with untiring vigilance. In fact Balban had become the guiding spirit of the Muslim rule, and when Mas'ud was deposed and his uncle Nasir-ad-din set upon the throne, the real authority was in the hands of the brilliant slave commander-in-chief.

The feebleness of the successors of Altamish had permitted a recrudescence of Hindu rebellion, and Balban's energies were devoted to constant campaigns against the ' infidels.' Year after year he led his troops through the Doab, or to the hills of Rantambhor, against Malwa or Kalinjar, or the raja of Ijari, and everywhere his arms were victorious. His reputation became so great that the other officers and chiefs, envious of his success, prejudiced the sultan against him and had him banished from court (1253). The leader of this intrigue was a renegade Hindu eunuch, and the envious officers found that they had exchanged the rule of a soldier for that of a schemer. There was universal discontent at the disgrace of the favourite, and the Turkish chiefs and the Persian officials of good family resented the despotism of the eunuch and his hired bullies. From all parts entreaties came to the banished general beseeching him to come back. The Turkish chiefs even rose in arms, and this demonstration procured the dismissal of Rihan the renegade and the restoration of Balban to all his honours (1254). Not only were men delighted at this act of justice, but it was observed that even the Almighty manifested His pleasure by sending down the long-needed rains. 'The success of Ulugh Khan shone forth with brilliant radiance; the garden of the world began to put forth leaf, and the key of divine mercy opened the doors of men's hearts.'

For twenty years in all Balban served the sultan indefatigably, and they were years full of rebellion, conspiracy, and Mongol alarms. His royal master led the life of a dervish, copied Korans to pay his modest needs, and lived in the simplest manner, attended by one wife, who cooked his dinner and was allowed no female servants. He was a kind and scholarly gentleman, who delighted in the society of the learned, but he was no king for India in the thirteenth century. Fortunately for him he had a deputy in Balban fully able to fill his place in the anxious cares of kingship. To this conspicuously able minister were due the two great measures of the reign: the organization of the frontier provinces and tribes under his able cousin Sher Khan, by which the attacks of the Mongols were successfully repelled ; and the steady suppression of Hindu disaffection — a perpetual and never-extinguished source of danger — in all parts of the kingdom. The constant jealousies and revolts of the overgrown Turkish chiefs demanded a strong hand to keep them down, and nothing but Balban's vigorous energy could have maintained the throne unimpaired through those twenty troubled years.

On Nasir-ad-din's death in 1266, the great minister, whose loyalty towards his gentle sovereign
had never wavered, naturally stepped into his place.
The same rule continued, but the mild influence of
the dervish sultan no longer softened the severity of
his vezir. The energetic minister became an implacable king. With ambitious Turkish khans treading on his heels, Hindus everywhere ready to spring
at the smallest opening for revolt, marauders infest-
ing the very gates of Delhi, assaulting and robbing
the bhistis and the girls who fetched water, above all
with the Mongols ever hammering on the doors of
the frontier posts, Balban had reason to be stern and
watchful, and if he carried his severity to extreme
lengths it was probably a case of his own life against
the rest. He suppressed with an iron hand the
forays of the hillmen who terrified the suburbs of
Delhi; his armies scoured the jungles about the capital, destroyed the villages, cleared the forest, and at
a sacrifice of 100,000 men turned a haunt of bush-
rangers into a peaceable agricultural district. By
building forts in disturbed parts and establishing
Afghan garrisons in block-houses, he freed the roads
from the brigands who had long practically closed
them. 'Sixty years have passed since then,' says
Barani, our chief authority for this reign, 'but the
roads have ever since been free from robbers.' Such
immunity was not attained by smooth words. Balban pounced upon a disturbed district like a hawk,
burnt and slew without mercy, till 'the blood of the
rioters ran in streams, heaps of slain were seen near
every village and jungle, and the stench of the dead

6

even spread to the Ganges.' Woodcutters were sent to cut roads through the jungles, and, like the reform of Marshal Wade in Scotland, the roadmaking did more to bring order among the wild tribes than even the massacre of their fighting men.

In spite of the suffering involved, such work as this was of lasting benefit to the kingdom. So was Balban's firm treatment of the Turkish landholders, who were assuming hereditary rights, and threatened to furnish forth a barons' war. Though these men were of his own kindred, and members, or sons of members, of the famous 'Forty' slaves, Balban had no mercy for them; he was with difficulty induced to mitigate the wholesale expropriation that he once contemplated, but it is clear that he did much to deprive the Turkish khans of their former power. He is said even to have poisoned his own cousin Sher Khan, the thirteenth century Lawrence of the Panjab, because he held almost royal authority in his arduous position; and many instances are recorded of his terrible severity towards officers whose conduct gave occasion for the exercise of stern justice.

Balban's one absorbing preoccupation was the danger of a Mongol invasion. For this cause he organized and disciplined his army to the highest point of efficiency; for this he made away with disaffected or jealous chiefs, and steadily refused to entrust authority to Hindus; for this he stayed near his capital and would not be tempted into distant campaigns. To realize the terror inspired by the Mongols one must read their description in the writings of Amir Khusru, a poet who lived at

the court under the patronage of Balban's cultivated
son Prince Mohammad. His picture of the Tatar
infidels, riding on camels, with their bodies of steel
and faces like fire, slits of eyes sharp as gimlets,
short necks, leathery wrinkled cheeks, wide hairy
nostrils and huge mouths, their coarse skins covered
with vermin and their horrible smell, is the car-
icature of fear. 'They are descended from dogs,
but their bones are bigger,' he says. 'The king
marvelled at their bestial faces and said that God

GOLD COIN OF BALBAN, STRUCK AT DELHI, A.H. 672 (A.D. 1273-4).

must have created them out of hell-fire. They
looked like so many sallow devils, and the people
fled from them everywhere in panic.' It was no
wonder that Balban kept his army ever on the
alert to drive such bogles away.

The only distant expedition the sultan made was
into Bengal, where 'the people had for many long
years tended to rebellion and the disaffected and
evil-disposed among them generally succeeded in con-
taminating the loyalty of the governors.' Barani's
opinion of the Bengalis has often been reiterated
in more recent times; but in the days of the early
Delhi kingdom the difficulty of communication

across imperfectly subdued country, and the absence of any sentiment of loyalty towards slave kings who had not yet founded a settled hereditary monarchy, may well have fostered ideas of independence in the great eastern province. Fifteen governors had successively ruled Bengal since Bakhtiyar the Khalji first carried the standard of Mohammad Ghori there in the first year of the thirteenth century; and their authority had been little curbed by the Delhi sultans. Altamish had put an end to the Khalji chiefs' ambitions and placed his own son in command of Bengal, but since then the weakness of the Delhi kings had left the governors to do as they pleased.

Tughril, the fifteenth governor, a favourite slave of Balban's, observing that the sultan was now an old man intensely preoccupied with the menace of the Mongols, and being fortified in his designs by recent successes in the wild country about Orisa, where the Bengal army had taken vast spoil, permitted 'the egg of ambition to hatch' in his head, and assumed the style and insignia of sovereignty. In vivid contrast to the cold severity of Balban, the usurper of Bengal was free and open-handed, a friend with all the people. 'Money closed the eyes of the clear-sighted, and greed of gold kept the cautious quiet. Soldiers and citizens forgot their fear of the sovereign power and threw themselves heart and soul into Tughril's cause.' The first army sent against him was defeated, as much perhaps by gold as by steel, and many of the Delhi troops deserted to the enemy. Their unlucky

general, Aptagin of the long hair, felt the full brunt
of Balban's fury, and was hanged at the gate of
Oudh, to the indignation of the cooler heads among
the people. A second expedition met with no
better fate.

Overwhelmed with shame and anger the old
sultan himself led a third campaign. Leaving the
marches over against the Mongols in the care of
Prince Mohammad, and placing trusty deputies in
charge of Delhi and Samana, he took his second
son Bughra Khan with him, and crossing the Ganges
made straight for Lakhnauti, in total disregard of
the rains which were then in season. Collecting
a fleet of boats, and, when none were to be had,
wading through mud and water under the torrential
rain of the tropics, the army pushed slowly and
steadily on to the eastern capital, only to find that
Tughril, not daring to face the sultan in person,
had fled with his troops and stores towards the
wilds of Jajnagar. 'We are playing for half my
kingdom,' said Balban, 'and I will never return to
Delhi, nor even name it, till the blood of the rebel
and his followers is poured out.' The soldiers knew
their master's inflexible mind, and resignedly made
their wills. The pursuit was vain for some time;
not a trace of Tughril or his army was to be found.
At last a party of scouts fell in with some corn-
dealers returning from the rebel's headquarters.
Chopping a couple of heads off untied the tongues
of the rest, and the enemy's camp was discovered.
A patrol of some forty men cautiously went forward and viewed the tents, with the men drinking

and singing and washing their clothes, the elephants browsing on the branches of the trees, the horses and cattle grazing. There was no time to go back for reinforcements,— Tughril would be off with the dawn,— and into this scene of idyllic peace the handful of troopers burst like a mountain spate Drawing their swords and shouting for Tughril they rode straight for his tent. He heard the clamour and leaping on a bare-backed steed galloped for the river, while his followers fled madly in all directions, persuaded that Balban and all his army were upon them. Tughril was checked by a dexterous shaft, and in an instant he was beheaded.

Then followed the punishment, conceived in Balban's comprehensive way. Gibbets were ranged along both sides of the long bazar of Lakhnauti, and on them were strung rows of rebels; the sons and kinsmen and followers of Tughril were killed and hung up to the horror of all beholders. Two days and more the work of retribution went on; even a beggar to whom the usurper had been kind was not spared, and old men told Barani half a century later 'that such punishment as was inflicted on Lakhnauti had never been heard of in Delhi, nor could anyone remember such a thing in all Hindustan.' When it was over the sultan sent for his son, Bughra Khan Mahmud, and made him take an oath to recover and hold the rest of Bengal, of which he was then and there appointed governor. Then he solemnly asked the prince, ' Mahmud, dost thou see?' The son did not understand. Again he said ' Dost thou see?' and the prince was still silent and amazed. A

third time the question was asked, and then the old
sultan explained : 'You saw my punishments in the
bazar? If ever designing and evil-minded men
should incite you to waver in your allegiance to
Delhi and to throw off its authority, then remember
the vengeance you have seen wrought in the bazar.
Understand me, and forget not, that if the governors
of Hind or Sind, Malwa or Gujarat, Lakhnauti or
Sonargaon, shall draw the sword and become rebels
to the throne of Delhi, then such punishment as has
fallen upon Tughril and his dependants will fall
upon them, their wives and children, and all their
adherents.

After this deadly warning, he tenderly embraced
his son with tears, and bade him farewell, knowing
perfectly that all counsels were thrown away upon a
prince whose whole soul was in his pleasures. Nevertheless Bughra Khan and five of his descendants ruled
in Bengal for more than half a century (1282–1339),
whilst in Delhi the house of Balban did not survive
his death three years. In suppressing a rebellion in
the remote eastern province, the sultan had really
founded his dynasty in the only part where it was free
to hold its own. He did not long enjoy the memories
of his terrible campaign. The death of his first-born,
the popular and promising 'martyr prince' Mohammad, in battle against the Mongols near Dipalpur, in 1285, broke his heart. During the day he
struggled against his grief, held his court with all
his wonted punctilious etiquette and splendour, and
transacted the business of State ; but at night he
wailed and cast dust upon his head.

In 1287 Balban died, after forty years of rule, half
as minister, half as king.   No one understood better
than he the conditions of kingship in India, or how
to impose himself upon his subjects.   He maintained a rich and ceremonious state among a people
always impressed by magnificence, and crowds of
Hindus would come long journeys to see his pomp
and majesty.   Even his private attendants were never
allowed to see him but in full dress.   That he never
laughed aloud is only to say that he was a well-bred
oriental gentleman who despised the levity of an
empty mind ; but neither did he permit anyone else
to laugh ; and never joking or indulging in the least
familiarity with any one, he allowed no frivolity in
his presence.   In his youth he had been fond of wine
and hazard, but all this was put aside when he came
to authority.   Throughout his forty years of power
he was never known to hold converse with vulgar
people or to give office to any but well-born men.
Slave as he was once, he came of a race of chiefs,
and no one showed more sensitiveness in preserving
the dignity of a king.   Balban, the slave, water-
carrier, huntsman, general, statesman, and sultan is
one of the most striking figures among many notable
men in the long line of the kings of Delhi.

CHAPTER V

FIRST DECCAN CONQUESTS

ALA-AD-DIN KHALJI

1290-1321

BALBAN was one of those men who leave no successors. His very dominance checked the growth of even imitators, much more rivals. He had extinguished the powerful group of slaves who were the true inheritors of Altamish. He had trained no school of great ministers. His hopes were centred in his eldest son, who died before him; he had no confidence in Bughra Khan, and when he found, on offering him the succession, that this frivolous prince preferred returning to his amusements in Bengal to waiting by his father's sick-bed for the splendid reversion of empire, Balban in his irritation left the throne to a son of his dead favourite, who never ascended it. A son of Bughra was set up by the chief officers, but never was a choice less fit. Kai-Kubad in his seventeen years had been so carefully brought up by tutors under his stern grandfather's eye that he had never been allowed to catch sight of a pretty girl or to sip a wine-cup. He had been taught all the polite arts and knew nothing of the impolite. This was the youth who suddenly found himself absolute master of all that the most luxurious city of India, all that India itself, could offer to youth and desire. The result may be left to the imagination. In less than three years he had drunk and debauched himself into a hopeless paralytic; and when a ruffian was sent to murder him, he found the pitiable young man in the chamber of mirrors in his lovely palace at Kilughari on the Jumna, lying at his last gasp, and then and there literally kicked him out of this world.

His father had come from Bengal to try and save him, though he was not himself of a didactic nature; but he found him amiable and hopeless, utterly under the spell of a clever vezir, who encouraged the fool in his folly in the hope of succeeding to the throne. But the vezir Nizam-ad-din overreached himself. The crippling of the kingdom was more serious than the paralysis of the sultan. The officers who remembered the stern order of Balban's rule found even greater severity but none of the order under the arrogant vezir. A series of murders, beginning with Balban's heir-designate, the son of the 'martyr prince,' followed by an insidious inquisition from which no man was safe, roused an opposition which developed into a war of races.

Besides the Turks who had held most of the offices of state since the days of Aybek, there were a large number of adventurers of other races in the service of the Slave Kings. Many of these were Af-

ghans, or Turks so mixed and associated with
Afghans that they had absorbed their character and
customs. These were known as Patans or Pathans,
a term used loosely, much as Moghul was in later
times, to describe the white men from the north-
west mountains. The clan of Khaljis, named after
the Afghan village of Khalj, though probably of
Turkish origin, had become Afghan in character,
and between them and the Turks there was no love
lost. Khaljis had conquered Bengal and ruled there,
and Khaljis held many posts in other parts. These
formed a strong party, and rallied round Jalal-ad-
din, the muster-master or adjutant-general, an old
Khalji who had been marked down for destruction
by the Turkish adherents of the vezir. The Khaljis
were not popular; but the vezir was hated: the
choice of evils, however, did not lie with the people,
and on the death of the paralytic sultan the reaction
against the Turks brought the Khaljis into power,
and set Jalal-ad-din upon the throne of Delhi. For
a time at least the Turks had lost the empire.

It is characteristic of the adaptability of the Indian people that although the Turks were foreigners
and their rule had been anything but conciliatory,
their suppression was resented as a wanton innovation. No Khalji, they said, had ever been a king,
and the race had no part or lot in Delhi. Conserva-
tive in everything, the Indian cherishes even his
oppressors. Nevertheless the Khalji dynasty lasted
thirty years, and included six sovereigns; and
amongst them was one great ruler, whose reign of
twenty years contributed powerfully to the extension

of the Muslim dominion in India. Jalal-ad-din Firoz
Shah himself was the mildest king that ever held a
sceptre. An old man of seventy years, preoccupied
with preparations for the next world, he utterly refused to shed blood even for flagrant crimes. When
Chhaju, a nephew of Balban, led an army against
the sultan and the rebels were defeated and captured, Firoz forgave them freely and even kindly
commended their loyalty to the fallen house. A
thousand Thugs were arrested, but Firoz would not
consent to the execution of even the members of a
society of assassins, and merely banished them to
Bengal. Traitors, conspirators, thieves, alike found
mercy and forgiveness at the hands of the long-
suffering king, who had never stained his soul with
blood save in open battle, and then—as against the
Mongols on the Indus in 1292—he had shown himself
valiant enough. The execution of a fakir suspected
of magic and sedition was his only act of capital
punishment, and the exception was unfortunate:
superstitious folk saw in the black storm that darkened the world on the day of the holy man's death
under the elephant's foot, and in the famine that
ensued, omens of the fall of the crown.

The invincible clemency and humility of the sultan
were incomprehensible and exasperating to his followers. His was no ideal of kingship for an Eastern
world. They resented his simplicity of life and
even his familiar evenings with the old friends of
his former obscurity. They did not appreciate his
love of wit and learning. What they wanted was a
fighting king, inexorable in his judgments and unsur-

passable in his pomp. Sedition grew apace, and the sultan's nephew, Ala-ad-din, who had married his uncle's daughter, put himself at the head of the malcontents. After a course of dissimulation—it was easy to deceive the kind-hearted unsuspecting old man—the nephew drew the sultan unarmed and unguarded into a trap (1296), and as Firoz was stooping and actually fondling the traitor, Ala-ad-din gave the signal and one of the basest murders in history was accomplished. The aged king was slashed, thrown down, and beheaded, and his white hairs cast at the feet of the nephew he had trusted.

'Although Ala-ad-din,' writes Barani in just horror, 'reigned successfully for some years, and all things prospered to his wish, and though he had wives and children, family and adherents, wealth and grandeur, still he did not escape retribution for the blood of his patron. He shed more innocent blood than ever Pharaoh was guilty of. Fate at length placed a betrayer in his path, by whom his family was destroyed, and the retribution that fell upon it never had a parallel in any infidel land.' Anxious as the historian is to vindicate the justice of heaven, it must be admitted that it was slow to take effect. For twenty years Ala-ad-din ruled Hindustan with unprecedented vigour, and broadened the borders of his kingdom. He had already a reputation as a soldier, and found no opposition worth mentioning to his accession. The 'Queen of the World' (Malika-i-Jahan), widow of Firoz, a woman who is described as 'the silliest of the silly,' did indeed set up one of his sons as king at Delhi; but

Ibrahim[1] was a mere stripling, and his more capable brother Arkali Khan was away in Multan. The whole family were secured under promise of safety, and once caught were blinded and shut up. The mouths of the people were closed with gold. As Ala-ad-din marched to Delhi, a catapult showered pounds of 'gold stars' among the crowd at every halt. Recruits flocked to such a Pactolian stream, and before he reached the capital he had a following of 56,000 horse and 60,000 foot. The officers and nobles of the late king, to their credit, wavered before they threw in their lot with his assassin; but gold and numbers told in the end.

In November, 1296, Ala-ad-din entered Delhi unopposed, seated himself with all pomp upon the throne, and took up his residence in the Red Palace. His politic conciliation of the late king's officers was abandoned as soon as the royal family were safely caged; but the new sultan's wrath curiously fell upon those of the officials and nobles who had deserted Firoz and taken his murderer's money. All these were arrested and locked up. 'Some were blinded and some were killed. The wealth which they had received from Ala-ad-din, and their property, goods, and effects were all seized. Their houses were confiscated to the sultan, and their villages were brought into the public exchequer. Nothing was left to their children; their retainers and followers were taken in charge by the amirs who supported the new régime, and their establish-

[1] He occupied the throne long enough to issue coins. See LANE-POOLE, *Catalogue of Indian Coins : Sultans of Delhi*, pp. 37, 38.

ments were overthrown.' The only three of the
officers of Firoz who were spared were three who
had never abandoned him nor taken gold from his
supplanter. 'They alone remained safe, but all the
other Jalali nobles were cut up root and branch.'[1] It
was a lesson for turn-coats.

Sultan Ala-ad-din, who entered upon his reign
with these trenchant measures, was first and fore-

GOLD COIN OF ALA-AD-DIN, STRUCK AT DELHI, A.H. 698
(A.D. 1298-9).

most a soldier. So illiterate was he that he did not
even know how to read. But he knew how to command an army and to carry it through an arduous
campaign. Shortly before the murder of his uncle
he had won great glory by his conquests in the Deccan. Hitherto the utmost stretch of the kingdom
of Delhi had been across the plains from the Indus
to Bengal, and from the Himalayas to the Vindhya
mountains. No Mohammedan ruler had ventured

[1] We have the details of this period from Ziya-ad-din Barani, whose
father and uncle were both in Ala-ad-din's employ, the one as deputy
at Baran, the other at Karra and Oudh. The historian had thus
ample means of information; nevertheless he is not always trust-
worthy.

to cross the Narbada river and the Satpura hills into
the great plateau of southern India — Maharashtra,
the land of the Marathas, the seat of ancient mon-
archies and of strange tongues. In 1294 however,
after successfully dealing with insurrections in Bandelkhand and Malwa, Prince Ala-ad-din set out with
eight thousand men from his government of Karra
on the Jumna, bent upon more ambitious schemes.
Forcing his way through the forests of the Vindhya
range, by difficult passes, and ill-provided with men
or supplies, the prince carried his small force 700
miles to Devagiri, the capital of the Maratha raja,
which he took and pillaged unresisted. He had
given out that he had quarrelled with his uncle the
sultan of Delhi and was seeking service with one of
the southern rajas. The ruler of Devagiri was taken
by surprise and fled to one of the hill forts. Here,
by another lie, Ala-ad-din procured his submission
and the cession of Elichpur, and thus the Muslims
made their first step into the Deccan. It was from
the boundless treasures won in this campaign that
the conqueror procured the 'golden stars' which
lighted his road to Delhi.

The way to the south, thus opened, was never
again shut, though in the earliest years of his reign
Ala-ad-din had other work to do. After the suppression of the nobles came the invasions of those
human locusts the Mongols, who from 1296 to 1305
made repeated incursions over the Indus. The
worst of these was in 1297, when Kutlugh Khwaja,
starting from the Oxus and coming down the passes,
marched upon Delhi, driving before him such a

crowd of fugitives that the streets were blocked and
a state of famine prevailed. The capital was in no
condition for defence ; but when urged to temporize
with the enemy, the sultan indignantly refused : ' If I
were to follow your advice,' he said, ' how could I show
my face, how go into my harim, what store would the
people set by me, and where would be the daring and
courage needed to keep down my own turbulent
subjects? No: come what may, to-morrow I march
into the plain of Kili.' There, at a short distance
from Delhi, he found 200,000 Mongols drawn up.
The sultan's right wing under his gallant general
Zafar Khan, who had lately taken Siwistan from the
Mongols by a brilliant *coup de main*, broke the
enemy's left and pursued them off the field for many
miles, mowing them down at every stride. But the
left, under Ulugh Khan, the sultan's brother, jealously refused to support him, and Zafar was cut off
by an ambush. Despising the Mongol leader's offer
of quarter, he shot his last arrows, killing an enemy
at every twang of the bow, and was then surrounded
and slain. Though the right wing of the Delhi army
was thus rashly but gallantly lost, its valour was not
thrown away. The Mongols had seen enough of
the Indian horsemen, and in the night they vanished.

The Mongol inroads and the long establishment
of these nomads on the frontier led to the settlement of many of the strangers in India, and their
quarters at Delhi became known as Mughalpur or
Mongol-town. They adopted Islam and were called
'the new Muslims.' Their fate was miserable.
They were kept in great poverty, and eventually

7

became a danger to the state. A conspiracy among them was discovered, and Ala-ad-din commanded that the whole of the 'new Muslims' should be destroyed in one day. The order was carried out. Thirty to forty thousand wretched Mongols were killed in cold blood, their houses plundered, their wives and children cast adrift on the world. Cruelty towards women and children was a new experience in India. 'Up to this time,' says Barani, 'no hand had ever been laid upon wives or children on account of men's misdeeds.' To cast them into prison in revenge for their men's rebellion was one of the unenviable inventions which made 'the crafty cruelty' of Ala-ad-din detested.

There was undoubtedly a great deal of popular ferment, which may well have taxed the never easy temper of the sultan and provoked severe retaliation. We read of a dangerous mutiny of the troops in 1298, after a successful campaign in Gujarat, where the Hindus had again become independent. Their raja was driven away into the Deccan, and the idol which had been set up at Somnath, in the place of the linga destroyed by Mahmud of Ghazni, was cast down and carried to Delhi to be trodden under the feet of the faithful. An attempt to wrest from the army the legal fifth of the immense booty seized in this campaign led to the mutiny; some of the chief officers were killed, including a nephew of the sultan, and the soldiers were allowed perforce to keep their spoil.

In spite of such checks, the wealth and prosperity of the sultan were unbounded. To quote the words of the contemporary Barani: ' In the third year of his reign Ala-ad-din had little to do beyond attending to his pleasures, giving feasts, and holding festivals. One success followed another ; dispatches of victory came in from all sides ; every year he had two or three sons born ; affairs of state went on to his satisfaction, his treasury was overflowing, boxes and caskets of jewels and pearls were daily displayed before his eyes, he had numerous elephants in his stables and seventy thousand horses in the city and environs. . . . All this prosperity intoxicated him. Vast desires and great aims, far beyond him—or a hundred thousand of his like,—germinated in his brain, and he indulged fancies which had never occurred to any king before him. In his conceit, ignorance, and folly, he completely lost his balance, formed utterly impossible schemes, and cherished the wildest desires. He was a man of no learning and never associated with men of learning. He could not read or write a letter. He was bad-tempered, obstinate, and hard-hearted ; but the world smiled upon him, fortune befriended him, and his plans were usually successful, so that he only became the more reckless and arrogant.' He dreamed of emulating the blessed Prophet and founding a new religion, and he contemplated setting up a viceroy in Delhi and then (he would say in his cups at one of his frequent carousals) ' I will go forth, like Alexander, in search of conquest, and subdue the world.' He caused his title to be proclaimed in the Friday prayers and engraved on coins and inscriptions as ' the second Alexander.'

There were wiser men than Ala-ad-din, however, at
the royal revels, and one of them, an uncle of the
historian whom we have quoted, ventured to give
the sultan good advice. He counselled him to leave
religion-making to the prophets, and instead of
dreaming of universal conquest to set about reducing
the many cities and districts of Hindustan—such as
Rantambhor, Chitor, Chanderi, Malwa, Dhar, Ujjayn
—which were still in Hindu hands ; to ' close the road
to Multan ' against the Mongols ; and to give up wine
and junketing. Instead of resenting this frank advice, the sultan promised to adopt it, and handsomely
rewarded the honest counsellor. The very first step
towards mastering the still unsubdued parts of Hindustan showed Ala-ad-din that he had been living in
a fool's paradise. Instead of conquering the world
in the rôle of Alexander, he found that the mere siege
of Rantambhor taxed all his energies ; and whilst it
was dragging on for many months, other events happened which caused reflection. He was very nearly
assassinated in a conspiracy headed by a nephew,
who, leaving the sultan for dead, sat himself upon the
throne, received the homage of the nobles, and was
even about to enter his uncle's harim when the eunuch
Malik Dinar faced him at the door and swore he
should not go in until he produced Ala-ad-din's head.
The head all too soon appeared, set alertly as ever on
its own shoulders, as the living sultan showed himself to the army on a neighbouring knoll. The rebel
Akat Khan was beheaded instead of his uncle ; the
conspirators were scourged to death with wire thongs,
and their wives and children sent into captivity.

Nor was this the only sign of the times. Two other nephews raised the flag of insurrection, and though overpowered and cruelly blinded in their uncle's presence, their failure did not discourage imitation. A mad revolt broke out at Delhi, led by a slave, who set up an unfortunate grandson of Altamish as sultan, opened the prison doors, and rioted unchecked for days. Though the revolt was more like a mummery of the Abbot of Unreason than a political movement, and was suppressed with little difficulty, it showed the uneasiness and ferment of the people. Four mutinies or insurrections in a few months pointed to something amiss, and the sultan determined to find out the causes of the discontent. After many consultations day and night with his chief counsellors, it was resolved that the main reasons were to be found in the sultan's disregard of the doings of the people; in the prevalence of convivial meetings where open political talk followed the wine-cup; in the seditious intimacy of the various amirs and notables; and in the fact that too many people had a superfluity of wealth with which they could suborn adventurers and set revolts on foot.

Whether these results were really the opinions of the council or merely the *ex post facto* deductions of the historian who records them, they were at least acted upon by the king. The evil effects of too much wealth among his subjects particularly impressed him: it was a disease admitting of easy and gratifying cure. 'The sultan,' says Barani, 'ordered that wherever there was a village held by proprietary right *(milk)*, in free gift *(in'am)*, or as a religious

endowment *(wakf)*, it should by one stroke of the
pen be brought under the exchequer. The people
were pressed and amerced and money was exacted
from them on every kind of pretext. Many were left
without any money, till at length it came to pass that,
excepting maliks and amirs, officials, Multanis *(i. e.,*
large traders from Multan) and bankers, no one possessed even a trifle in cash So rigorous was the con-
fiscation that, beyond a few thousand tankas, all
the pensions, grants in land, and endowments in the
country were appropriated.   The people were all so
absorbed in obtaining the means of living that the
very name of rebellion was never mentioned.'

In the next place he organized a universal system
of espionage. ' No one could stir without his knowledge, and whatever happened in the houses of nobles, great men, and officials, was communicated to
the sultan by his reporter.' Nor were the reports
shelved ; they led to unpleasant explanations. ' The
system of reporting went to such a length that nobles dared not speak aloud even in " palaces of a
thousand columns," and if they had anything to say
they communicated by signs.   In their own houses,
night and day, the reports of the spies made them
tremble. No word or action that could provoke
censure or punishment was allowed to escape. The
transactions in the bazars, the buying and selling,
and the bargains made, were all reported to the sultan and were kept under control.'

Nor was this all. Remembering the warning of
his counsellors on the political influences of social
revels, ' he prohibited wine-drinking and wine-selling

as well as the use of beer and intoxicating drugs. Dicing was also forbidden. Many prohibitions of wine and beer were issued. Vintners and gamblers and beer-sellers were turned out of the city and the heavy taxes which had been levied upon them were abolished and lost to the treasury. The sultan directed that all the china and glass vessels of his banqueting room should be broken, and the fragments of them were thrown before the Badaun gate, where they rose in a heap. Jars and casks of wine were brought out of the royal cellars and emptied at the same gate in such abundance that mud and mire was produced as at the rainy season.' The sultan himself renounced all wine-drinking, and many of the better sort followed his example, but of course there was a great deal of clandestine bibbing among the dissolute, and these when detected were thrown into pits dug outside the Badaun gate, where many perished miserably. It was found impossible to wholly suppress the use of wine, and the sultan was obliged to wink at a certain amount of drinking, provided that it was private and the liquor brewed at home ; but public drinking was for the time stamped out.

Still further to discourage conspiracy and privy understandings, the sultan gave commands that ' noblemen and grandees should not visit at each other's houses, or give feasts, or hold meetings. They were forbidden to form alliances without consent from the throne and they were also prohibited from allowing people to resort to their houses. To such a length was this last prohibition carried that strangers could not gain admittance into a noble-man's house. Feasting and hospitality fell into total disuse. Through fear of the spies the nobles kept themselves quiet; they gave no parties and had lit-tle communication with each other. No man of a seditious, rebellious, or evil reputation was allowed to come near them. If they went to the palaces, they could not lay their heads together and sit down cosily and tell each other their troubles.'[1]

Besides this more than Russian system of espion-age among the Muslims, great and small, the sul-tan devised special measures against his Hindu subjects. The Hindu was to be so reduced as to be left unable to keep a horse to ride on, to carry arms, to wear fine clothes, or to enjoy any of the luxuries of life. He was taxed to the extent of half the produce of his land, and had to pay duties on all his buffaloes, goats, and other milch-cattle. The taxes were to be levied equally on rich and poor, at so much per acre, so much per animal. Any col-lectors or officers taking bribes were summarily dis-missed and heavily punished 'with sticks, pincers, the rack, imprisonment and chains.' The new rules were strictly carried out, so that one revenue officer would string together twenty Hindu notables and enforce payment by blows. No gold or silver, not even the betel nut, so cheering and stimulative to pleasure, was to be seen in a Hindu house, and the wives of the impoverished native officials were reduced to taking service in Muslim families.

[1] BARANI, *Tarikh - i - Firoz - Shahi*, ELLIOT and DOWSON, iii, 181–188.

Revenue officers came to be regarded as more deadly than the plague ; and to be a government clerk was a disgrace worse than death, insomuch that no Hindu would marry his daughter to such a man.

All these new enactments were promulgated without any reference to the legal authorities. Ala-ad-din held that government was one thing and law another, and so long as what he ordered seemed to him good he did not stop to inquire whether it was according to law. One day however he saw the learned kazi of Biana at court, and addressing him said he had some questions to ask to which he required truthful replies. 'The angel of my fate seems to be at hand,' cried the kazi in alarm, 'since your Majesty wishes to question me on matters of religion '—that is, religious law. The sultan promised not to kill him, and a curious conversation ensued.

Ala-ad-din wished first to know the legal position of Hindus, and the kazi replied 'They are called payers of tribute (*kharaj ghuzar*), and when the revenue officer demands silver from them, they should, without question and with all humility and respect, tender gold. If the officer throws dirt (or spits) into their mouths, they must unreluctantly open their mouths wide to receive it. By doing so they show their respect for the officer. The due submission of the non-Muslims (*zimmi*) is exhibited in this humble payment and by this throwing of dirt into their mouths. The glorification of Islam is a duty, and contempt of the Religion is vain. God holds them in contempt, for He says " keep them under in subjection." To keep the Hindus in abasement is especially a religious duty, because they are the most inveterate enemies of the Prophet.'

The sultan said that he did not understand a word of the learned man's argument, but he had taken his measures to reduce the pride of the Hindus, and had succeeded in making them so obedient that 'at my command they are ready to creep into holes like mice.' 'O Doctor,' he went on, 'thou art a learned man, but hast no experience of the world. I am an unlettered man, but I have seen a great deal. Be assured then that the Hindus will never become submissive and obedient till they are reduced to poverty. I have therefore given orders that just sufficient shall be left to them from year to year of corn, milk, and curds, but that they shall not be allowed to accumulate hoards of property.'

So far the law and the sultan were not at variance. When they spoke of the punishment of corrupt revenue officers, there was still not much difference; but when the sultan touched upon the delicate question of his own claim upon war-booty and upon the public treasury, the kazi said, ' The time of my death is at hand. If I answer your question honestly you will slay me, and if I give an untrue reply I shall hereafter go to hell.' Nevertheless he spoke out boldly and told Ala-ad-din that all treasure won by the armies of Islam belonged to the public treasury and not to the sultan, and that if he wished to follow the highest example of the most enlightened caliphs he would draw no more from the treasury for him-

self and his family and establishment than was al-
lotted to each fighting man in the army. This reply
excited the sultan's wrath and he said 'Dost thou
not fear my sword, when thou tellest me that all my
great expenditure on my harim is unlawful?' The
kazi replied, 'I do fear your Majesty's sword, and I
look upon this turban as my winding sheet; but
your Majesty questions me about the law, and I answer to the best of my ability. If however you ask
my advice in a political point of view, then I say that
whatever your Majesty spends upon your harim no
doubt tends to raise your dignity in the eyes of
men ; and the exaltation of a king's dignity is essential to good policy.'

After many questions and answers, the sultan said
to the kazi, 'You have declared my proceedings in
these matters to be unlawful. Now see how I act.
When troopers do not appear at the muster, I order
three years' pay to be taken from them. I place wine-
drinkers and wine-sellers in the pits. If a man de-
bauches another man's wife I effectually prevent him
from again committing such an offence and the woman I cause to be killed. Rebels, good and bad, old
hands or novices, I slay ; their wives and children I
reduce to beggary and ruin. Extortion I punish
with the torture of the pincers and the stick, and I
keep the extortioner in prison, in chains and fetters,
until every halfpenny is restored. Political prisoners I confine and chastise. Wilt thou say all this is
unlawful?'

Then the kazi rose and went to the entrance of the
room, placed his forehead on the ground, and cried

with a loud voice,—' My liege, send your unworthy servant to prison, or order me to be cut in two, but *all* this is unlawful and finds no support in the sayings of the Prophet or in the expositions of the learned.' The sultan said nothing, but put on his slippers and went into his harim. The kazi went home, took a last farewell of his family, and performed the ablutions required in one about to die. Then he bravely returned to court ; when to his amazement the sultan gave him his own robe and a thousand tankas, with these words, ' Although I have not studied the Science or the Book, I am a Muslim of a Muslim stock. To prevent rebellion, in which thousands perish, I issue such orders as I conceive to be for the good of the state and the benefit of the people. Men are heedless, contumacious, and disobedient to my commands. I am then compelled to be severe to bring them into obedience. I do not know whether this is lawful or unlawful : whatever I think to be for the good of the state or opportune for the emergency, that I decree.'

We have given most of Barani's account of this interview and of Ala-ad-din's methods of administration because they present a valuable picture of Muslim rule in India, and such intimate views are rare in Eastern chronicles. The historian may perhaps have described what he himself thought rather than what the sultan or the kazi really said; but as his relations were officials in Ala-ad-din's service, he had good means of knowing the truth. The sultan did not stop at repressive measures : he interfered with trade, and even meddled with the laws of supply and

demand. The occasion for these innovations was
presented by an external danger. Another invasion
of the Mongols in 1303, when they again threatened
Delhi, camped on the Jumna, blocked the roads, and
occupied the suburbs for two months, alarmed the
sultan. The Mongols retired without taking the capital, but not on account of any success of the Indian
army. Never in fact had Delhi been less protected.
The sultan had just returned from taking the Rajput stronghold of Chitor, the siege of which in the
rainy season had almost prostrated his troops. A
second army sent to the Deccan to conquer Warangal in the same unfavourable season had suffered even
more severely, and returned diminished and discouraged. There was no force at his command capable
of meeting the Mongols in the field, and their departure without conquering the capital was regarded
as nothing less than a miracle.

This narrow escape concentrated Ala-ad-din's care
upon his defences. Abandoning for the time all
thought of further conquest, he settled himself at
his new palace-fortress of Siri—one of the royal suburbs which, like Kilughari, afterwards 'Newtown,'
(Shahr-i-nau), were growing up round the capital
— and set to work at preparations for repelling
attack. He repaired and added to the forts of
Delhi, constructed siege-engines, stone-slings and
mangonels, collected arms and stores. Strong garrisons were placed at Samana and Dipalpur, which
had become the Muslim outposts on the threatened
north-west frontier — for the Mongols still practically held the Panjab—and tried generals were set

in command of all the posts on the Mongol track.
The main difficulty was how to increase the army
and maintain it in efficient order,— well-mounted,
well-armed, well-trained, and well-supplied with
archers. The pay of the soldier was fixed at

THE GATEWAY OF ALA-AD-DIN IN THE MOSQUE AT DELHI.

234 *tankas* (nearly £24), with an addition of 78
tankas (£8) for those who contributed two horses.
In order to enable the soldier to live on this
pay, support his family, and furnish himself with
horses and arms, the sultan ventured upon experiments in political economy. He resolved to keep

down the cost of necessaries, and enacted that thenceforth there should be a fixed price for food. The principal items were thus fixed in the new tariff : Wheat, 7½ *jitals* (nearly 3d) per *man* (about a quarter, 28 lbs.) ; barley, 1½d ; rice, 2d ; pulse, 2d ; lentil, 1d. This scale of prices was maintained as long as Ala-ad-din lived. As a matter of fact it may be taken to represent the average open market price in country towns, and the sultan's measures were evidently intended to counteract the tendency to inflated prices at the metropolis caused by an inadequate supply of provisions.

To increase this supply and encourage larger importation he gave orders that the ' Khalisa ' or crown villages of the Doab and some other parts should pay their taxes in kind, and with these contributions he accumulated vast stores of grain in Delhi, from which in times of scarcity corn was sold at the tariff price to the inhabitants. The carriers of the kingdom were registered, and encouraged to bring corn from the villages at the fixed price. Any attempts at regrating or holding up corn and selling at enhanced prices were sternly put down. Inspectors watched the markets, and if prices rose by so much as a farthing the overseer received twenty stripes with a stick ; the offence seldom recurred. Short weight was checked by the effectual method of carving from the hams of the unjust dealer a piece of flesh equivalent to the deficit in the weight of what he had sold. Everything was set down in the tariff : vegetables, fruits, sugar, oil, horses, slaves, caps, shoes, combs, and needles ; and we learn that a serving girl cost 5 to 12 tankas, a concubine 20 to 40, slave labourers 10 to 15, handsome pages 20 to 30, and so forth.

These various measures show that the sultan, though he might be wrong-headed and disdainful of the law, was a man of sense and determination, who knew his own mind, saw the necessities of the situation, met them by his own methods, and carried out those methods with persistence. They were undoubtedly successful. We hear of no more rebellions, and when next the Mongols tried issues with the sultan's new army they were effectually defeated. 'The armies of Islam were everywhere triumphant over them. Many thousands were taken prisoners, and were brought with ropes round their necks to Delhi, where they were cast under the feet of elephants. Their heads were piled up into pyramids or built into towers.' It is related in sober fact that the blood and bones of the Mongols formed part of the building materials of the new walls and gates and defences with which the sultan improved the capital.[1] On one of the occasions of a Mongol inroad not a man went back alive, and the enemy ' conceived such a fear and dread of the army of Islam that all fancy for coming to Hindustan was washed out of their breasts. All fear of the Mongols entirely departed from Delhi and the neighbouring provinces. Perfect security was everywhere felt, and the rayats carried on their agriculture in peace.'[2] This was largely due to the

---

[1] It was after these repeated successes that the unfortunate Mongols who had settled in the suburbs of Delhi were massacred in Mughalpur as related above.   [2] BARANI, *l. c.*, iii, 199.

successful frontier fighting of Ghazi Malik, afterwards Sultan Taghlak, the governor of the Panjab, a worthy successor of Sher Khan.

Freed by these reforms from the fear of conspiracy and invasion, Sultan Ala-ad-din resumed his plans of conquest. He had reduced two great Hindu fortresses, Rantambhor and Chitor, though at enormous cost. He now turned again towards the Deccan. An army under Malik Kafur Hazardinari (the ' five-hundred guinea man '), a handsome castrato who had fascinated the sultan, was sent in 1308 to recover Devagiri, where the Yadava ruler, Rama Deva had reasserted his independence and neglected to pay the tribute he promised at the time of Ala-ad-din's conquest fifteen years before. The campaign was successful. Kafur, assisted by the muster-master Khwaja Hajji, laid the country waste, took much booty, and brought the rebel Hindu and his sons to Delhi. The sultan treated the captive raja with all honour, gave him a royal canopy and the style of ' Kings of Kings,' and presenting him with a lac of tankas (£10,000) sent him back to govern Devagiri as his vassal.

In the following year Kafur and Hajji were dispatched on a more ambitious errand : they were ordered to take the fort of Warangal, in Telingana, towards the eastern Ghats, the capital of the Kakatiya rajas. On the march through his territories Rama Deva displayed the dutiful behaviour of a rayat, assisted the army in every way, and contributed a contingent of Marathas, thus justifying the sultan's confidence. The mud fort of Warangal was taken by assault, the stone fort was invested, and

8

the raja surrendered his treasures and agreed to pay tribute. Kafur returned to Delhi with a booty of a hundred elephants, 7,000 horses, and quantities of jewels. In 1310 the same generals pushed their way to the Malabar coast, took the old capital of Dvara-samudra, almost as far south as Mysore, destroyed the great temple of the golden idols in Ma'bar,[1] bringing home in the early part of 1311 no less than 612 elephants, 20,000 horses, coffers of precious stones and pearls, and 96,000 *mans* of gold, which, taking the *man* at no more than ¼ cwt., amounts to 1200 tons of gold. Considering the vast wealth of the Hindu shrines, which had never before been despoiled in the Deccan, the sum, though doubtless exaggerated, is not absolutely incredible. The treasure was brought to the palace of Siri, and the sultan presented the officers of the fortunate campaign with gifts of gold by the hundredweight. The rajas of Devagiri and Warangal paid their trib-

---

[1] Kafur founded a mosque on the coast. If it was the same mosque ' built by the officers of Sultan Ala-ad-din ' at ' Seet Bunda Ramessar,' which Firishta says was repaired by the Bahmanid Sultan Mujahid about 1378, it must have been on the Malabar or west coast of India. ' Ramessar ' cannot be Ramesvara, which is on the Coromandel coast opposite Ceylon. Cape Ramas, south of Goa, as suggested by Briggs, seems a more probable identification. Ma'bar, which Wassaf defines as extending from Kulam (Quilon) to Nilawar (Nileswara) has usually been identified with the Coromandel or east coast. But this Persian traveller, who wrote about 1300, not only defines Ma'bar as above stated, but describes it immediately after Gujarat, and states that Persian horses were exported ' to Ma'bar, Kambayat (Cambay), and other ports in their neighbourhood' (ELLIOT and DOWSON, iii, 33). The fact that Kafur marched on to Ma'bar from Dvara-samudra agrees with Wassaf's definition.

ute, and the northern part of the Deccan acknow-
ledged the suzerainty of Delhi.

This was the climax of Ala-ad-din's reign. He
had done much. The Mongols were no longer the
terror of the Panjab. The army was never stronger,
as its victories in the Deccan proved, and never
cheaper, owing to the regulated price of provisions.
Rebellion had ceased to raise its head, and the severity of its repression had procured a security to
the agriculturist and safety of the roads such as had
never been known before. The control of the markets not only insured cheap food at the capital but
honest dealing, according to Barani,—but the eulogy
is probably relative. Temperance had been forced
upon the people, and, with the example of the sober
court, men of learning and piety abounded. Such
results testify to the greatness of a remarkable king.

The inevitable and swift reaction came from the
sultan's own faults, exaggerated by an increasing disease. His violent temper led him to displace experienced governors; his infatuation for Kafur bred
envy and disunion and caused the death or imprisonment of trusted counsellors. His sons, prematurely
emancipated from the schoolroom, took to drink and
debauchery. The disputes of the nobles and the
riotous behaviour of the heir encouraged revolts on
all sides. In the midst of the confusion Ala-ad-din
died (January, 1316) of a dropsy. A bloody and
unscrupulous tyrant, none may refuse him the title
of a strong and capable ruler.

The death of the strong man was followed by the
results too common in Eastern history. There was

no one fit to stand in his place. The favourite Kafur
seized upon the government, and set up Shihab-ad-
din Omar, a child of six years, on his father's throne.
Two elder sons of the late king were deprived of
sight with atrocious cruelty. The chief queen was
robbed and turned out of the palace. The miscreant
was even plotting a general massacre of the great
nobles, when one night some foot soldiers fortunately
contrived to murder him in his bedroom. His regency had lasted scarcely more than five weeks.
Another son of Ala-ad-din, after acting for a few
months as governor over his infant brother, sent him
away blinded, and took the throne himself in April,
1316, with the title of Kutb-ad-din Mubarak Shah.

No more violent contrast to the stern and capable
father could be imagined. Mubarak was an easy-
going good-tempered youth of seventeen, the slave
of his own pleasures, and everything reverted to the
old lax way. The genial new king opened the gaols
and let seventeen thousand prisoners loose; presented the army with six months' pay; distributed
his largesse and grants promiscuously. All the new
taxes and penalties were abolished, and all dread of
the sultan and of the revenue officer's scourge vanished. 'Men were no longer in doubt and fear
of hearing " Do this, but don't do that; say this,
but don't say that; hide this, but don't hide that;
eat this, but don't eat that; sell such as this,
but don't sell things like that; act like this,
but don't act like that." ' Everyone took his ease
and indulged his tastes, like his sovereign. The
wine-shops were re-opened and all the world drank.

Prices went up, the new tariff was forgotten, and the bazar people, rejoicing at the death of their persecutor, cheated and fleeced as they listed. Labourers' wages rose twenty-five per cent.; bribery, extortion, and peculation flourished. The Hindus, relieved of the recent exactions, were 'beside themselves with joy. They who had plucked the green ears of corn because they could not get bread, who had not a decent garment, and had been so harassed and beaten that they had not even time to scratch their heads, now put on fine apparel, rode on horseback, and shot their arrows.' In short everyone did as he pleased and enjoyed himself to the full, and India was her old happy-go-lucky self again.

The sultan set his subjects a bad example. Utterly careless and unspeakably depraved, he threw himself heart and soul into all the wretchlessness of unclean living. Openly by night and by day he displayed his contempt for decency. So eager was the demand at court for mistresses that the price of a pretty girl, who could be bought in the late reign for a couple of pounds, ran up to as much as £200. Like his father the young sultan had a vile favourite, a Hindu Parwani, a pariah of the lowest class from Gujarat, whom he styled Khusru Khan, and under his corrupt influence Mubarak became more shameless than ever: his very speech became foul and obscene, he tricked himself in woman's clothes, and let his major domo indulge his horseplay upon the nobles in full court stark naked. No more was the sultan seen at the public prayers in the mosque of his forefathers; the fast of Ramazan was openly violated.

With this wholesale abandonment of religion and morals the reckless youth's temper began to show the ferocity of his vindictive father. When Hari-pala Deva, the son of the late Rama Deva, rebelled at Devagiri, Mubarak had him flayed alive. When the king's cousin Asad-ad-din, indignant at the way things were going, got up a conspiracy and was be-trayed, not only were the plotters beheaded in front of the royal tent, but twenty-nine young brothers of the leader, children wholly innocent of the plot, were slaughtered like sheep, and the women of the family were turned out homeless into the streets. His own brothers did not escape his fury. Three of them, including the ex-child-king, were in the fort of Gwaliar, blinded and helpless. All three were mur-dered. The governor of Gujarat was executed for no fault; the new Hindu raja of Devagiri, Yak-lakhi, revolted, and had his nose and ears cut off; the old and tried nobles of the late sultan, by the intrigues of the Hindu pariah, were disgraced, ban-ished, blinded, imprisoned, and scourged. Finally one night in March, 1321, the favourite murdered his master, and the headless trunk of Mubarak Shah was seen by the light of torches falling from one of the palace windows. He amply deserved his fate.

Then began a hideous reign of terror. Khusru mounted the throne as Sultan Nasir-ad-din, 'the Helper of the Faith,' and there followed an orgy of blood and violence such as had never before been heard of in India. The harim of the sultan was brutally ravished; everyone worth killing was killed in the palace; three days after the murder of his sovereign Khusru took to wife the queen of his victim, a Hindu princess to whom such an alliance was an unspeakable profanation ; the wives and daughters of the royal family and of the great nobles were delivered over to the scum of Khusru's pariahs ; ' the flames of bloodshed and brutality reddened the sky.' The holy Koran was desecrated ; idols were set up in the mosques. The reign of an unclean pariah was as revolting to the Hindus themselves as to the Muslims. Had a Rajput attempted to rally the still powerful forces of his countrymen and to make a bid for the throne, the chaos of the times might have given him a chance of success. The stubborn defence of Rantambhor and Chitor showed that the Hindu chiefs were far from subdued. But no Indian of any race or creed, save the outcast sweepers of his own degraded and despised class, would follow a Parwani.

The hope of the Muslims lay in one man, the only man of whom the Hindu upstart went in abject fear. This was Taghlak, the warden of the marches, who had held the frontier against the Mongols since the great days of Ala-ad-din's victories, and had routed them in a score of battles.[1] Taghlak placed himself at the head of all that was left of the old nobility and set out from his frontier post to save Delhi from its obscene·devourer. The affrighted pariah collected all the troops he could muster, emptied the

[1] Ibn-Batuta in 1340 saw an inscription of Taghlak's on the mosque at Multan which ran ' Twenty-nine times have I fought with the Tatars and routed them and hence am I called al-Malik al-Ghazi ' (Ed. DEFREMERY, iii, 202).

treasury of every farthing, and scattered all the hoard among the soldiers. Most of the Muslims took his money, heartily cursed the giver, and went to their homes: they were not the men to take up arms against Ghazi Taghlak, the champion of the faith. With his Hindus and such few contemptible Mohammedans as his gold could buy, Khusru attempted to withstand his enemy's march; but his forces were utterly routed, the Parwanis were slaughtered wherever they were found, and their abject master was caught hiding in a garden, and beheaded (August, 1321). So ended four months of the worst tyranny that India ever knew.

Taghlak assembled the nobles and officers and bade them bring forward any scion of the royal family that might have survived, and set him on the throne. There was not one left. 'O Ghazi Malik,' they shouted with one voice, 'for many years thou hast been our buckler against the Mongols and hast warded them away from our country. Now thou hast done a faithful work which will be recorded in history : thou hast delivered the Muslims from the yoke of Hindus and pariahs, hast avenged our benefactors and earned the gratitude of rich and poor. Be our king.' And they all did homage to the new sultan.

CHAPTER VI

A MAN OF IDEAS

MOHAMMAD TAGHLAK

1321–1388

THE old soldier did not belie his reputation. The trusty warden of the marches proved a just, high-minded, and vigorous king. Under his firm hand order was restored as if by magic. Everything possible was done to repair the misfortunes of the unhappy ladies of the late court, and to punish their persecutors. Orders were given to reduce the taxation on agricultural lands to a tenth or eleventh of the produce, and to encourage the tillers to greater production. The Hindus were more heavily taxed, yet not to the verge of poverty. In the verse of Amir Khusru:

'Wisdom and prudence in all that he did were revealed;
  The faculties' hoods seemed under his crown concealed.'

Peace and prosperity once more reigned in Hindustan, and two expeditions under Taghlak Shah's eldest son Prince Jauna, then known as Ulugh

Khan, recovered the Deccan provinces as far as Telingana, which the recent troubles had encouraged to revolt. Taghlak himself led his army to Bengal, which had never been even nominally subject to Delhi since the death of Balban, and there he received the homage of the provincial viceroy of Lakhnauti, Nasir-ad-din (grandson of Balban's son Bughra Khan), and carried in chains to Delhi his recalcitrant brother Bahadur Shah, who styled himself king in eastern Bengal. On his return from this expedition the gallant old sultan met his death (1325) by the fall of a roof which crushed him beneath its ruins. His body was found arched over his favourite child whom he strove in his last moments to protect. There seems little doubt that the catastrophe was treacherously planned by his eldest son.[1]

It is in this son, Prince Jauna, who ascended the throne as the Sultan al-Mujahid Mohammad ibn Taghlak, that the main interest of the Karauna[2] dynasty abides. In each of the three dynasties that ruled India throughout the thirteenth and fourteenth centuries there was one conspicuously remarkable figure. Among the slave kings it was Balban, the man of action; among the Khaljis it was Ala-

---

[1] It is so asserted by the Moorish traveller Ibn-Batuta, who was at Delhi sixteen years later, and had his information from an eye-witness. See DEFREMERY'S ed., iii, 212–214.

[2] Karauna is evidently Marco Polo's *Caraonas* (ed. YULE, i, 99), explained as meaning half-breeds, 'sons of Indian (possibly Biluchi) mothers by Tatar fathers.' The Karawina, described by Wassaf as the artillerymen of the Chaghatai army in Khurasan, may be the same race, and the Mongols used to nickname the Chaghatai Turks Karawanas (ROSS, *Tarikh-i-Rashidi*, 76*, 77*).

123   FORT OF TAGHLAKABAD, AT DELHI, ENCLOSING TOMB OF TAGHLAK SHAK.

ad-din, the crude but daring political economist;
among the Karaunas it was Mohammad Taghlak,[1]
the man of ideas. The history of the East, as we
have said, centres in its kings, and the history of
Eastern dynasties is apt to consist of the rise of one
great man and the decay of his successors. Mohammad Taghlak was the most striking figure in mediæval India. He was a man with ideas far beyond his
age. Ala-ad-din had brought a vigorous but uncultivated mind to bear upon the problems of government ; Mohammad Taghlak was even more daring
in his plans, but they were the ideals of a man of
trained intellect and tutored imagination. He was
perfect in the humanities of his day, a keen student
of Persian poetry—the Latin of Indian education,—
a master of style, supremely eloquent in an age of
rhetoric, a philosopher, trained in logic and Greek
metaphysics, with whom scholars feared to argue, a
mathematician and a lover of science. The contemporary writers extol his skill in composition and his
exquisite calligraphy, and his beautiful coinage bears
witness to his critical taste in the art of engrossing
the Arabic character, which he read and understood
though he could not speak the language fluently.

In short he was complete in all that high culture
could give in that age and country, and he added to
the finish of his training a natural genius for original
conception, a marvellous memory, and an indomitable will. His idea of a central capital, and his plan
of a nominal token currency, like most of his schemes,

---

[1] So commonly called, for Mohammad-i-Taghlak, the Persian
equivalent of the Arabic Mohammad ibn (son of) Taghlak.

were good ; but he made no allowance for the native dislike of innovations, he hurried his novel measures without patience for the slow adoption of the people, and when they grew discontented and rebelled he punished them without ruth. To him what seemed good must be done at once, and when it proved impossible or unsuccessful his disappointment reached the verge of frenzy, and he wreaked his wrath indiscriminately upon the unhappy offenders who could not keep pace with his imagination. Hence with the best intentions, excellent ideas, but no balance or patience, no sense of proportion, Mohammad Taghlak was a transcendent failure. His reign was one long series of revolts, savagely repressed ; his subjects, whom he wished to benefit and on whom he lavished his treasure, grew to loathe him ; all his schemes came to nothing, and when after twenty-six years he died of a fever on the banks of the Indus, he left a shattered empire and an impoverished and rebellious people.

Yet he began his reign with everything in his favour. He followed a deeply revered father, and he had a high reputation of his own. He was known to be a great general, and his private life was temperate and even austere. All India was quiet, and the distant provinces had been recovered. The suspicion that his father's sudden end was deliberately planned by the son may have set the people against him ; but neither Barani nor Firishta support the story, and it is not certain that it was generally believed. Even if it were, such murders were too common to form an ineffaceable stigma. Mohammad

Taghlak failed by his own mistaken government, not on account of an initial crime.

As a rule he never consulted anybody, and formed his projects unassisted; but one day he sent for the historian Barani, who was often in attendance at court, and frankly discussed affairs with him. ' My kingdom is diseased,' he complained, ' and no treatment cures it. The physician cures the headache, and fever follows; he strives to allay the fever, and something else supervenes. So in my kingdom disorders have broken out; if I suppress them in one place, they appear in another; if I allay them in one district, another becomes disturbed. What have former kings said about these disorders?' The man of history cited instances of the abdication of kings in favour of their sons, or of a sovereign's retirement from the affairs of state, which were left to wise vezirs. The sultan seemed to approve the idea of abdication, adding ' At present I am angry with my subjects and they are aggrieved with me. The people are acquainted with my feelings, and I am aware of their misery and wretchedness. No treatment that I employ is of any benefit. My remedy for rebels is the sword. I employ punishment and use the sword, so that a cure may be effected by suffering. The more the people resist, the more I inflict chastisement.'

The series of tortures and executions described by Ibn-Batuta is too horrible to relate, and the frequent scenes at Delhi, which the Moorish traveller witnessed, where the trained elephants, with tusks armed with iron blades, tossed the victims in the air, trampled them under foot, and carved them into slices, make one's blood run cold. The sultan's own brother and nephew did not escape his ferocity: suspected of treason the former was beheaded in the presence of his brother; the nephew fled to the raja of Kampila, brought destruction upon his protector, and when caught himself, was flayed and roasted alive, and his cooked flesh sent to his family. One can hardly believe that such enormities could have been committed by a man of Mohammad Taghlak's refinement.

Apart from such monstrous barbarities, his great mistake — a capital error in an Eastern country — was that he could not let well or ill alone. He was too clever not to see the ills, but not clever enough to know that they were better undisturbed. *Quieta non movere* was never his motto: rather was it 'be instant in season and (especially) out of season.' On the whole his was a fine principle, a high ideal; but the reaction when he found his ideal unattainable was violent and deplorable. Ibn-Batuta knew him well in the latter part of his reign, and was well able to judge his character. This is his portrait of the sultan :—

'This king is of all men the one who most loves to dispense gifts and to shed blood. His gateway is never free from a beggar whom he has relieved and a corpse which he has slain. Tales are spread abroad among the people of his generosity and courage, as of his bloodshed and vindictiveness towards offenders. With all this he is the humblest of men and the most eager to show justice and truth. The rites of religion find full observance with him, and he is strict in the matter of prayer and in punishing its neglect. . . . But what is pre-eminent in him is generosity.'

The boundless prodigality of the sultan was indeed one of the causes of his troubles. Even the wealth of India, reinforced by the spoils brought back from the Hindu cities of the Deccan, now again under control, could not meet the extravagance of his

GOLD COIN OF MOHAMMAD TAGHLAK, STRUCK AT DELHI,
A.H. 726 (A.D. 1326).

generosity and the magnificence of his court. To foreigners he was specially hospitable, preferring them to natives, says the Moorish traveller, who himself enjoyed the sultan's high favour and was presented with fiefs and large sums of money, appointed to a judgeship, and finally sent as Mohammad's ambassador to China. When distinguished strangers came to Delhi, the sultan would settle upon them the revenues of so many villages or districts, which maintained them in luxury during their visit and enabled them to go home in affluence. The almost incredible largesse he scattered among these visitors and among learned men, poets, officials, and *umadwars* of all degrees, impoverished the treasury which the tranquil prosperity of his father's brief reign had replenished, and the immense expeditions which the sultan prepared for visionary foreign conquests completed the ruin of his finances. His project of conquering Persia kept a huge army standing idle, and another dream of invading China led to a disastrous check in the passes of the Himalayas where money and men were spilt like water.

The drain on the treasury compelled fresh taxation, and there is no doubt that an oppressive fiscal system in a country where the margin of agricultural profit is minute was the chief rock upon which Mohammad Taghlak's government split. The first project which the sultan formed (says Barani), and which led to the ruin of the country and the decay of the people, was an attempt to get five or ten per cent. more tribute from the lands in the Doab, the fertile plain between the Ganges and the Jumna. He introduced oppressive cesses and made stoppages from the land returns until the backs of the rayats were broken. The cesses were collected so rigorously that the peasants were reduced to beggary. The rich became rebels, and the lands fell out of cultivation. The effects spread to other provinces; the peasants became alarmed, lost confidence, abandoned their lands, burned their stacks, turned their cattle loose, and took to the jungles. Irritated at the failure of the revenue the sultan hunted the wretched Hindus like wild beasts, ringed them in the jungles as if they were tigers, and closing in massacred them wholesale. The Doab, Kanauj, and all the country as far as Dalamau, were laid waste and

9

every man captured was killed and his head hung on
the rampart of a town.   Landowners and village
chiefs were sacrificed as well as humble rayats.   A
deficiency of the seasonable rains aggravated the
distress, and famine stalked about the land and
mowed down the unhappy people for years.

It was partly the melancholy condition of Hindustan, but still more the inconvenience of a distant
northern capital to an empire which was spreading
more and more in the Deccan, that induced the
sultan to take the step of transferring the seat of
government to Devagiri, which he now renamed
Daulatabad, 'the empire-city,' in the Maratha country not far from Poona.   The insecurity of the roads,
as well as the long distances, made Delhi an unsuit-
able centre, and we find that sometimes the revenue
of the Deccan was allowed to accumulate for years
at Daulatabad from sheer inability to transport it
safely to the capital.   Whether the Maratha city
would have been more convenient may be questioned, at least for the eastern part of the empire,
but for the west and south it might have answered
well enough.   There was nothing preposterous in
the sultan's plan.   The Deccan provinces — for it
was now divided into four — extended as far south
as Kulbarga near the Bhima tributary of the Krishna
river, and though it is not easy to define their eastward boundary it probably reached to the Godaveri,
though Telingana was rather a tributary state than
a part of the empire.

Had he contented himself with merely shifting
the official court, the change would have been rea-

sonable and practical. But he must needs transport the whole population of Delhi summarily and *en masse* to the new capital. What this meant may be realized when it is remembered that the Delhi which Ibn-Batuta described was a vast city, ten miles across, composed of successive suburbs built round the forts and palaces of different kings. There was old Delhi, the city of the Ghazni rulers; near by stood Siri, afterwards named the Dar-el-Khilafa, 'Abode of the Caliphate,' founded by Ala-ad-din; Taghlakabad was the suburb built by the sultan's father, whose palace was roofed with glittering gilt tiles (*karamida mudhahhaba*); and Jahanpanah, 'the Refuge of the World,' was the name given to the new city which Mohammad Taghlak dominated from his stately palace. The great wall of old Delhi, which astonished the Moorish visitor by its thickness and its ingenious arrangement of guardrooms and magazines, had twenty-eight gates; and the great mosque, the Kutb Minar, and the splendid palaces, excited the admiration of the traveller who had seen all the cities of the East and their wonders. He never tires of expatiating on the grandeur of the royal receptions and stately pageants in the 'thousand columned' hall of 'the World's Refuge.' Yet the Delhi he saw was a city slowly recovering from what seemed to be a deathblow. All the people had been forcibly removed years before, and the place was still comparatively empty. The heart-broken inhabitants were made to give up their familiar homes and cherished associations, and, taking with them their servants and their children and such belongings as they

could carry, to trudge the weary march of seven
hundred miles to a strange country which could
never replace the beautiful city where they were born
and to which they were bound by every tie of love
and memory.   Many died on the way, and of those
who reached Daulatabad few could resist the home-
sickness and despondency that kill the Indian in
exile.   They were chiefly Muslims, but they were
forced to live in an 'infidel' country, and they gave
up the ghost in passive despair.   The new capital
became the nucleus of the cemeteries of the exiles.

The ill-considered plan had failed: Daulatabad
was a monument of misdirected energy.   The long
road, a forty days' journey, between Delhi and the
new capital, laid out with infinite care, bordered
with trees all the way like an avenue in a park, with
frequent inns and rest-houses, only beckoned the
exiles home.   The sultan, who had the wisdom to
recognize his failure, ordered the people back to
Delhi, but few survived to return.   He imported
'learned men and gentlemen, traders and landholders' from the country to repopulate the deserted
capital; but they did not flourish, and it was long
before Delhi recovered its prosperity.   The Moor
found the great suburbs sparsely occupied and the
city still seemed almost deserted.

It is but just to the hasty sultan to admit that he
did his best to remedy some of his mistakes.   If he
could not repeople Delhi at a stroke with the rapidity
with which he had emptied it, he did much to mitigate the distress caused by famine and excessive
taxation.   He abolished (in 1341) all taxes beyond

the legal alms and the government tithes, and himself sat twice a week to receive the complaints of the
oppressed. He distributed daily food to all the
people of Delhi for six months in a time of scarcity,
and he organized an excellent system of government
loans to agriculturists which would have been of
great service but for the dishonesty of the overseers.
To meet the heavy drain upon the treasury he made
his famous experiment of a token currency, which
raised a storm as furious as that which raged round
Wood's halfpence in the days of Swift. He may
have taken the idea from the paper-money issued by
Khubilai Khan in China, or from the paper notes
with which a Mongol khan of Persia had recently
endeavoured to cheat his subjects. But Mohammad
Taghlak's forced currency was not intended to de-
fraud, and as a matter of fact accidentally enriched the
people, whilst the substitution of minted copper for
paper was a new idea. The copper token was to
pass at the value of the contemporary silver tanka,
and of course its acceptance depended upon the
credit of the public treasury. Mohammad Taghlak
has been called 'the Prince of Moneyers,' and there
is no doubt that he devoted much attention to his
coinage and dealt with it in a scientific way. 'So
important indeed,' says the greatest authority on
Indian numismatics,[1] 'did he consider all matters
connected with the public currency that one of the
earliest acts of his reign was to remodel the coinage,
to adjust its divisions to the altered relative values of

[1] E. Thomas, *Chronicles of the Pathan Kings of Delhi* (1871),
207, 233.

the precious metals, and to originate new and more
exact representations of the subordinate circulation.
The leading motive . . . seems to have been
the utilization of the stores of gold which filled the
sultan's treasuries; and, without proposing to introduce a definite gold standard, which under the surrounding circumstances would doubtless have proved
impracticable, he appears to have aimed at a large
expansion of the currency of the land by direct
means, associated with an equitable revision of the
basis of exchange between gold and silver, which
had been disturbed by the large accessions of the
former from the Deccan, unaccompanied by any
proportionate addition to the supply of the latter.'

He was thus an expert in currency questions, and
when he introduced his copper tokens he was taking
a step of which he should have known the consequences. The curious point is that, whilst no doubt

BRASS MONEY OF MOHAMMAD TAGHLAK STRUCK AT DELHI,
A. H. 731 (1330–31 A.D.)

fully aware that the value of the token depended
upon the credit of the treasury, he forgot that
it was absolutely essential to the success of his
innovation that none but the state should issue
the tokens. In those days however there was no
milling or other device of costly machinery to dis-

tinguish the issues of the royal mint from private
forgeries. To forge in gold was expensive, but any
skilled Hindu engraver could copy the inscriptions
and strike copper tokens of the value of tankas in
his own behalf. The result was natural. 'The promulgation of this edict,' says Barani, 'turned the
house of every Hindu into a mint, and the Hindus
of the various provinces coined crors and lacs[1] of
copper coins. With these they paid their tribute,
and with these they purchased horses, arms, and fine
things of all kinds. The rajas, village headmen, and
landowners grew rich upon these copper coins, but
the state was impoverished. In those places where
fear of the sultan's edict prevailed, the gold tanka
rose to be worth a hundred of the [token] tankas.
Every goldsmith struck copper coins in his work-
shop, and the treasury was filled with these tokens.
So low did they fall [after a time] that they were
not valued more than pebbles or potsherds. The
old coin, from its great scarcity, rose four-fold and
five-fold in value. When trade was interrupted on
every side, and when the copper tankas had become
more worthless than clods, the sultan repealed his
edict, and in great wrath he proclaimed that whoever
possessed copper coins should bring them to the
treasury and receive the old ones in exchange.
Thousands of men from various quarters who possessed thousands of these copper coins, and caring
nothing for them had flung them into corners along
with their copper pots, now brought them to the

---

[1] It is hardly necessary to explain that a lac (*lakh*) is 100,000, and
a cror (*karor*) 100 lacs.

treasury and received in exchange gold tankas and silver tankas, etc. So many of these copper tankas were brought to the treasury that heaps of them rose up in Taghlakabad like mountains,'—and there they were seen a century later in the days of Mubarak Shah II. How the treasury contrived to meet this extraordinary run on its reserve is not explained. As Mr. Thomas pointed out, if good money was paid for every token, true or forged (and there was no means of distinguishing good from bad), the sultan's temporary loan from his own subjects must have been repaid with more than even oriental rates of interest.

All these innovations harassed and annoyed the people and made the sultan unpopular. The failure of his schemes embittered him and his extreme severity towards all who contravened his enactments brought widespread discontent and rebellion. There were other causes for insurrection. The provincial officials were no longer the old feudal landowners, attached by ties of race and gratitude to their Turkish sovereigns. The Turks had been displaced ; the triumph of the Khaljis had loosened the old bonds that knitted the governing class together; a new dynasty that was neither pure Turk nor Khalji was in power, and the officers governing the provinces were hungry adventurers, often foreigners, Afghans, Persians, Khurasanis, Mongols, whom the sultan overwhelmed with costly gifts. These men had none of the old loyalty, such as it was, and it was from them, known as 'the foreign amirs' that the revolts came which shattered the empire.

In the early years of his reign Mohammad Taghlak had ruled a state wider, larger, and more splendid than any of his predecessors. Whilst even the great Ala-ad-din struck his coins only at Delhi and Deva-giri, the name and titles of Mohammad Taghlak shone upon the issues of the mints of Delhi, Agra, Tirhut (called Taghlakpur), Daulatabad, Warangal (called Sultanpur), Lakhnauti, Satgaon and Sonar-gaon in Bengal. A contemporary writer gives a list of twenty-three provinces subject to the sultan of Delhi, from Siwistan, Uchh, Multan, and Gujarat, by the Indus, to Lakhnauti in Bengal and Jajna-gar in Orisa, and from Lahore near the Himalayas to Dvara-samudra and the Malabar coast. Never again till the time of Aurangzib did a king of Delhi hold so wide a sway. Piece by piece the empire dropped away. One province after another re-volted, and though the sultan was usually victorious and punished the rebels without mercy, he could not be everywhere at the same time, and whilst one insurrection was being crushed, another sprang up at the other end of his dominions. We hear of re-volts in Multan, in Bengal, in Ma'bar, at Lahore, again in Multan, then at Samana, now at Warangal and next near Oudh, at Karra and in Bidar, at Devagiri and in Gujarat. Some of them were never suppressed, and Bengal and the Deccan were lost to the kingdom.

It was in vain that Mohammad Taghlak invoked the shade of a great name and obtained the sanction of the Abbasid caliph of Cairo to his title as ortho-dox king of India. In vain he received the mantle and diploma of investiture (1343), and welcomed a beggarly descendant of the famous caliphs of Baghdad with peculiar solemnity and humble deference to his splendid court at Delhi and even set the sacred foot upon his own proud neck. Nothing could restore the loyalty of the people or of their governors. Experiments and innovations had harassed them and brought much suffering; frequent executions and even massacres had exasperated them. No one trusted the changeable and impetuous king, whose fiery temper had been maddened by disappointment and revolts and who punished small and great offences with the same merciless ferocity. The end came whilst he was putting down a rebellion in Gujarat and Sind. He pursued the chief rebel towards the mouth of the Indus; but he was already ill with fever, and, still full of eager plans for crushing the Sumras of Thatta and seizing the rebel leader whom they were sheltering, Mohammad Taghlak died on the banks of the river in March, 1351. He had brought exceptional abilities and a highly-cultivated mind to the task of governing the greatest Indian empire that had so far been known, and he had failed stupendously. It was a tragedy of high intentions self-defeated.

After his death India recovered like a sick man after an exhausting fever, and the troubles subsided as the waves after a storm. The disturbing force was gone, and the people showed that they could be quiet enough if they were let alone. Mohammad Taghlak left no sons, but his cousin Firoz Shah was at once elected to the throne by the chiefs of the army then fighting in Sind, and after defeating the rebels he had no difficulty in making his accession sure. An attempt to set up a pretended son of the late sultan at Delhi collapsed on his approach, and thenceforward during the thirty-seven years of his reign there was not a single rebellion. This was certainly not due to any vigour of the sultan. Firoz was a man of forty-five, whose mother was a Hindu princess of Dipalpur, who nobly gave herself to his father in order to save her people from the exactions with which they were vindictively oppressed when the Raja Mal Bhatti at first proudly refused to give a Rajput princess to a mere half-bred Turk. Their son had been carefully brought up by his brave uncle, the warden of the marches, and had been trained in the art of government by that talented but wrong-headed projector Mohammad Taghlak, with whom he lived as a son for many years. Probably the lessons of his preceptor were read backwards; at all events Firoz reversed his predecessor's policy in every detail.

It was characteristic of the merciful and pious disposition of the new king that, after burying his cousin with all honour, he sought out the victims of his ferocity or their representatives and endeavoured as far as possible to indemnify them for their sufferings and losses. When this was done he collected the attested documents in which they admitted the reparation they had received and expressed themselves satisfied. All these papers he placed in the tomb of the tyrant, in the pious hope 'that God would show

mercy to my patron and friend.' It was a gracious
and beautiful act. Firoz possessed in an overflowing
degree the milk of human kindness, that supreme
gift of sympathy and tenderness which made the
whole Indian world his kin. He has been charged
with weakness and fatuity, but it was a weakness
that came very near the Christian ideal of love and
charity, and it brought peace and happiness to a land
which had been sorely tormented. Like his name-
sake, Firoz the Khalji, the new sultan had a horror
of bloodshed and torture. He had seen too much
of both under his cousin's rule, and he resolved that
they should cease. 'The great and merciful God,'
he wrote in his own touching memoirs, 'taught me,
His servant, to hope and seek for His mercy by
devoting myself to preventing the unlawful slaying
of Muslims and the infliction of any kind of torture
upon them or upon any men.'

So gentle a king was not made for the glories of
conquest; he abhorred war and clearly was no
general; if not content to leave the revolted
provinces alone, he made little effort to recover
them. The Deccan was allowed to become independent under Hasan Gangu, the founder of the
Bahmanid dynasty, whose sultans ruled all the
provinces south of the Vindhyas for 180 years.
Bengal also remained independent, though Firoz
twice attempted to bring it back under subjection.
On the first campaign (1353) he was absent from his
capital eleven months, and after winning a great
battle, in which 180,000 Bengalis are said to have
been slain, he refused to storm the fort of Ikdala in

which the king of Bengal had taken refuge, for fear
of shedding more of the blood of the faithful, and
sadly returned to Delhi. In the second expedition,
six or seven years later (1359–60), though he had
70,000 cavalry, infantry 'past numbering,' 470 elephants, and all the paraphernalia of war, he concluded
a treaty of peace with the Bengal king, and then proceeded to lose himself and his army whilst elephant-
hunting in Padmavati, in the wilds of Jajnagar, and
only after great privations and much difficulty found
his way back to Delhi, where no news had been
received of him for six months. He had been away
two years and a half.

A later expedition to conquer Thatta, which
Taghlak had failed to subdue, occupied about the
same length of time. With 90,000 horse and 480
elephants Firoz marched to Bhakkar. Part of the
force descended the Indus in 5000 boats, the rest
marching along the bank. Famine and pestilence
reduced the horses, and after a battle with the
Samma Jam or ruler of Sind, who had a large army
and had never owned an overlord, the sultan made a
'strategic retreat' towards Gujarat, pursued by the
enemy, who captured his boats. On the retreat all
the horses died; treacherous guides inveigled the
army into the salt marshes of Kachh, and they lost
themselves in the desert. Again for six months the
sultan and his army disappeared from human ken;
not a word of them reached Delhi, and the vezir had
to forge cheering dispatches to relieve the public
anxiety. The sultan however doggedly held to his
purpose, refitted his army in Gujarat, sent thrice to

Delhi for reinforcements, and in a second invasion, after some trouble in crossing the Indus, succeeded in occupying Sind, and starved the jam into surrender. The native ruler was brought to Delhi in all honour, and his son was made jam in his stead. This was the only victorious exploit of the reign of Firoz, except the reduction of Nagarkot, and it was won at great cost. The sultan had again been away from his capital for two years and a half.

In any other reign there would undoubtedly have been a revolution and a rival king during these long absences. But Firoz possessed a treasure in his vezir, a converted Hindu of good family from Telingana, named Makbul Khan, who had held the highest offices under the dangerous favour of Mohammad Taghlak. Over Firoz the wise though illiterate Hindu gained such influence that the sultan used to say that Khan-i-Jahan, 'lord of the world,' as he was entitled by virtue of his office, was the real king of Delhi. So fond was the sultan of his invaluable vezir that he allowed an income of over a thousand a year to every son that was born to him, and yet more by way of marriage portion to each daughter; and as Makbul was an uxorious person, who kept two thousand ladies in his harim, ranging from olive Greeks to saffron Chinese, these endowments must have reached a considerable sum. But the vezir was worth his money. As the sultan's deputy and *alter ego* he held the state securely while his master was away, stood always between him and official worries, and administered the kingdom with exceptional skill and wisdom. If the borders were more limited than before, the smaller area was better developed and made more productive.

It was doubtless due to Makbul's influence, seconded by the Rajput blood which Firoz inherited from Bibi Naila, that the new régime was marked by the utmost gentleness and consideration for the peasantry. It will be remembered that the preceding sultan had instituted a system of government loans in aid of the agriculturists. These loans the rayats, who had not yet recovered from the distress caused by Mohammad Taghlak's exactions, were wholly unable to repay. By the advice of the vezir the official records of these debts were publicly destroyed in the sultan's presence, and the people were given a clean bill. Taxation was brought back to the limits prescribed by the law of the Koran, and any attempts at extortion were sternly punished. 'Thus,' says Afif, the panegyrist of the reign, who was a frequent attendant at the court of Firoz, 'the rayats grew rich and were satisfied. Their homes were filled with corn and goods, horses and furniture; everyone had plenty of gold and silver; no woman was without her ornaments and no house without good beds and divans. Wealth abounded and comforts were general. The whole realm of Delhi was blessed with the bounties of God.'

Nor was this all. The sultan was an enthusiastic builder. He had a passion for naming and founding towns. When a son (Fath Khan, ' victory-lord ') was born to him on his first march to Delhi after his accession, he immediately laid the foundations of a town on the site of the happy event and called it

Fathabad, 'the city of Fath' or 'of victory.' On his Bengal campaigns he rechristened Ikdala ' Azadpur,' and Panduah ' Firozabad,' and founded the new city of Jaunpur (Jaunanpur) in honour of his cousin the late king. In the province of Delhi he not only built Fathabad and Hisar Firoza, but also a second Firozabad on the Jumna, ten miles from the capital, which became the Windsor of his London, where he chiefly resided, and whither the people of Delhi used to resort in crowds, making holiday by the river, along whose banks the new city spread for six miles. Here he set up one of the two Asoka pillars which he had removed from their original places. He had famous architects in Malik Ghazi Shahna and Abd-al-Hakk, who employed an immense staff of skilled workmen, all duly paid from the treasury after the plans had been approved and the necessary grants assigned.

One result especially of these new foundations was of incalculable benefit to the country. To supply his new city of Hisar Firoza the sultan constructed (1355) a double system of canals, from the Jumna and the Sutlej, one of which, 'the old Jumna canal,' still to this day supplies the district with irrigation along two hundred miles of its ancient course, and now brings the water to Delhi. A later historian, Firishta, credits Firoz with not less than 845 public works, canals, dams, reservoirs, bridges, baths, forts, mosques, colleges, monasteries and inns for pilgrims and travellers, to say nothing of repairing former buildings, such as the Kutb Minar and many of the tombs of the kings of Delhi. Curiously not a single

road is mentioned, though that was the greatest
want of India. Of all these, the canals were the

TOMB OF FIROZ SHAH AT DELHI.

chief blessing to the people. By the improved irrigation, they were able to get in two harvests instead
of one. The superintendence of the canals was in-

10

trusted to skilled engineers who examined the banks during the rainy season and floods and reported on their condition. In return for this benefit the sultan levied a water-rate of ten per cent. on the outlay. Another wise step was the reclaiming of waste lands by the government, the proceeds of which were devoted to the support of religion and learning. Firoz annually allowed more than a third of a million pounds (36 lacs) to learned men and pious endowments, and a million (100 lacs) was distributed every year in pensions and relief to the poor. The sultan was not only a great builder but a large gardener. He planted twelve hundred gardens near Delhi and many elsewhere, and the produce, among which white and black grapes of seven varieties are mentioned, brought in £8000 net profit to the treasury. The three sources of water-dues, reclaimed lands, and market gardens added nearly thirty thousand pounds to the annual revenue, which Afif reckoned at six crors and eighty-five lacs of tankas (£6,850-000) throughout the reign—about a third of the revenues of Akbar two centuries later. Of this the fertile Doab alone contributed £800,000.

It is not clear whether this revenue includes the rents of the villages and lands which were assigned to public officials as salary, but it probably does not. This method of paying public servants was strongly condemned by the sultan Ala-ad-din, as tending to feudal power and fostering rebellion ; and Firoz was the first to adopt it generally. During his reign it worked well, but it may be questioned whether it did not contribute to the break-up of the kingdom which ensued after his death. The grants indeed often amounted to viceroyalties of great power, and we find large districts and even provinces assigned to eminent nobles. Thus Karra and Dalamau were granted to Mardan Daulat with the title of 'King of the East'; Oudh and Sandila and Koil formed separate fiefs; Jaunpur and Zafarabad were given to another amir; Gujarat to Sikandar Khan, and Bihar to Bir Afghan. All these nobles were expected to defend their frontiers and manage their internal affairs. Another deduction which must be considered in estimating the revenue was due to the sultan's system of allowing his great fief-holders so much for every well-grown, good-looking, and well-dressed slave, whom they furnished for the service of the court.[1] When the feudatories, that is, most of the high officers of the state, came to pay their annual visit to the capital—a kind of rent-audit— they brought not only presents for the sultan, of horses, elephants, camels, mules, arms, gold and silver vessels, etc., but also from ten to a hundred slaves apiece, for whom a corresponding deduction was allowed from their taxes or rents. The chief who brought the most valuable contribution was held in most esteem, and thus the system of annual presents to the king, which became so onerous a tax under the Moghul emperors, began to prevail. The slaves were well educated at court, and trained either for the army, for palace employment, or for

[1] These slaves were captured in war, doubtless against insubordinate Hindu chiefs; we read of '400 slaves, children of chiefs, and Abyssinians' presented by the governor of Gujarat in 1376.

mechanical trades. There were 40,000 of them on guard at the palace, and 12,000 artisans, in Delhi, and altogether not less than 180,000 slaves were supported by the government. They had a depart-ment of their own, with a treasury, muster-master, and distinct officials. When the sultan went abroad he was escorted by thousands of these slaves,—arch-ers, swordsmen, halberdiers, and packmen mounted on buffaloes. Never before had slaves been so largely employed, though Ala-ad-din had mustered over 50,000.

The court to which these pampered servants min-istered was luxurious but orderly. It is true the sultan was somewhat addicted to wine, and on one occasion, in the midst of the Bengal campaign, the general Tatar Khan discovered his sovereign in an undignified position, lying half-dressed on his couch, with a mysterious sheet concealing something under the bed. Tatar Khan saw what was the matter, and both were speechless with surprise. At last he be-gan a little sermon on the wickedness of indulgence at such a time of anxiety. The sultan inquired what he meant, and asked innocently if anything untoward had happened. The khan pointed to the hidden wine cups under the bed and looked solemn. Firoz said he liked a modest drop now and then to moisten his throat, but Tatar was not to be molli-fied. Then the sultan swore that he would drink no more wine whilst the khan was with the army. So the general thanked God and went out. But Firoz soon afterwards bethought him that the khan was much needed at the other end of the kingdom, and sent him there in all haste. Several times the sultan was lectured by holy men on his weakness, but he worked off his excesses by vigorous hunting, to which he was enthusiastically devoted, and the vice cannot have gone to such lengths as to interfere with affairs of state—at least so long as the able Hindu vezir was there to control them.

The testimony of all contemporary chroniclers shows that Firoz was adored by the people. It was not only that he reformed abuses, checked extortion, reduced taxation, increased irrigation, and enlarged the markets and opportunities of labour: he was 'a father to his people,' took care of the needy and unemployed, refused to dismiss aged officials but let their sons act for them,—'the veteran,' he said, 'may thus stay at home in comfort, whilst the young ride forth in their strength';—he contrived the marriages of poor Muslims who could not otherwise afford the usual dowries, and provided state hospitals for the sick of all classes, native and foreign. Kindly to the Hindus, he yet sternly forbade public worship of idols and painting of portraits, and taxed the Brahmans, who had hitherto been exempt.[1] A devout Muslim, he kept the fasts and feasts and public prayers, and in the weekly litany the names of his great predecessors were commemorated as well as his own and that of the caliph who had sanctioned his authority. When an old man he went on pilgrimage to the shrine of the legendary hero Salar

[1] The poll-tax (*jizya*) on non-Muslims was £4, £2, or £1, according to their rank ; the Brahmans were taxed at rather more than the third rate.

Mas'ud at Bahraich, humbly shaved, as an act of
piety. He never did anything without consulting
the Koran, and even selected a governor in accord-

GOLD COIN OF FIROZ SHAH, A. H. 788 (A. D. 1386).

ance with a *fal* or lucky omen in the sacred book.
Making every allowance for the exaggeration of the
court chronicler, his panegyric, written after the
sultan's death, is probably not misplaced : ' Under
Firoz all men, high and low, bond and free, lived
happily and free from care. The court was splendid.
Things were plentiful and cheap.[1] Nothing untoward happened during his reign. No village remained waste, no land uncultivated.'

His old age was troubled by the loss of his great
vezir, who died in 1371 ; three years later the death
of the crown prince Fath Khan shook the aged
sultan grievously. He surrendered all authority
into the hands of the late vezir's son, the second
Khan-i-Jahan, and when the latter fell by the influence of Prince Mohammad in 1387, the old king
transferred the royal elephants to the prince and
allowed him to rule as he pleased. Unfortunately
Mohammad was given to pleasure, and his mis-

---

[1] Some prices may be quoted: Wheat 3d. (8 *jitals*) the quarter
(*man*); barley 1½d., grain 1¼d. the quarter ; sugar 1d. to 1¼d. the
sir or ¾ lb.

government excited a formidable rebellion of the slaves who formed so important a faction in Delhi. Firoz himself had to come forward to quell the revolt, which instantly subsided at his appearance; and the prince fled. The sultan next appointed his grandson Taghlak Shah II, son of Fath Khan, to administer the realm, and very soon afterwards died (Sept., 1388), 'worn out with weakness,' at the age of ninety. No king since Nasir-ad-din had so appealed to the affections of his subjects; 'none had shown himself so just, and merciful, so kind and religious—or such a builder.' In the brief and modest memoirs which the sultan left, he recites some of the successful efforts he made to repress irreligion and wickedness, and to restore good government, just law, kindness, and generosity to the people, in the place of torture and bloodshed and oppression. 'Through the mercy which God has shown to me,' he says, 'these cruelties and terrors have been changed to tenderness, kindness, and compassion. . . . I thank the All-Bountiful God for the many and various blessings He has bestowed upon me.'

CHAPTER VII

DISINTEGRATION

PROVINCIAL DYNASTIES

1388–1451

THE long and prosperous reign of Firoz Shah had assuaged the troubles of the people, but it had not strengthened the authority of the crown. Firoz was loved, perhaps respected, but certainly not feared. A generation had grown up who knew nothing of the inexorable despotism of a Balban, an Ala-ad-din, or a Mohammad Taghlak, and the dread of the sovereign was like a forgotten dream. The people did not rebel, because they were contented and had nothing to gain by revolution. The success of the reign was due to the personal character of the sultan and his prudent vezir: there was nothing to warrant the expectation that similar tranquillity would follow the accession of a new ruler. On the contrary, there were elements of the sultan's own creating that made for disintegration.

The system of depending upon a powerful body of slaves for civil and military service led to far-reaching consequence. Many of these slaves were converted—or nominally converted—Hindus, and to some of these renegades were assigned the great fiefs of the empire. However sincere their loyalty to Firoz their master, they were bound by no such ties to his successors, and their influence tended to encourage that Hindu independence which had been fostered by the sultan's mild rule. The intermarriage of the royal family and other dignitaries with Hindus could produce no real amalgamation between peoples effectually sundered alike by race, religion, and social custom. The Hindus paid tribute when compelled, but their free tribes and aristocratic chiefs were always eager to shake off the yoke of the foreigners, and in the years following the death of Firoz one of the most notable features of the disturbed period is the large part played in politics by Hindu leaders, whether slaves converted to the court religion, or rajas who had asserted their independence but were not above concerting insurrections with their renegade fellow-countrymen. Thus on the one hand we see the great provinces held in fief by successful courtiers, slaves, often renegade Hindus, whose power tended to become hereditary and to develop independent dynasties ; on the other, a universal revival of the old Hindu chiefships and of the independence of the hill tribes.

A strong ruler might possibly have stemmed the tide which was engulfing the power of Delhi, but even he must have bent and broken before the storm which burst upon India ten years after the death of Firoz. In those ten years there was no

king of even moderate capacity. Fath Khan, the
hope of his father, was dead; the next son, Zafar,
was also gone. The old sultan's grandson Taghlak II
was young and foolish, addicted to wine and dissipation, and the amirs and palace slaves rose and
killed him before he had lolled on the throne five
months. Another grandson Abu-Bekr was opposed
by his uncle Mohammad, the prince whom the
slaves had expelled from his regency under Firoz,
and who had since established some sort of authority
from Samana to Nagarkot in the Panjab, and after
several unsuccessful efforts secured Delhi in 1390.
His four years' reign was vexed by a series of rebellions; the Hindu chiefs were everywhere in revolt,
the great feudatories under no control; and the persecution and banishment of the foreign slaves (whose
nationality was tested by a Hindi shibboleth) did
nothing to mitigate their disruptive influence.
Mohammad's son Humayun, proudly entitled
'Alexander' (Sikandar Shah), died after a reign
of six weeks, and though his brother Mahmud sat
on the throne for eighteen years (1394–1412), that
throne was for some time set up at Kanauj, and
even when at Old Delhi, his cousin Nasrat Shah, son
of Fath Khan, held a rival court at the new capital
of Firozabad close by; thus there were two kings at
Delhi, and both were mere puppets in the hands
of ambitious amirs.

Such was the chaotic state of the kingdom of
Delhi when Timur descended upon it with his
ninety-two regiments of a thousand horse each. The
great conqueror, whose career is familiar to all in the

pages of Gibbon, had already overrun all Persia and
Mesopotamia to the frontier of the Ottoman empire in Asia Minor on the west, and occupied Afghanistan on the east, before the wealth of India drew
him to the invariable road of Central Asian invaders.
When he laid the project before his council of war
there was strenuous dissuasion. Five great rivers to
cross, dense jungles, fierce warriors led by terrible
rajas couched in forest fastnesses like wild beasts in
their lairs, and mailed elephants with deadly armed
tusks—these, said the chiefs, were obstacles enough.
But others recalled the example of Mahmud the
Idol-breaker with far inferior forces, and Timur's
sons urged the surpassing riches of India and the
pre-eminence of such a possession, whilst the men of
religion dwelt on the duty of the Holy War against
the infidels. The objectors still insisted that even
if successful their hardy race would surely degenerate and their descendants grow soft and effeminate
even as the natives of Hindustan—a prediction
verified two centuries later;—but Timur was not to
be put off. 'My object,' he wrote or caused to be
written in his memoirs, 'my object in the invasion of
Hindustan is to lead a campaign against the infidels,
to convert them to the true faith according to the
command of Mohammad (on whom and his family
be the blessing and peace of God), to purify the
land from the defilement of misbelief and polytheism,
and overthrow the temples and idols, whereby we
shall be *ghazis* and *mujahids*, champions and soldiers
of the faith before God.' His will prevailed over the
doubting men of war, and the venture was resolved.

An advanced force under his grandson Pir Mohammad, who held Kabul, descended upon the
Indus at the close of 1397, and besieged Multan.
Timur himself, confirmed in his resolution by his
forerunner's report of the distracted state of the
country, left Samarkand in March, 1398, struggled
through the 'stony girdles of the earth,' through ice
and snow, descended appalling precipices in pursuit
of the infidel tribes, and crossed the Indus at Attok,
where Jalal-ad-din had swum the river when es-
caping from Timur's ancestor Chingiz Kaan. 'On
the eastern bank of the Hyphasis, on the edge of the
desert, the Macedonian hero halted and wept':
the Tatar conqueror indulged no such sensibility
but threw a pontoon across the Chinab, and, joined
by his grandson, who had now taken Multan, pressed
steadily eastward.   Fearful stories of the plundering
and massacring of the people preceded him, and the
inhabitants of Dipalpur fled to the protection of
the Rajput fortress of Bhatnir, in vain, for Timur
stormed it and slew 10,000 Hindus in an hour.
Sirsuti was found deserted, Fathabad was empty,
everyone had hurried panic-stricken into the jungle.
In December the invading host stood encamped on
the plain of Panipat, the battle-field of Delhi, but
there was no man to oppose them.   A week later
Timur was before the capital.

On the 17th December, 1398, the decisive battle
was fought.   Timur crossed the Jumna and carefully
surveyed the ground.   He took unusual precautions
to allay the terrors of his troopers, who were ex-
travagantly nervous about the invincible elephants

of the enemy. He issued calthrops ('claws of iron')
to the troops to throw before these alarming beasts,
and defended the camp with a strong abatis of brush-
wood and trees, behind which he placed the women,
stores, and cattle, as well as 'the good and learned
men of the army' who, on being consulted where
they would wish to be stationed during the battle,
modestly expressed a wish to be 'placed with the
ladies.' The immense number of Hindu prisoners,
reckoned at 100,000, could not safely be left in the
camp, and Timur ordered them all to be slain in
cold blood. Then taking an augury from the Koran,
and scouting the warnings of the astrologers, he set
out his forces for battle.

The Indian army under Ikbal Khan and the sultan Mahmud did not refuse the challenge. They
mustered 10,000 horse and 40,000 foot, with 125
elephants in mail with poisoned blades fastened to
their tusks and howdahs fitted with hand-grenades
and fireworks to frighten the horses. The battle
was ordered on each side in the usual manner:
vaward, rearward, centre, right and left wings.
Timur rode to a neighbouring knoll and recon-
noitered them as they approached, then bowed himself on the earth and prayed to God for victory.
He mounted in full assurance that his prayer was
heard. Completing his arrangements, he strengthened his vaward and right wing, and the signal for
the battle was given by the roll of drums. A well-
concealed flanking movement took the Indian ad-
vance-guard in the rear and scattered them. The
right wing under Pir Mohammad drove in the Indian

left by a steady discharge of arrows, and followed it up with the sword.   The left, equally successful, pursued the enemy's right up to the gates of Delhi. The Indian centre still held out under Ikbal and the sultan, but Timur sent orders to pick off the mahauts and wound the riderless elephants.   The Indian soldiers, says the conqueror, 'showed no lack of courage, but bore themselves manfully in the fight'; they were out-numbered and out-generalled, however, and finally took to flight.   The sultan and Ikbal Khan escaped with difficulty to the city, trampling their own men under the elephants in the crush, and that night they fled to the mountains, basely leaving their wives and children behind.   The victory was complete, and Timur, pitching his camp by the tomb of Firoz, gave thanks to God with tears.

The leading men came out and surrendered the city on the following day, and in deference to the pleading of the ulama and other wise and pious Muslims the conqueror accepted a ransom for the lives of the people.   There was to be no sack and no massacre.   Unfortunately the collection of the ransom led to brawls on the 26th, and Timur's humane intentions were frustrated.   It was no doubt difficult to restrain a great army of Turks, who had been accustomed for years to slaughter and pillage wherever they went.   For three days the unhappy city was turned into a shambles.   'All my army, no longer under control, rushed to the city and thought of nothing but killing, plundering, and making prisoners.'   Every man got from twenty to a hundred captives, many of whom Timur sent to

Samarkand to teach the famous handicrafts of India
to his own people. There were immense spoils of
rubies, diamonds, pearls, gold and silver ornaments
and vessels, silks and brocades. Only the quarter
inhabited by the sayyids and ulama—the heads of
the Muslim religion—escaped the general sack.
Siri, Jahanpanah, and old Delhi had been completely gutted. 'Although I was wishful to spare
them, I could not succeed, for it was the will of God
that this calamity should fall upon the city.'

After a fortnight of state functions, feasts and
levees, it occurred to Timur that he had come to
Hindustan to wage a Holy War upon the infidels,
and that he ought to be stirring (Jan. 1, 1399). After
entering the fort of Firozabad on the Jumna, and
praying in its mosque, he took Mirat by storm,
massacred the men, took the women and children
prisoners, and razed the town to the earth. He
then pushed north to Hardwar, where he had heard
of the image of the sacred cow from whose mouth
the Ganges was supposed to flow and whither the
Hindus made pilgrimage to the mysterious source
of the holy river. Such superstition roused the
zealot's passion, and the wretched Indians were
made to pay dearly for the legend. Crossing the
Ganges, after a veritable orgy of slaughter, the
soldier of the faith prostrated himself in gratitude
to God, and felt that he had accomplished his mission
in Hindustan. He had come, he said, for two purposes: to war with infidels for the sake of the
rewards of the next world, and to seize this world's
riches, since 'plunder in war for the faith is as

lawful to Muslims as their mother's milk, and the consumption of that which is lawful is a means of grace.' Lacs of infidels had been dispatched 'to the fires of hell,' and the zealous warriors of Islam were laden with spoils. Enough had been done, and it was time to turn homewards and see what was going on at the other end of Asia. Fighting his way through the Siwalik hills, beneath Mussooree, driving the heathen into the Himalaya valleys, plundering and burning villages as he proceeded, seizing Nagarkot and Jammu, and detaching a force to take Lahore, Timur and his invincible host marched beneath the sloping eaves of India, and, after a final rhinoceros hunt, disappeared up the Afghan valleys. In March the fearful visitation was over.

When the Scourge of God had departed, men came out of their hiding-places like the hare when the hunter has passed. Fortunately, in his haste to return to Samarkand, Timur had been able to harry but a small part of India; but wherever his army had trampled, from the Indus to the Ganges, over the whole of the Panjab, desolation and famine were left behind. Thenceforward, until the days of the Moghul empire, Delhi never regained her old ascendancy. For a time Ikbal Khan, the vezir, held the capital, drove out Nasrat Shah, and made vigorous efforts to put down the growing hostility of the Hindu chiefs, who were now independent at Etawa, Gwaliar, and many other strongholds. Sultan Mahmud found Delhi insupportable with all the power in the vezir's hands, and set up a separate court at Kanauj, until the death of Ikbal in a battle with Khizr Khan, the viceroy of Multan, in November, 1405, set him free and enabled him to return to the capital and rule a kingdom which had shrunk to little more than the Doab and Rohtak. The next six or seven years were spent in a struggle between the great feudatories, in which the dissolute and incompetent sultan played a sorry part, and when Mahmud died in 1412 there was no king left at Delhi. The government was conducted by the Lodi amir Daulat Khan, but he made no assumption of royal dignity.

Nor did his successor assume the title of king. Khizr Khan, the founder of the dynasty of Sayyids, who claimed descent from the family of the Arabian Prophet, had prudently cast in his lot with Timur when the 'noble Tartarian' invaded India; and on taking the command at Delhi, in May 1414, he made no pretension to be more than Timur's deputy. There is no evidence however that this allegiance was anything more than a politic fiction, whilst the coinage issued by Khizr bore the names of Firoz and other defunct kings of the late dynasty as guarantees of its authenticity. The history of the Sayyid dynasty, which numbered four rulers, consisted mainly in a perpetual struggle to retain some sort of control of the small territory still attached to the kingdom of Delhi. How small this was will be realized when it is stated that almost yearly campaigns were undertaken to extort the annual tribute from the Hindu raja of Katehr (Rohilkhand, north-east of Delhi), from Mewat on the south, and from Etawa in the Doab. We read of frequent rebellions in the north-west at Sirhind and Jalandhar, generally headed by Jasrath, a Gakkar leader of the Murree hills; of revolts at Koil (Aligarh), Badaun, Etawa; of pursuits of rebels into the mountains of Rupar near Simla on the north; of invasions and intrigues by the Timurid governor of Kabul, and by the rulers of Malwa and of Jaunpur.

'Khizr's seven years' tenure of power presents but few incidents of mark; there is a seeming oriental want of energy to sustain an accomplished triumph, an air of ease which so often stole over the senses of a successful owner of a palace in Delhi; and so his vezir and deputy, Taj-al-mulk, went forth to coerce or persuade, as occasion might dictate, the various independent chiefs, whether Muslim or Hindu, whose states now encircled the reduced boundaries of the old Pathan kingdom. There were of course the ordinary concessions to expediency, so well understood in the East, submission for the moment in the presence of a superior force, insincere professions of allegiance, temporizing payments of tribute, or desertion of fields and strongholds easily regained; but there was clearly no advance in public security or in the supremacy of the central government. The inevitable law of nature had, no doubt, been asserting itself anew in the ready recovery of the free Hindu tribes as against the effete dominancy of the domesticated Muslims; but this process had been in continuous action from the day when the thin wedge of Mohammedanism first thrust itself amid the overwhelming population of India, whose almost Chinese attachment to ancient ideas would have resisted far more persuasive arguments than the sharpest edge of a scimitar or the most eloquent exhortations of the latest inspired preacher of Islam. Added to this normally antagonistic element there had intervened in higher quarters an amalgamative process of intermarriage with Hindu females and an admission of Hindu converts upon very easy terms to all the honours of Mohammedan nobility; so that any prestige the conquering race might once have claimed was altogether subdued if not degraded by these inconsistent concessions; and it required something more revolutionary than the accession of a local sayyid to perpetuate a new dynasty.'[1] The murder of Khizr's successor Mubarak Shah by his vezir, followed by the dispatch of that minister whilst he was attempting to assassinate the next sultan, led to worse anarchy and paved the way for the accession, in 1451, of the Afghan Bahlol Lodi and a new line, whose rule for a time restored somewhat of the faded splendour of Delhi.

The rest of India was split up into numerous independent states, whose annals are for the most part unwritten or unworthy of record. Petty rulers, like Ahmad Khan of Mewat, held the land to within a dozen miles of Delhi to the south; and Darya Khan, the Lodi, matched him in his government of Sambhal on the north. There were independent chiefs in the Doab and at Biana, Hindu rajas at Kampila and Patiala and other places which had formerly owned the sovereignty of Delhi. Out of the ruck of small principalities, Hindu and Muslim,

[1] THOMAS, *Chronicles of the Pathan Kings*, 327, 328.

some half dozen great dynasties stand forth in Bengal, Oudh, Malwa, Gujarat, and the Deccan.

BENGAL. The governors of Bengal had long attained independence, and assumed the style and authority of kings ; and since the days of Mohammad Taghlak there had been scarcely an attempt at interference from Delhi, beyond the futile and half-hearted campaigns of the pacific Firoz. Within its own borders, however, Bengal was often divided against itself. Rival kings ruled eastern and western Bengal from the two cities of Sonargaon (near Dhaka) and Satgaon (close to Hugli), until these after a long struggle were united to Lakhnauti under Ilyas Shah in 1352 and the provincial capital was fixed at Panduah, to which Firoz gave his own name. Firozabad remained the capital of the whole province till 1446, when the seat of government was removed again to Lakhnauti, which now received the name of Gaur, and later the epithet of Jannatabad or ' Paradise-town.' Very little is recorded of the annals of the numerous rulers of Bengal who governed the province, together with part of Bihar, and latterly Jajnagar, Orisa, Tipara, Kamrup, and Chittagong, from the days of Mohammad Ghori (1202) to the conquest by Akbar in 1576. Some were Khaljis, some were Turks ; a Hindu established a brief dynasty which was converted to Islam ; and at the close of the fifteenth century a series of Abyssinian kings, derived from the African bodyguard imported by the eunuch sultan Barbak, held the throne ; the latest kings were Afghans. Provincial as these

GOLDEN MOSQUE AT GAUR.

sovereigns were, they maintained great state and luxury, and the remains of their architecture bear witness to their taste.

JAUNPUR. For splendour of architecture, however, the 'Kings of the East,' or Sharki Maliks of Jaunpur, stand supreme in the period before the Moghul empire. Upon the decline of the Delhi kingdom the eunuch Sarwar, who became Khwaja-i-Jahan and vezir under the last sultans of the house of Taghlak, was sent in 1394 into 'Hindustan'—the land of Hindus, a term used specifically to denote the country about Benares and Oudh, where the Hindus were still practically independent — and took up his residence at Jaunpur, the new city founded on the Gumti opposite Zafarabad by his late master Firoz. He soon 'got the fiefs of Kanauj, Karra, Oudh, Sandila, Dalamau, Bahraich, Bihar, and Tirhut into his own possession, and put down many of the infidels, and restored the forts which they had destroyed. The Almighty blessed the arms of Islam with power and victory. The raja of Jajnagar and the king of Lakhnauti now began to send to Khwaja-i-Jahan the [tributary] elephants which they had formerly sent to Delhi.' Thus began the dynasty of the 'Kings of the East,' which subsisted in conspicuous power for nearly a century. Their dominions stretched along the plain from Kanauj to Bihar, and from the Ganges to the Himalaya Tarai, and occupied most of the country corresponding roughly with the later kingdom of Oudh between the dominions of Delhi and Bengal.

MINAR OF FIROZ II AT GAUR (1488).

167

Jaunpur, the town of Jauna, *i. e.* Mohammad Taghlak, supplanting the many-templed Hindu city of
Ratagarh (afterwards named by the Muslims Zafarabad, 'triumph-town'), was the first Mohammedan

FORT OF JAUNPUR, EAST GATE.

stronghold planted in the very midst of the most
Hindu part of northern India. Mahmud of Ghazni
had never reached this point, but legend records
the triumphant march of his nephew, the youthful
and heroic Salar Mas'ud, who ravaged the land up
to the gates of Benares and threw down the temples
of Ratagarh. He met his death in battle with the

Hindus, and dwells for ever in the reverent memory of the Muslims, who for centuries visited his grave at Bahraich, where the martyr prince is said to have appeared to the aged sultan Firoz and warned him of his approaching end.[1] On the site of the temple where Ramachandra slew the giant demon Kavala-vira, still the scene of Hindu worship, Firoz built the fort which developed into the populous capital of the Sharki kings. Sarwar's successors, descended from his adopted sons, the children of Karanfal (*i. e.* ' Clove '), a slave water-bearer of Firoz's court, not only maintained the integrity of their dominions and resisted the attacks of Ikbal Khan and the Delhi troops, but made Jaunpur a seat of learning, a refuge for men of letters in those days of confusion and strife, and an example of noble building.

Ibrahim Shah, who reigned from 1401 to 1440, was the most distinguished figure among the six ' Kings of the East.' He not only repelled alike the military and the diplomatic advances of Mahmud, the sultan of Delhi, but even invaded the capital himself in 1413 during the confusion which ensued upon Mahmud's death, retiring however when Khizr Khan appeared upon the scene. The Sayyids tried conclusions with Ibrahim in 1427, but after a well-fought battle beside the Jumna peace was ratified by the marriage of Bibi the daughter of Mubarak Shah to the crown prince of Jaunpur. An invasion by the king of Malwa in 1435 was rewarded by the capture

---

[1] See A. FÜHRER and E. W. SMITH, *The Sharqi Architecture of Jaunpur*, 2—16, to which the following account of Sharki history is indebted.

of Kalpi, which had been a bone of contention between the three kingdoms of Delhi, Jaunpur, and
Malwa; but thenceforward to his death Ibrahim
reigned in peace, an energetic and benevolent prince,
beloved of his people, a zealous Muslim, and an en-

ATALA DEVI MOSQUE, AT JAUNPUR.

lightened patron of art and learning.   The beautiful
Atala mosque built in 1408 is his chief monument.
Its characteristic feature, a lofty inner gateway of
simple grandeur, recalling the propylon of Egyptian
temples, supplied the place of a minaret, and concealed from the quadrangle the too dominating

outline of the great dome which covered the house of prayer. The graceful two-storeyed colonnades, five aisles deep, round the spacious quadrangle, broken by minor domes and gateways, the fine ashlar masonry of its plain buttressed exterior, the exquisite and rich, yet never intricate, floral ornament surrounding its doors and windows and prayer-niche, its geometrical trellis screens and panelled ceilings, are typical of a pure style of Saracenic art, with scarcely a trace of Indian influence. Even in such a land of precious stones of architecture, the Atala Masjid remains a gem of the first water.

Ibrahim's successor Mahmud, whose eighteen years' reign was from time to time disturbed by the necessity or temptation to take part in the struggle then centred round the decayed power of Delhi, which he besieged in 1452, also left a monument in the mosque of the Lal Darwaza, or Ruby Gate, so called from the vermilion entrance to the palace of his wife Bibi Raji, who built the adjacent mosque; and their son Husain completed the magnificent Jami' Masjid or cathedral mosque, which Mahmud had begun and of which the foundation had been laid as far back as the last years of Ibrahim. This glorious building, the sister and the rival of the Atala mosque of his grandfather, is a worthy memorial to a king whose ambition, urged by a high-spirited wife, another princess of Delhi, soared to the possession of the throne of Mohammad Taghlak; and whose campaigns extended his frontier till they embraced Etawa, Sambhal, and Badaun, made the raja of Gwaliar his vassal, and spread the terror of his arms over Orisa.   The new Afghan king of Delhi, Buhlol, was too strong for him in the end, and a fatal battle near Kanauj in 1477 deprived Husain of all his possessions.   He was allowed to dwell for some years at the city which he and his ancestors had embellished, and then fled to Bihar, whilst his supplanter, the son of Buhlol, laid low his beautiful capital, demolished the stately palaces, destroyed the royal tombs, and was with difficulty dissuaded from razing even the mosques to the ground.   The kingdom of Delhi once more touched the frontier of Bengal.

MALWA.   At the time when the new state of Jaunpur was beginning to wedge itself between Delhi and Bengal, two other powerful kingdoms broke away from the central power under local dynasties in Malwa and Gujarat.   One of Firoz Shah's great fiefholders, Dilawar Khan, a descendant of the Ghori kings, who held the fief of Dhar among the spurs of the Vindhya range, made himself independent in 1401 during the confusion that followed Timur's invasion, and soon extended his authority over the greater part of the ancient Hindu kingdom of Malwa, which had resisted the encroachments of the Muslims up to the time of Balban, but had since been a province more or less subject to the kings of Delhi.   The old capital, Ujjain, had been a famous seat of Indian learning, but the new dynasty deserted it for a new city which Hushang the son of Dilawar built at Mandu on a small plateau among the Vindhya slopes.   The situation of Malwa,

hedged in by warring states, Delhi and Jaunpur on
the north and the rising power of Gujarat on the

TOWER OF VICTORY AT CHITOR.

west, involved the new state in frequent wars, and
its kings in turn attacked one or other of their
neighbours. The murder of Dilawar's grandson

Mohammad in 1435 by his vezir, Mahmud the Khalji, set the assassin on the throne, and Mahmud raised the kingdom of Malwa to its greatest strength. Though his siege of Delhi was unsuccessful, his campaigns against Jaunpur, the Rajputs, and the Deccan resulted in the acquisition of Kalpi on the Jumna, Ajmir and Rantambhor in Rajputana, and Elichpur south of the Satpura range. His perpetual conflicts with the rana of Chitor, however, ended in a crushing defeat in 1440, the memory of which is still revived by the lofty Pillar of Victory which Rana Kumbho set up at his capital. After this, Rajput influence gradually became supreme in Malwa; Rana Sanga defeated the second Mahmud as effectually as Rana Kumbha had humbled the first; and Medini Rao, the lord of Chanderi, managed the kingdom as chief minister of the nominal sovereign, until the invasion of India by Babar, involving the defeat of the Rajputs and the death of Medini Rao, gave Bahadur Shah of Gujarat the opportunity to take possession of Malwa in 1531.

GUJARAT. An inaccessible position, beyond the great desert and the hills connecting the Vindhyas with the Aravali range, long preserved Gujarat from the Mohammedan yoke. Only by sea was it easily approached, and to the sea it owed its peculiar advantages, its favouring climate and fertile soil, and the wealth which poured in from the great commercial emporia of Cambay, Diu, and Surat. The greater part of the Indian trade with Persia, Arabia, and the Red Sea passed through its harbours, besides a busy coasting trade. 'The benefit of this trade overflowed upon the country, which became a garden, and enriched the treasury of the prince. The noble mosques, colleges, palaces, and tombs, the

GOLD COIN OF GHIYAS SHAH OF MALWA A. H. 880 (A. D. 1475-6).

remains of which still adorn Ahmadabad and its other cities to this day, while they excite the admiration of the traveller, prove both the wealth and the taste of the founders.'[1] Not till the reign of Ala-ad-din at the close of the 13th century did it become a Muslim province, and a century later it became independent again under a dynasty of Muslim kings. Their beginning resembled the birth of the Malwa state. Firoz Shah in 1391 granted the fief of Gujarat to Zafar Khan, the son of a converted Rajput, and five years later the fiefholder assumed the royal canopy. He soon enlarged his dominions, at first but a strip between hills and sea, by the annexation of Idar to the north and Diu in Kathiawar, plundered Jhalor, and even took possession of Malwa for a short space in 1407, setting his brother on the throne in the place of Hushang the son of Dilawar. His successor Ahmad I founded the

[1] ERSKINE, *History of India*, i, 21.

fortress of Ahmadnagar, and also Ahmadabad, which has ever since been the chief city of Gujarat, and recovered Bombay and Salsette from the Deccan kings. Mahmud I not only carried on the traditional wars of his dynasty with Malwa on the east and Khandesh on the south, but kept a large fleet to subdue the pirates of the islands.

Nor were Asiatic pirates the only disturbers of his coast. The first of the three great waves of European invasion was already beating on the shores of Gujarat. Vasco da Gama had reached the Malabar ports in 1498, and the effects of the new influence were soon felt further north. The Portuguese had no more intention at first of founding an eastern empire than the later Dutch and English companies. The hostility of the Muslim traders compelled them to protect their agents, and a commercial policy was necessarily supported by military power. The position of invaders was forced upon the Portuguese, as it was later on upon the English. The collision was brought about by the spirited action of the last Mamluk sultan of Egypt. Kansuh el-Ghuri, realizing the imminent jeopardy of the great Indian trade which supplied so much of the wealth of Egypt, resolved to drive the Portuguese from the Arabian Sea. His appeal and threats to the pope had no effect, and there remained the resort to arms. The Mamluks had long maintained a fleet in the Red Sea, and Admiral Husain was dispatched in 1508 to Gujarat with a well-equipped war squadron manned with sailors who had often fought with Christian fleets in the Mediterranean.

He was joined by the fleet of Gujarat, commanded
by the governor of Diu, in spite of the efforts of the
Portuguese captain, Lourenço de Almeida, to prevent their union; and the combined fleet was in
every respect superior to the flotilla of Christian
merchantmen which boldly sailed out of the port of
Chaul to the attack. The Portuguese were defeated
in a running fight which lasted two days, and the
young captain, son of the famous viceroy, was
killed. 'His ship was surrounded on every side;
his leg was broken by a cannon-ball at the com-
mencement of the action; nevertheless he had himself placed upon a chair at the foot of the mainmast,
and gave his orders as coolly as ever. Shortly afterwards a second cannon-ball struck him in the breast,
and the young hero, who was not yet twenty-one,
expired, in the words of Camoens, without knowing
what the word surrender meant.' He was avenged
a few months later when on Feb. 2, 1509, his
father, the viceroy Francisco de Almeida, utterly
defeated the combined fleet of Egypt and Gujarat
off Diu. In the following year the king of Gujarat
offered Albuquerque, the conqueror of Goa, the
port of Diu, and a Portuguese factory was there
established in 1513, though the celebrated fortress
of the Christian invaders was not built till 1535.[1]

Though unable to withstand the Portuguese — or
perhaps not unwilling to see his powerful deputy
at Diu humiliated—Bahadur was one of the most
brilliant figures among the warrior kings of Gujarat.

[1] See LANE-POOLE, *History of Egypt in the Middle Ages*, 352;
MORSE STEPHENS, *Albuquerque*, 36–38.

12

The Rajputs of the hills and the kings of the Deccan owned his superiority, and in 1531 he annexed Malwa. A Rajput rising and the advance of the Moghuls under Humayun the son of Babar for a time destroyed his authority, as will presently be seen, but he recovered it bravely, only to fall at last,

GOLD COIN OF MAHMUD SHAH OF GUJARAT, A. H. 946 (A. D. 1539-40).

drowned in a scuffle with the Portuguese whom he had admitted to his coast. The final absorption of Gujarat in the Moghul empire in 1572 belongs to a later chapter.

DECCAN. Nothing has been said of the affairs of the Deccan since the reign of Mohammad Taghlak, after whose time no king of Delhi had ever held authority south of the Vindhyas. The rebellions which embittered the last years of that too ingenious sovereign had nowhere been more successful than in his favourite province of the south. The revolt of the 'new amirs' in Sind, which hastened his end, was but a part of a larger movement, and its centre was in the Deccan. Here a brave and capable Afghan, Hasan Gangu, who had risen from menial service at Delhi to high command in the southern armies, placed himself at the head of the disaffected, and defeated the royal troops near Bidar. No attempt was made to suppress the revolt, for the king was too deeply engaged in endeavouring to restore order nearer home; and Hasan Gangu became king of the Deccan (1347). His dominions included almost all that the campaigns of Ala-ad-din and Mohammad Taghlak had won from the Hindu rajas of the great southern plateau. The valley of the Tapti was independent under the separate dynasty of the kings of Khandesh, an offshoot of Gujarat, who maintained their distinct though limited power at their new capital Burhanpur from 1370 to the conquest of Akbar in 1599. But the rest of the Deccan, from Elichpur in Berar down to the Krishna and Tungabhadra rivers, and across from the Arabian Sea to Mahur, Ramgir, and Indore on the frontier of Warangal, was under the rule of the new dynasty of the Bahmanids, founded by Hasan Gangu. On the east the Hindu kingdom of Warangal barred his access to the Bay of Bengal; and on the south, beyond the Krishna, stretched the great empire of Vijayanagar, the last bulwark of Hindu power in the Deccan, which, gathering together the fragments scattered by the tumultuous assaults of Mohammad Taghlak, formed a mighty state, able to parry every onslaught of the Muslims for two centuries to come.

Hasan Gangu Zafar Khan fixed his capital at Kulbarga, near the Bhima, and gave it the name of ' the fairest city,' Ahsanabad; and here his descendants ruled till 1526 over most of what is now called the Bombay Presidency and the Nizam's Territory. On the north, beyond an occasional dispute with Gujarat,

there was little trouble ; but the kingdom of Warangal or Telingana, supported by the raja of Orisa,
was a standing menace to the Muslim power,
though Mohammad I reduced it to tributary submission varied by intermittent hostilities. In 1422
Ahmad Shah I invaded Warangal, captured its prince,
and shot him from a catapult on the walls into a
flaming wood-pile which he had prepared below.
The heavy loss he suffered on his march back did
not discourage him, and three years later he extinguished the native dynasty and annexed their territory ; but the fact that the Hindus of Warangal
ventured to retaliate in 1461, and even marched as
far as Bidar, shows that the annexation soon became
little more than nominal.

The power of the Bahmanid dynasty must have
been overwhelming to have reduced the empire of
the Carnatic to even occasional subjection. The raja
of Vijayanagar ruled not only what was afterwards
known as the kingdom of Mysore but the whole
country between the Krishna (or rather its tributary,
the Tungabhadri) and the Kaveri, stretching from
coast to coast, from Mangalore on the west to Con-
jeveram on the east, and from Karnal on the north
to Trichinopoli on the south. Yet this great Hindu
empire was repeatedly forced to pay tribute to the
Bahmanids, and never succeeded in winning a victory over them. Vijayanagar coveted the triangle
of land between the upper course of the Krishna and
the Tungabhadri river, known as the Raichur Doab,
with its fortresses of Mudkal and Raichur, and the
campaigns of the 14th and 15th centuries centred in

this territory : but the Bahmanids steadily kept their grip on it, and never permanently lost a fortress or a mile of ground. In the earliest campaign the raja led 30,000 horse, 100,000 foot, and 3,000 elephants, to the assault of Mudkal in the debatable land, and for the moment triumphed in the capture of the fortress and the massacre of the Muslims (1366). But Mohammad I, the son of Hasan Gangu, was soon on his track. Standing on the banks of the Krishna he vowed that he would neither eat nor sleep till he had crossed in face of the enemy and avenged his slaughtered saints. He crossed, and the raja fled ; abandoning his camp and 70,000 men, women, and children, on whom the sultan wreaked his vengeance without mercy. The Bahmanid kings had no bowels of compassion, and it is related of one of them that whenever the number of Hindus massacred at one time reached 20,000 it was his habit to indulge in a feast.

Mohammad continued his march to Adoni and even to the capital Vijayanagar itself, which he vainly besieged for a month. This campaign, in which he repeatedly vanquished the enemy, and laid the Carnatic waste, is said to have cost the lives of half a million Hindus, and it was only after ambassadors had urgently pleaded with him that the sultan consented to forego his custom of indiscriminate slaughter and pledged his successors, somewhat ineffectually, to the like clemency. Another campaign waged by his son Mujahid in 1378 was undertaken for the possession of the strong fortress of Bankapur, south of Dharwar, and after several victories and hunting the raja from place to place, and after restoring the mosque on the sea-coast which Kafur had founded nearly seventy years before, Mujahid led his army back to the Krishna with over 60,000 prisoners, chiefly women. He was murdered on his way home by his uncle Dawud, but the change of rulers made no difference in the superiority of the Muslim kingdom. Vijayanagar paid an annual tribute, or if it withheld it there was war and humiliation.

The most signal discomfitures of the Hindus occurred in the reign of Firoz the son of Dawud. On

GOLD COIN OF FIROZ, STRUCK AT AHSANABAD, A.H. 807 (A.D. 1404–5).

the first occasion (1398) Vijayanagar was the aggressor, the object being as usual the regaining of Mudkal and Raichur. Firishta tells a quaint story of how a grave kazi and his friends insinuated themselves into the not very fastidious favour of the nautch girls of the enemy's camp, and disguised as dancing women contrived to get themselves smuggled into the presence of the raja's son, whom they diverted with a sword-dance which ended in the plunging of their daggers into the prince's breast. This catastrophe, followed up by a night attack, caused the flight of the raja, and Vijayanagar had to

pay £400,000 to get the enemy over the border. In
1406, as the annual tribute had not been rendered,
Firoz again invaded the Carnatic. The war was
provoked by the raja, who, hearing of a lovely but
coy maiden in Mudkal, marched upon the fortress to
secure her, but instead of succeeding in his amorous
quest not only found the maiden fled but learnt that
the army of Kulbarga was on his track. Firoz took
Bankapur, which his predecessor had vainly coveted,
and did not retire till the enemy had again suffered
the loss of 60,000 prisoners. Not only did the raja
surrender the fortress; he even yielded a princess to
the sultan's harim — an humiliating degradation for
a Hindu sovereign — together with immense treasure, and was actually obliged to admit his foe as a
guest within the walls of the capital. An interesting feature of the Bahmanid wars was the adoption
of the 'Rumi,' i. e. Ottoman, custom of forming a
laager of linked wagons to protect the camp. As we
shall see, Babar employed this mode of defence with
the addition of chained gun-carriages. Other campaigns followed in 1419, 1423, 1435, and 1443, accompanied by the usual Bahmanid victories and
massacres, the destruction of temples and Brahman
colleges, and general devastation, and ending in the
invariable submission and tribute of the Hindu state.[1]

The unsuccessful siege (1459) of Devarakanda in

---

[1] The history of Vijayanagar may be read in the recent valuable
work of Mr. ROBERT SEWELL, *A Forgotten Empire*, in which the
annals of Firishta are supplemented by the records of oriental and
Portuguese travellers, and the campaigns are examined with much
topographic learning.

the Telugu country by the Bahmanid Humayun—an oriental Nero — shows that the power of the dynasty was limited by Hindu chiefs to the east; but the conquests of Mohammad II between 1476 and 1481, when Rajamandari, Kandapali, and Kandavid were wrested from the raja of Orisa, the sultan's arms triumphed over Masulipatan, and Belgaon was added on the west, raised the kingdom of Kulbarga to its greatest glory and extent. The pride was very shortly followed by the fall, but the blow did not come from rival empires. The kingdom broke up from internal causes. The succession of two young sons of Humayun under a regency weakened the royal authority, and though the wise administration of a great minister, Mahmud Gawan, and a decade of vigorous campaigns of aggression secured a vast extension of territory and an unprecedented degree of prosperity, the unjust execution of the minister and the subsequent demoralization of king and state led to the disruption of an empire that had outgrown its cohesion. A recent division into large provincial governments hastened the dissolution. During the reign of Mohammad's youthful son, Mahmud Shah II, the various provinces shook off the parent's yoke. Imad-al-mulk was crowned king in Berar (1484); Yusuf Adil Shah proclaimed the independence of the newly created government of Bijapur in 1489; Nizam-al-mulk prepared the way for the separation of Junair. Thus the most important provinces in the north, west, and south-west were lost; and early in the 16th century (1512) Telingana, never very firmly held, followed

the rest and declared its independence. Mahmud
Shah, once a captive, next a refugee, died at Bidar,
which had for some time superseded Kulbarga as
the dynastic capital, in 1518, and with him the
power of the Bahmanids came to an end, though
three sons and a grandson mounted a nominal throne
during the next eight years.

Their dominions were divided among the Adil
Shahs of Bijapur (1489–1686), the Kutb Shahs of
Golkonda (1512–1687), the Barid Shahs of Bidar
(1492–c. 1609), the Nizam Shahs of Ahmadnagar
(1490–1595), and the Imad Shahs of Berar (1484–
1572). Of these dynasties we shall hear again when
we come to the Deccan wars of Aurangzib. It is
now time to turn to a new invasion of India from
the north-west, which gradually converted a country
divided among numerous petty dynasties into a
united and powerful empire, and founded the long
line of the great Moghuls which endured to the days
of the Mutiny.

BOOK III

THE MOGHUL EMPIRE

1526–1764

CHAPTER VIII

THE COMING OF THE MOGHULS

THE EMPEROR BABAR

1451–1530

THE Muslims of India had grown effete. The old hardy vigour which had enabled the hills-men to trample upon the rich and ancient civilization of the Hindus was extinct. A race of conquerors had become a squabbling crowd, jostling each other for the luxuries of thrones, but wanting the power to hold a sceptre. The respect which belonged to a caste of foreigners, who kept themselves apart and observed strict rules of religious and social law, had been degraded when those laws were lightly es-teemed, when the harims of the Muslims were filled with native women, when Hindus who nominally professed Islam were promoted to high office,—when the Mohammedan domination, in short, had become the rule of the half-caste. The empire of Delhi had disappeared. The greater provinces had their separ-ate kings, the smaller districts and even single cities and forts belonged to chiefs or clans who owned no higher lord. The king's writ was no more supreme; it was the day of the little princes, the Muluk-at-tawaif or Faction-Kings.

Something, it is true, had been done to restore the vanished power of Delhi during the century that followed the collapse of the Taghlak dynasty after the invasion of Timur. The Sayyids utterly failed, but their successors the Lodi Afghans showed at first both energy and wisdom. Buhlol, who supplanted the last of the feeble Sayyids in 1451, was a good soldier and a simple man, who was content to let the world know that he was king without parading the pomp of monarchy. He took the minor principalities round Delhi in hand, and after a stubborn war of over a quarter of a century succeeded (as we have seen) in recovering Jaunpur and its territories and restoring the old frontier of his kingdom as far as Bihar. His son Sikandar, succeeding him in 1488, completed his task by subduing Bihar, where Husain the last king of Jaunpur had taken refuge, and by a treaty of alliance with the king of Bengal it was arranged that the dominion of Delhi should march with that of Bengal as in former times. The Rajputs of Dholpur, Chanderi, and Gwaliar submitted; and Sikandar's kingdom, including the Panjab, the Doab, Jaunpur, Oudh, Bihar, Tirhut, and the country between the Sutlej and Bandelkhand, began to recall the earlier supremacy of Delhi.

The resemblance was only on the surface, however, and, as Erskine has pointed out in his judicious history,[1] 'these extensive possessions, though under

[1] W. ERSKINE, *History of India under Baber and Humayun*, i, 406.

one king, had no very strong principle of cohesion.
The monarchy was a congeries of nearly independent
principalities, jagirs, and provinces, each ruled by an
hereditary chief, or by a zemindar or delegate from
Delhi; and the inhabitants looked more to their
immediate governors, who had absolute power in
the province and in whose hands consequently lay
their happiness or misery, than to a distant and
little-known sovereign. It was the individual, not
the law, that reigned. The Lodi princes, not merely
to strengthen their own power, but from necessity,
had in general committed the government of the
provinces and the chief offices of trust to their own
countrymen, the Afghans; so that men of the Lodi,
Fermuli, and Lohani tribes held all the principal
jagirs; which from the habitual modes of thinking
of their race they considered as their own of right
and purchased by their swords rather than as due
to any bounty or liberality on the part of the
sovereign.'

A throne depending on the allegiance of 'an aristocracy of rapacious and turbulent chiefs' demands
politic concessions on the part of the monarch.
Afghans above most men resent an undue assumption of superiority and tolerate with difficulty the
tedious etiquette and obsequious ceremony of a
formal court. Their king must be their chief, a
bon camarade and admitted leader in arms, but
he must not give himself airs or show a want of
respect for the free and outspoken clansmen upon
whose swords his dominion rests. Unfortunately the
new sultan of Delhi, Ibrahim son of Sikandar, who

succeeded his father in 1518, was a man of forms and a stickler for royal prerogative. He made the great Afghan chiefs stands motionless in his presence with folded hands and vexed them with petty rules of etiquette. Dreading their power—already displayed in the support given by an influential faction to his brother Jalal, who had been nominated to the government of Jaunpur and made a rash and unsuccessful effort to share a divided crown—instead of attempting to disarm them by favour and concession, he sought to reduce them to a sense of their inferiority by treating his lower subjects with the same degree of consideration that he showed to the Afghan nobles. When discontent arose, and revolt after revolt sprang up, he endeavoured to quench the rising conflagration by the blood of some of the leading amirs.

The result was still wider disaffection. The eastern districts about Oudh, Jaunpur, and Bihar, where Afghan influence was especially strong, rose in arms and chose Darya Khan, of the Lohani tribe, as their chief. In the Panjab, Daulat Khan, a son of one of the half dozen Afghan nobles who had set the Lodi dynasty on the throne of Delhi seventy years before, rebelled in alarm at the execution of some of the leading chiefs. The rule of sultan Ibrahim had become intolerable even to his own nation, and his uncle Ala-ad-din fled to Kabul to solicit the aid of its king, the descendant of Timur, in wresting the crown of Delhi from its ill-advised possessor.

The king of Kabul was not the man to shrink from an adventure of any kind; the wilder and the

more daring it seemed, the better he liked it. Babar
is perhaps the most captivating personality in
oriental history, and the fact that he is able to
impart this charm to his own Memoirs is not the
least of his titles to fame. He is the link between
Central Asia and India, between predatory hordes
and imperial government, between Timur and Akbar.
The blood of the two great scourges of Asia, Mongol
and Turk, Chingiz and Timur, mixed in his veins,
and to the daring and restlessness of the nomad
Tatar he joined the culture and urbanity of the
Persian. He brought the energy of the Mongol, the
courage and capacity of the Turk, to the subjection
of the listless Hindu; and, himself a soldier of
fortune and no architect of empire, he yet laid the
first stone of the splendid fabric which his grandson
Akbar completed.

' His connexion with India began only in the last
twelve years of his life. His youth was spent in
ineffectual struggles to preserve his sovereignty in
his native land. His early manhood, passed in his
new kingdom of Kabul, was full of an unsatisfied
yearning for the recovery of his mother country.
It was not till the age of thirty-six that he abandoned
his hope of a restored empire on the Oxus and
Iaxartes, and turned his eyes resolutely towards the
cities and spoils of Hindustan. Five times he invaded the northern plains, and the fifth invasion
was a conquest. Five years he dwelt in the India
he had now made his own, and in his forty-eighth
year he died.

' His permanent place in history rests upon his
13

Indian conquests, which opened the way for an imperial line ; but his place in biography and in literature is determined rather by his daring adventures and persevering efforts in his earlier days, and by the delightful Memoirs in which he related them. Soldier of fortune as he was, Babar was not the less a man of fine literary taste and fastidious critical perception. In Persian, the language of culture, the Latin of Central Asia, as it is of India, he was an accomplished poet, and in his native Turki he was master of a pure and unaffected style alike in prose and verse. The Turkish princes of his time prided themselves upon their literary polish, and to turn an elegant *ghazal*, or even to write a beautiful manuscript, was their peculiar ambition, no less worthy or stimulating than to be master of sword or mace. Wit and learning, the art of improvising a quatrain on the spot, quoting the Persian classics, writing a good hand, or singing a good song, were highly appreciated in Babar's world, as much perhaps as valour, and infinitely more than virtue. Babar himself will break off in the middle of a tragic story to quote a verse, and he found leisure in the thick of his difficulties and dangers to compose an ode on his misfortunes. His battles as well as his orgies were humanized by a breath of poetry.

‘ Hence his Memoirs are no rough soldier's chronicle of marches and countermarches, " saps, mines, blinds, gabions, palisadoes, ravelins, half-moons, and such trumpery "; they contain the personal impressions and acute reflections of a cultivated man of the world, well-read in Eastern literature, a close and

THE EMPEROR BABAR.

195

curious observer, quick in perception, a discerning judge of persons, and a devoted lover of nature,— one, moreover, who was well able to express his thoughts and observations in clear and vigorous language. The man's own character is so fresh and buoyant, so free from convention and cant, so rich in hope, courage, resolve, and at the same time so warm and friendly, so very human, that it conquers one's admiring sympathy. The utter frankness and self-revelation, the unconscious portraiture of all his virtues and follies, his obvious truthfulness and fine sense of honour give the Memoirs of this prince of autobiographers an authority which is equal to their charm.

'The line of emperors who proceeded from Babar's loins is no more. The very name of Mongol has lost its influence on the banks of Iaxartes ; the Turk is the servant of the Russian he once despised. The last Indian sovereign of Timur's race ended his inglorious career an exile at Rangoon almost within our own memory ; a few years later the degenerate descendants of Chingiz Kaan submitted to the officers of the Tsar. The power and pomp of Babar's dynasty are gone ; the record of his life — the *littera scripta* that mocks at time — remains unaltered and imperishable.' [1]

Babar's earlier career must be read elsewhere : it began far away from India, in the country beyond the Oxus where the descendants of Timur struggled for the remaining fragment of the vast empire which

[1] See LANE-POOLE, *Babar* (Clarendon Press, 1900), from which much of the present chapter is derived.

had broken up as soon as his iron hand was stiffened in death. Timur's conquests were too recent, too hasty, to be organized into settled empire. They were like a vast conflagration driven before the wind, which destroys the herbage for a while, but when the flame has passed the earth grows green again. Even in the original home, the Oxus land, a single century saw the downfall of Timur's dynasty: the fire had only left some embers, which smouldered awhile, but, lacking the kindling and stirring of the great incendiary, finally died out. After that, the sole relic of Timur's vast dominions was the little kingdom which an exiled prince of his own brave blood set up among the crags and passes of the Afghan hills — whence came the great Moghuls[1] and the glories of Delhi and Agra.

It was among these embers of the great fire that Babar, in 1494, at the age of eleven, found himself suddenly king of the province of Farghana beside the Iaxartes, by right of inheritance in the sixth generation from Timur. No boy had ever to face

---

[1] ' Moghul ' — more accurately Mughal — is the Arabic spelling of Mongol, and is specially applied to the emperors of India descended from Babar and sometimes called in Europe the Babarids. They were however of mixed race ; Babar himself was a Turk on his father's side, though a Mongol on his mother's, and he abhorred the very name of Moghul. His descendants introduced a strong Rajput strain by their marriages with Hindu princesses. The term Moghul is also applied to the followers of the Moghul emperors, and came to mean any fair man from Central Asia or Afghanistan, as distinguished from the darker native Indians. The various foreign invaders, or governing Muslim class, Turks, Afghans, Pathans, and Moghuls eventually became so mixed that all were indifferently termed Moghuls.

such perilous paths as those which led the young king of Farghana to the heights of his soaring ambition. He would reign where Timur reigned at Samarkand, and there hold sway over the empire of his ancestor : nothing less would content him. But the road to empire lay among jealous kinsmen, treacherous chiefs, mutinous retainers, and the ever-growing power of the hostile Uzbeg tribes. Twice did Babar seat himself upon Timur's throne, and twice was he expelled to wander a homeless exile among the hills, dwelling in the shepherds' huts, or suffering the ungracious protection of his mother's Mongol relations in the northern steppes. Ten years of ceaseless effort, brief triumph, sore defeat, and grinding misery, all borne with that courage and sanguine hope that were among his finest qualities, ended in his retreat to Kabul, where he took the little throne which had been held by Timur's lineage ever since his raid into India. Here Babar made himself a kingdom, small compared with the dominion of the present amir of Afghanistan, but not easy to hold, with its turbulent and jealous tribes and rocky barriers.

But a mountain chiefship was no fit ambition for a king who had twice ruled Samarkand. Babar's dreams still reverted to the land of his forefathers, and only the disastrous failure of his third attempt to recover Timur's capital in 1512 convinced him that the true road to empire led down the passes into the rich plains of Hindustan. His thoughts had often turned towards the east whilst he was bringing into order the restless tribes of his mountain realm, and several times his expeditions led him very near the

Indian frontier; but he had been twenty years at
Kabul before he carried his thoughts into decisive
action and began his campaign of conquest. An attack in 1519 on Bajaur, in the Indian borderland
near Chitral, with which recent history has made us
familiar, was merely a preliminary step, though followed by the occupation of Bhira on the Jehlam. Babar had thus set his foot upon the Panjab, and claimed
it in right of his ancestor Timur's conquest a hundred and twenty years before; but it was no more
than a claim, for the moment he turned back to
Kabul the Indians recovered the territory, and Babar's occupation, with a couple of thousand horse,
was but a raid. It was not till 1524 that he entered
resolutely upon the campaigns which ended in the
conquest of Hindustan.

The appeal of Alam Khan Ala-ad-din, the uncle of
sultan Ibrahim, already noticed, was but the spark
that kindled a long-prepared train. The claimant to
the throne of Delhi appeared at Kabul to urge a
petition that was already granted in Babar's own
mind. No more propitious moment could be desired. India was seething with faction and discontent. Babar was strong and prepared, and at his
side was a member of the Lodi family to sanction
his plans and invite adhesion. The emperor was
soon on the march, and following his previous route
to Bhira was quickly in the neighbourhood of Lahore.
The insurgent governor, Daulat Khan, had already
been driven out by the Delhi army, but he was
amply avenged by the Kabul troops, who routed
the enemy with heavy slaughter, and chased them

through the streets of Lahore, plundering and burning the bazar. Babar rested only four days in the
capital of the Panjab, and then pressed on at his best
speed to Dipalpur, where he stormed and sacked the
town, and massacred the garrison. He appointed
some of his most trusty officers to defend the province, and having established 'sultan' Ala-ad-din at
Dipalpur (with a veteran Mongol to watch him), the
emperor returned to Kabul to beat up reinforcements.

Babar set out on his final invasion of India in November, 1525. His eldest son, Humayun, brought
a contingent from Badakhshan, and Khwaja Kalan,
trustiest of generals, led the troops of Ghazni.
Daulat Khan, after deceiving the invaders with pretended support, was now in the field against them
at the head of 40,000 men, and the old Afghan had
girded on two swords in token of his resolve to win
or die. Nevertheless this valiant army broke and
vanished at Babar's approach with a far less numerous force, and the emperor continued his advance.

'The decisive battle was fought on April 21,
1526, on the plain of Panipat—the historic site
where the throne of India has been thrice won.
For several days Babar was busy with his preparations. He collected seven hundred gun-carts, and
formed a laager by linking them together with
twisted bull-hides, to break a cavalry charge, and by
arranging hurdles or shields between each pair to
protect the matchlock men.[1] Then two marches
more brought the army to Panipat. Here he had

[1] Baggage-wagons were probably used to supplement gun-carriages
in forming a breastwork. Babar frequently mentions that the ar-

the town on his right, his left was defended by ditches and abatis of trees, while he placed his cannon and matchlocks in the centre. He was careful to leave gaps in his line a bowshot apart, through which 100 or 150 men could charge abreast.

'On the 20th of April a night surprise was attempted upon the Afghans' position, and though it failed, owing to the confusion of the troops in the darkness, it had the effect of drawing the enemy out of his camp. Sultan Ibrahim, elated by the ease with which this attack had been driven back, brought his army out at dawn on the 21st in battle array. It was said to muster 100,000 men and 100 elephants. The moment Babar detected the movement of the enemy, his men were ordered to put on their helmets and mail, and take up their stations. His army was drawn up behind his laager in the usual order, right and left centre, right and left wing, advance guard, and reserve; but in addition he had placed flanking parties of Mongols on the extreme right and left, with orders to execute their famous national manoeuvre, the *tulughma*—a rapid wheel charging the enemy's rear—of which Babar well knew the tremendous effect.

rangement of his chained carriages was copied from the ' Kumi,' i. e. Osmanli, order of battle. At the battle of Khaldiran in 1514, between the Osmanlis and the Persians, the former not only chained their guns together, but 'set up their usual breastwork of baggage-wagons and camels in front of the Janizaries,' thus using a wagon laager in the centre as well as chained guns at the extremities of their line of battle. Mr. Oman tells me that the use of war-carts, formed and manœuvred in hollow squares, was invented by the Hussites in the Bohemian wars to resist the German cavalry.

'The army of Delhi came straight on, at a quick march, without a halt from the start. They seemed to be aiming at Babar's right, and he sent up the reserve to its support. As the enemy came up to the ditches, abatis, and hurdles, they hesitated, and the pressure of the troops behind threw them into some confusion. Taking advantage of this Babar sent out his Mongol flankers through the gaps in the laager, and they galloped round the enemy and poured their arrows into the rear. Part of the emperor's left wing, advancing incautiously, got into difficulties; but the general's eye was on them, and they were promptly supported from the centre. Meanwhile the right was also hard pressed and Babar sent forward his right centre to their assistance. The master-gunner, Ustad Ali, made pretty practice with his *firengi* pieces, in front of the line, and was admirably seconded by Mustafa, the cannoneer on the left centre. The enemy was now engaged on all sides, front, flanks, and rear; and their charges, which seemed ineffective to men who had stood up to the Mongols' swoop, were easily repulsed and driven back upon their centre, which was already too crowded to be able to use its strength. In this jammed confusion they lay at the mercy of the hardy Turks and Mongols, who fell upon the strangled ranks with deadly effect.

'By noon the great army of the king of Delhi was broken and flying for dear life. Sultan Ibrahim himself lay stark on the field, amidst some fifteen thousand of his dead. They brought his head to

Babar, and prisoners, elephants, and spoil of all sorts began to come in from the pursuers. " The sun had mounted spear-high when the onset began, and the battle lasted till mid-day, when the enemy were completely broken and routed, and my people victorious and triumphant. By the grace and mercy of Almighty God this difficult affair was made easy to me, and that mighty army, in the space of half a day, was laid in the dust." Two detachments were at once dispatched to occupy Delhi and Agra, and on Friday, April 27, the public prayer was said in the mosque of the capital in the name of the new Emperor, the first of the ·' Great Moguls." '

The spoil of the royal treasuries at Delhi and Agra was immense and the first business was to divide the booty among the expectant troops. To his eldest son Humayun, who had played his part like a man in the great battle, he gave seventy lacs (of dams, i. e. about £20,000) and a treasure which no one had counted. His chief Begs were rewarded with six to ten lacs apiece (£1,700 to £2,800). Every man who had fought received his share, and even the traders and camp-followers were remembered in the general bounty. Every man and woman, slave and free, young and old, in Kabul, was sent a silver coin in celebration of the victory. When Humayun brought his father the glorious diamond, one of the famous historical jewels, valued at 'half the daily expenses of the world,' which the family of the late Raja Vikramajit had given him in gratitude for his chivalrous protection, Babar

gave it back to the young prince.[1] He had no love
for wealth or precious stones, except to give away,
and his prodigal generosity in distributing the immense spoil of the Delhi kings gained him the
nickname of 'the Kalandari' — the begging-friar
He was content with fame.

Babar was now king of Delhi, but not yet king of
Hindustan, much less of India. Even of the dominions of Delhi, which then stretched from the Indus
to Bihar, and from Gwaliar to near the Himalayas,
he was only nominally master. The Lodi dynasty,
indeed, was dethroned, and its king slain, but that
king left a brother to claim the crown, and the land
remained unsubdued east and south of Agra. The
people were hostile to the strangers of uncouth
tongue, and each town and petty ruler prepared for
obstinate resistance. The strongholds of the Doab
and Rajputana were all fortifying against attack,
unanimous in rejecting the newcomers. In spite of
the surfeit of treasure, Babar's troops were like to
starve. 'When I came to Agra,' he says, 'it was
the hot season. All the inhabitants fled from terror,
so that we could find neither grain for ourselves nor
fodder for our beasts. The villages, out of mere
hatred and spite to us, had taken to anarchy, thiev-
ing, and marauding. The roads became impassable.
I had not had time, after the division of the treasure,
to send fit persons to occupy and protect the different parganas and stations. The heats this year

---

[1] Perhaps the famous Koh-i-nur : see an interesting article by Mr.
H. Beveridge in the *Calcutta Review*, 1897, in which the history of
this diamond is traced, and Ball's *Travels of Tavernier*, ii, app. i.

chanced to be unusually oppressive, and many men dropped at about the same time, as though struck by the *samum*, and died on the spot.'

The troops began to murmur. They longed for the cool air of Kabul, and even made ready to return. They looked upon India as a buccaneer looked on a gallion: the prize money secured, they wished to make sail. They had to deal with an obstinate man, however, and Babar summoned the chief officers together and made them a speech. He recalled their past toil and labours together, the weary marches and grievous hardships, and reminded them that all these had been endured for the sake of the great reward which was now theirs. 'A mighty enemy had been overcome, and a rich and powerful kingdom was at their feet. And now, having attained our goal and won our game, are we to turn back from all we have accomplished and fly to Kabul like men who have lost and are discomfited? Let no man who calls himself my friend ever again moot such a thing. But if there be any one of you who cannot bring himself to stay, then let him go.' Thoroughly ashamed, the murmurers dared not say a word. There are few acts more splendidly heroic in Babar's career than this bold resolve to stay where he was— in the middle of India, among hostile nations, and a discontented soldiery — and the reward of his firmness soon appeared. Not only his own people but many of his enemies were won over. First an Afghan officer came with a valuable contingent of two or three thousand retainers from the Doab. Then a powerful chief was won by the emperor's clemency to his captured sons.　Meanwhile Sambhal was taken by guile; and Humayun led an army against the insurgent Afghans in the east, who were advancing into the Doab, but immediately broke up on his approach and fled over the Ganges.　The young prince pursued, took Jaunpur and Ghazipur, and leaving strong divisions to hold his conquests, marched back by way of Kalpi to support his father against a pressing danger.

For Babar was now coming to the grip with the only formidable rival left in Hindustan.　The great Rana Sanga of Chitor, the revered head of all the Rajput princes, commanded a vast army.　One hundred and twenty chieftains of rank, with 80,000 horse and 500 war elephants, followed him to the field. The lords of Marwar and Amber, Gwaliar, Ajmir, Chanderi, and many more, brought their retainers to his standards; and the battered old hero, who counted eighty wounds in his body, and had lost an arm and an eye in the wars, was not to be denied when his drums beat to battle.　The famous Rana was now marching on Biana.　The emperor sent on a light detachment towards the threatened fortress, with orders to hang on the enemy and harass him; and himself set out with his main body in battle array on February 11, 1527.　All his campaigns hitherto had been against fellow Muslims; now, for the first time, he was marching against 'heathens'; it was the Jihad, the Holy War.　Moreover these 'heathens' were fighting men of the first class. Babar had some experience of the warlike capacities of various races.　He knew the Mongol wheeling

swoop, the Uzbeg charge, the Afghan skirmish, and
the steady fighting of his own Turks; but he was
now to meet warriors of a higher type than any he
had encountered. 'The Rajputs, energetic, chivalrous, fond of battle and bloodshed, animated by a
strong national spirit, were ready to meet face to face
the boldest veterans of the camp, and were at all
times prepared to lay down their life for their
honour.'

'The emperor camped at Sikri — afterwards
Akbar's exquisite palace-city of Fathpur — where he
was joined by the garrison from Biana. These men
had already received a lesson from the Rajputs, of
whose bravery and daring they spoke with deep
respect. The enemy was evidently not one that
could be trifled with. An outpost affair soon confirmed this impression: an incautious advance by
one of the amirs was instantly detected by the
Rajputs, who sent the Turks flying back to camp.
Being now in touch with the enemy, the emperor
put his army in battle array. As before at Panipat,
he ranged the gun-carriages, and probably the baggage-wagons, so as to cover his front, and chained
them together at a distance of five paces. Mustafa
from Turkey ordered his artillery admirably in the
Ottoman manner on the left wing, but Ustad Ali had
a method of his own. Where there were no guns
or wagons, a ditch was dug, backed by portable
wooden tripods on wheels, lashed together at a few
paces apart.' These preparations took twenty-five
days, and were designed to restore the confidence of
the troops, who were almost in a panic at the reports

of the numbers and courage of the Rajputs and at the foolish predictions of a rascally astrologer.

It was at this crisis that Babar renounced wine, broke his drinking cups, poured out the stores of liquor on the ground, and calling his dispirited officers together, addressed them: 'Gentlemen and Soldiers, — Every man that comes into the world must pass away: God alone is immortal, unchangeable. Whoso sits down to the feast of life must end by drinking the cup of death. All visitors of the inn of mortality must one day leave this house of sorrow. Rather let us die with honour than live disgraced.

> With fame, though I die, I am content,
> Let fame be mine, though life be spent.

God most high has been gracious in giving us this destiny, that if we fall we die martyrs, if we conquer we triumph in His holy cause. Let us swear with one accord by the great name of God that we will never turn back from such a death, or shrink from the stress of battle, till our souls are parted from our bodies.'

The response was enthusiastic. Every man seized the Koran and took the oath, and the army began to pluck up heart. Babar resolved to advance upon the enemy. On New Year's Day, March 12, he writes:— 'I advanced my wagons [and guns] and tripods with all the apparatus and machines that I had prepared, and marched forward with my army in order of battle — right wing, left wing. and centre in their places. In front were the wagons, gun-carriages, and tripods on wheels, and behind came Ustad Ali Kuli

with a body of his matchlock men, to prevent the
communication being cut off between the artillery
and the infantry behind, and to enable them to advance and form into line. When the ranks were
formed and every man in his place, I galloped along
the line, encouraging the begs and men of the centre, right, and left, giving special directions to each
division how to act, and to each man orders how to
proceed and engage. Then, when all was arranged,
I moved the army on in order of battle for a couple
of miles, when we camped.' On Saturday March
16, 1527, the two armies met at Kanwaha. The
battle began by a desperate charge of the Rajputs
upon the emperor's right, which he instantly supported from his reserves, whilst opening fire with his
artillery from the centre. It was impossible to stop
a Rajput charge, however; they came on, wave after
wave, against the cannon, and the fight grew more
and more desperate. After several hours of hand
to hand conflict Babar sent orders to his flanking
columns to wheel and charge in the famous Mongol
tactics, whilst at the same time he ordered his guns
forward and sent out the household troops at the
gallop on each side of his centre of matchlock-men,
who also advanced firing. This combined manœuvre
shook the enemy. Few Indians will fight when
taken in the rear. The Rajputs were pressed into a
disordered crowd, and nothing but their indomitable
gallantry prolonged a battle that was fast becoming a
massacre. Ustad Ali's 'huge balls' did fearful execution, and at last the splendid chivalry of India gave
up hope, forced its way through the encompassing

14

Turks, and fled in every direction, leaving heaps of slain upon the fields. Many chiefs had fallen, and the heads of the noble Rajputs rose in a ghastly tower erected by their conqueror. Sanga escaped, severely wounded, and died soon after, but no raja of his line ever again took the field in person against an emperor of Babar's house.

Within a year the invader had struck two decisive blows, which shattered the power of two great forces. At Panipat the Mohammedan Afghans went down; Kanwaha crushed the confederacy of the bravest Hindus. The storming of the fortress of Chanderi, the stronghold of Medini Rao, the great Rajput vezir of Malwa, completed the overthrow. When the upper fort was carried, the desperate garrison killed their women and children, and rushing forth naked threw themselves upon the Muslim swords, and such as came through leaped over the ramparts to certain death. There was no more trouble with the Rajputs.

It was otherwise with the Afghans. Beaten at Delhi they were still strong in Bihar, and had even resumed the offensive when they saw the emperor absorbed in the Rajput campaign. But their time of retribution was at hand, and as soon as Chanderi had fallen Babar set out in February, 1528, to reduce the eastern province. The Afghans fell back from Kanauj at his approach, and awaited him on the further bank of the Ganges. Babar set up his camp opposite and ordered a pontoon to be thrown across the sea-like stream. 'The Afghans mocked at so wild a project, but the bridge went on; and the

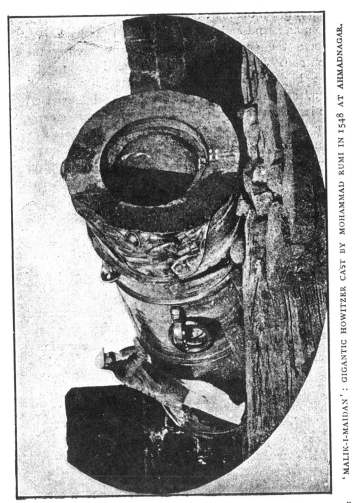

'MALIK-I-MAIDAN': GIGANTIC HOWITZER CAST BY MOHAMMAD RUMI IN 1548 AT AHMADNAGAR.

skilful fire of the matchlocks and artillery, discharged from an island and from a battery on the bank, protected the engineers who were constructing the pontoon. Ustad Ali even succeeded in firing off the big cannon called 'Dig Ghazi' ('victorious gun,' a title it had won in the battle of Kanwaha) no less than sixteen times a day, which was clearly a record performance at that time. On March 13 the bridge was finished, and some of the infantry and the Panjab troops were sent over to skirmish. On the three following days the artillery and the whole of the imperial forces were safely got across, but the enemy, after stubbornly fighting, decamped. They were hotly pursued nearly as far as Oudh, with the loss of their families and baggage, and many were overtaken and slain. The Afghan army was utterly dispersed for the time, and Babar returned to Agra for the rainy season.'

The city was a very different place from the Agra he had found. He delighted in running water, and had sunk wells and built tanks among the tamarinds beside the Jumna, and planted roses and narcissi in regular parterres. In India a 'garden' includes a dwelling, and Babar's Charbagh with its marble pavilions and beds of roses must have been a delightful palace. The Indians, who had never seen this sort of pleasure-ground, called it 'Kabul.'

' He was not left long in repose. The Afghans in Bihar were not yet quelled. Mahmud Lodi, the brother of sultan Ibrahim, had arrived among them, and they flocked to the standard of their hereditary king. Jaunpur and most of Bihar declared for him, and the many factions laid aside their rivalries for the moment to support the last chance of an Afghan restoration. Babar received this news in the middle of January, 1529, whilst he was staying at Dholpur, preparing for a predatory campaign in Sind. He at once returned to Agra and led his army out. At the news of his approach the large army of the Afghans, numbering, it was said, a hundred thousand men, melted away: the Lodi pretender fled from before Chunar, to which he was laying seige; Sher Khan escaped from Benares; and as Babar pressed on to Buxar, several of the Afghan leaders came in to offer their submission; and their prince, finding himself almost deserted, sought protection with the Bengal army.'

The kingdom of Bengal, as we have seen, had long been independent of Delhi, and Babar had no immediate intention of subduing it, so long as it did not interfere with him. But the protection it was affording to the rebels was not the act of a friendly power, and the massing of the Bengal troops on the frontier was ominous. ' Reinforced by 20,000 men from Jaunpur, Babar resolved to force the passage of the Gogra in face of the Bengalis. He made unusually elaborate preparations, for he knew the enemy were skilful gunners, and were in great force. Ustad Ali was to plant his cannon, *firengi* pieces, and swivels on a rising ground at the point between the two rivers, and also keep up a hot fire from his matchlock-men upon the Bengali camp on the east bank of the Gogra. A little below the junction of the rivers, Mustafa was to direct a cannonade from his artillery, supported by matchlocks, on the enemy's flank, and upon the Bengal flotilla which lay off an island. The main army was formed up in six divisions, four of which, under the emperor's son Askari, were already north of the Ganges. These were to cross the Gogra by boats or fords, and keep the enemy busy while the artillery was being carried across, and a strong force was sent ahead to divert their attention. The fifth division, under Babar himself was to support Ustad Ali's batteries above the confluence, and then to cross the Gogra under cover of the guns; whilst the sixth went to the support of Mustafa's artillery on the right bank of the Ganges.

'On Sunday and Monday, May 2 and 3, 1529, these two divisions crossed the Ganges and on Tuesday they marched on to the Gogra. Ustad Ali at the confluence was making excellent practice with his *firengis* upon the Bengal vessels in the river. Meanwhile news came that Askari had got his divisions over the Gogra, and on the morning of Thursday, May 6, the battle began. The Bengal army, as was foreseen, moved up the river to meet Askari, and Babar at once ordered the fifth and sixth divisions to cross anyhow, swimming, in boats, or on bundles of reeds, and take the enemy in the rear. The movement was brilliantly carried out in the face of a determined resistance. Attacked in front and rear and flank, the enemy broke and fled. Good generalship had once more guided valour to victory. The result was the collapse of the Afghan rebellion, and the conclusion of a treaty of peace with Bengal. In three battles Babar had reduced northern India to submission.'

It was his last exploit. The year and a half of life that remained to him he spent chiefly at Agra, endeavouring to set his new empire in order. For permanent organization there was really no time. A large part of his dominions was under very loose control and the polity of Hindustan under his rule was simply the strong hand of military power. In the more settled regions the lands and towns were parcelled out in fiefs among his officers or jagirdars, who levied the land-tax from the cultivators, the duties from the merchants and shopkeepers, and the poll-tax from the Hindus, and paid fixed contributions in money and military service to the emperor. But the large zamindars or landholders were often so powerful that their dependence on the crown was little more than nominal, and India was still, as Erskine observes, 'rather a congeries of little states under one prince than one regular and uniformly governed kingdom.' The tribes of the frontier and hill districts can hardly be said to have submitted in more than form, and in Sind on the west and Bihar on the east the king's writ was lightly regarded. All the different provinces, however, according to a list in Babar's Memoirs, west to east from Bhira and Lahore to Bahraich and Bihar, and north to south from Sialkot to Rantambhor, contributed to the revenue, which is stated at fifty-two crores of tankas or dams, which comes to £2,600,000 for the regular revenue from land-tax. Three quarters of a century later his grandson Akbar drew a revenue of over £18,000,000 from the same source, though from a considerably larger area.

It was probably during the comparative leisure of his last year that Babar wrote that valuable description of Hindustan which displays his undiminished interest in natural history, and his singular quickness of observation. Though he had conquered his new empire he did not love it. 'The country and towns of Hindustan,' he writes, 'are extremely ugly. All its towns and lands have a uniform look; its gardens have no walls; the greater part of it is a level plain.' He found 'the ·plains' monotonous after the mountain scenery of Kabul and the well-watered orchards of Farghana. 'Hindustan, ' he adds, 'is a country that has few pleasures to recommend it. The people are not handsome. They have no idea of the charms of friendly society. They have no genius, no intellectual comprehension, no politeness, no kindness or fellow-feeling, no ingenuity or mechanical invention in planning or executing their handicrafts, no skill or knowledge in design or architecture. They have no good horses, no good flesh, no grapes or musk-melons, no good fruits, no ice or cold water, no good food or bread in their bazars, no baths, or colleges, or candles, or torches — never a candlestick!'

He would not have written this sweeping and wholly unjust condemnation had he lived longer in India and seen more of its people; and he does indeed admit that there are advantages, such as the abundance of workmen, and the 'pleasant climate during the rains'; but, on the whole, to him 'the chief excellency of Hindustan is that it is a big country with plenty of gold and silver.' One can see that even from his throne at Agra he looks back with regret to his own land, the land of melons and cool waters, and remembers with the pang of the exile the joyous days he spent beside the Kabul river.

He was not the man he had been. Fever and a wandering restless life, joined to frequent bouts of drinking and constant use of opium, had undermined a wonderful constitution. Yet between his fits of fever his vigour remained extraordinary. He could take up a man under each arm, and run with them round the battlements of a fortress, leaping the embrasures: and even in March, 1529, he notes: 'I swam across the river Ganges for amusement. I counted my strokes, and found that I swam over in thirty-three strokes. I then took breath, and swam back to the other side. I had crossed by swimming every river I had met, except only the Ganges.' He was also constantly in the saddle, and often he did his eighty miles a day. All this did not make for long life, and Babar's snapped with the suddenness of an overstrained spring. He passed away in his beautiful garden palace at Agra, on the 26th of December, 1530,—a man of only forty-eight, a king of thirty-six years crowded with hardship, tumult, and strenuous energy — but he lies at peace in his grave in the garden on the hill at Kabul, 'the sweetest spot' which he had chosen himself, surrounded by those he loved, by the sweet-smelling flowers of his choice, and the cool running stream; and the people still flock to the tomb and offer prayers at the simple mosque which an august descendant built in memory of the founder of the Indian Empire.

CHAPTER IX

THE EBB OF THE TIDE

HUMAYUN

1530–1556

IT was no easy throne that Babar left to his eldest
son in December, 1530, nor was Humayun man
enough to fill it. Though only twenty-three years
of age, he was not without experience; he had commanded under his father in the Indian war, and governed the outlying province of Badakhshan beyond
the Hindu Kush. Babar had lavished good advice
upon the son whom he loved above all things.
'His presence,' he once wrote, 'opened our hearts
like rosebuds and made our eyes shine like torches.
His conversation had an ineffable charm, and he
realized absolutely the ideal of perfect manhood.'
The young prince was indeed a gallant and loveable
fellow, courteous, witty, and accomplished as his
father, warm-hearted and emotional, almost quixotic
in his notions of honour and magnanimity, personally brave,—as indeed were all the princes of his
house,—and capable of great energy on occasions.

218

But he lacked character and resolution. He was incapable of sustained effort, and after a moment of triumph would bury himself in his harim and dream away the precious hours in the opium-eater's paradise whilst his enemies were thundering at the gate. Naturally kind, he forgave when he should have punished; light-hearted and sociable, he revelled at the table when he ought to have been in the saddle. His character attracts but never dominates. In private life he might have been a delightful companion and a staunch friend; his virtues were Christian, and his whole life was that of a gentleman. But as a king he was a failure. His name means 'fortunate,' and never was an unlucky sovereign more miscalled.

The qualities most essential at the time of his accession were a firm grasp of the military situation and resolution to meet it. It was a position that called for boundless energy and soldierly genius. Babar, as we have seen, had not conquered Hindustan: he had only reduced to partial submission a territory comprising little more than what we should now call the Panjab and North-West Provinces. He had not annexed Bengal to the east, nor the great provinces of Malwa and Gujarat, now united under one king, to the south. The many chiefs of Rajputana were cowed but not subdued, and in most of the outlying parts of the kingdom the Moghul power was but slightly recognized. Numerous Afghan officers still held powerful fiefs, and these men had not forgotten that the kings of Delhi had been Afghans but a few years before. When a member of the deposed dynasty appeared amongst them in Bihar, there were all the materials for a formidable insurrection. Thus even in his inherited dominions—about an eighth part of all India—Humayun was not secure from rivals and revolts.

Nor was he safe from the hostility of his own family. Babar had particularly commended his other sons to Humayun's kindness, and never was forbearance more cruelly tried. There was not one of his three brothers who did not intrigue against him. Kamran, the next in age, had been already ruler of Kabul under his father, and not only retained his western province but annexed the Panjab, always professing his allegiance to Humayun, whose pre-occupations no less than his brotherly kindness induced him to tolerate the usurpation. It was short-sighted policy, however, for with Kamran practically independent on the north-west frontier the main recruiting ground of the Moghul army was cut off. Hitherto the fighting strength of the Muslims in India had been nourished and restored by the hill tribes of Afghanistan and the men of the Oxus. Now that source was dammed, and Humayun was forced to depend upon the army already in India, which was constantly depleted by loss in battle, or by natural causes, without any resources of reinforcement, and was suffering the inevitable degeneration that overtakes a hardy race when exposed to the luxuries of wealth and the influence of an enervating climate.

Kamran, a surly ill-conditioned traitor, unworthy of Babar's seed, was the most formidable of the

BABAR, HUMAYUN, AKBAR, AND JAHANGIR.

221

brothers. Askari and Hindal, ever weak and shifty, were dangerous only as tools for ambitious men to play upon. Their repeated treachery towards their too magnanimous brother was of a piece with their general worthlessness. Two cousins, Mohammad Zaman and Mohammad Sultan, also made their futile bids for a throne which not one of the family was then great enough to hold. Humayun was too gentle to do the only prudent thing, to make an end of them, and to this beautiful but unwise clemency he owed part of his misfortunes. But his worst enemy was himself. Instead of taking a statesmanlike view of the situation, meeting the most pressing danger first, and crushing one antagonist before he engaged another, he frittered away his army in divided commands, and deprived it of its full strength; he left one enemy unsubdued behind him while he turned to meet another; and when victory by chance rewarded his courage, rather than his tactics, he reposed upon his laurels and made merry with his friends whilst his foes used the precious time in gathering their forces for a fresh effort. Had he brought the whole of his strength to bear upon each enemy in turn he must have been successful; for Babar's troops were still the men who had won Delhi and defeated Sanga, and Babar's generals were still in command of their divisions. But Humayun weakened their valour and destroyed their confidence by division and vacillation, neglected the counsels of the commanders, and displayed such indecision that it is a marvel that any army still adhered to his falling fortunes.

There were three ominous clouds on his horizon when he came to the throne. On the north-west was his brother Kamran; but as he professed loyalty, however insincerely, Humayun was fain to let him alone. On the east were the Afghans in Bihar, with a brother of the late Lodi sultan of Delhi at their head. On the south was Bahadur Shah, the king of Gujarat and Malwa, actively pressing his triumphs over the Rajputs and rapidly approaching within striking distance of Agra. He too had a pretender to put forward in the person of the cousin already named, Mohammad Zaman. Of the two chief perils the king of Gujarat was the more imposing, but the Afghan confederacy the more dangerous adversary. Humayun was perpetually hesitating between the two. First he marched to Bihar and easily disposed of Mahmud the Lodi in a decisive victory near Lucknow in 1531. Instead of following up his success by crushing the routed Afghans with his utmost strength, he abandoned the siege of Chunar, Sher Khan's stronghold in Bihar, accepted a purely perfunctory submission, and left thus the most capable, unscrupulous, and ambitious man in the whole Afghan party free to mature his plans and strengthen his power whilst the emperor was away at the other end of Hindustan.

It was the fear of the king of Gujarat that induced this fatal retreat. Bahadur Shah undoubtedly was aiming at the conquest of Delhi, but he was not ready for it yet, and such raids or expeditions as he had encouraged the pretenders to the throne to lead against Agra and Kalinjar had been easily repulsed by the imperial troops. When Humayun, abandoning the fruits of his victory at Lucknow, arrived in Malwa at the close of 1534, he found Bahadur busily engaged in the siege of the great Rajput fortress of Chitor. Instead of attacking at once, and by his timely interference probably winning to his side the inestimable friendship of the Rajput chiefs, he must needs stand by till the quarrel was fought out.[1] It was admirable chivalry to call a truce while his Muslim enemy was waging what might be termed a Holy War against Hindu 'infidels,' and one cannot help respecting Humayun's quixotic observance of a Mohammedan scruple of honour; *mais ce n'était pas la guerre.* Profiting by the emperor's fine feelings, Bahadur stormed Chitor; the Rajput women eagerly rushed upon the swords of their husbands and fathers to escape the shame of Muslim harims; the men sallied forth to be slaughtered; and the conquerer turned to meet his complaisant foe, who amiably awaited the issue.

Flushed with recent victory the Gujaratis might probably have overwhelmed Humayun's army, on which the irritation as well as the revels of the delay had exerted their usual influences; but the triumph of the heavy artillery in the siege of Chitor had given undue weight to the advice of the Ottoman engineer, the 'Rumi Khan,' who had worked the guns with the help of Portuguese and other European gunners; and, as with Sir John Burgoyne before Sevastopol, the voice of the engineer prevailed over the bolder counsels of the cavalry leaders. At the Rumi Khan's motion, instead of falling in-

[1] *Tabakat-i-Akbari*, E. and D., v, 191.

stantly upon the imperial troops, the army of Gujarat penned itself up in a fortified camp. The enemy, as the engineer foretold, confronted by the big guns, could not get in; but on the other hand the defenders could not get out. The open country around was in the hands of the Moghul archers, whose arrows gave short shrift to any men of Gujarat who ventured outside the ditch. Famine rendered the camp untenable, and at last in the dead of night Bahadur slunk away with only five followers. His army, discovering the desertion, immediately dispersed, and Humayun, on seeking the cause of the unusual hubbub, found himself in undisputed possession of the vast camp and all the spoils of the enemy. On this occasion he showed unwonted energy; pursued the king of Gujarat to Mandu, and on to Champanir, and Ahmadabad, and thence to Cambay, one flying out as the other entered in; till Bahadur at last found refuge in the island of Diu. Malwa and Gujarat—two provinces equal in area to all the rest of Humayun's kingdom—had fallen like ripe fruit into his hands. Never was conquest so easy.

Never, too, was conquest more recklessly squandered away. The vast spoils of the Gujarat camp, of Champanir, and of Cambay, utterly demoralized the Moghuls. The emperor had shown energy and decision in the pursuit; he had proved his mettle when he himself took part in scaling the fort of Champanir by means of iron spikes, the forty-first man to reach the battlements. Then came the reaction. Instead of insuring the efficient control

15

and administration of his new acquisitions, Humayun devoted himself to festivities in Malwa, while his brother **Askari**, as viceroy of Gujarat, revelled at Ahmadabad, and even boasted in his cups that he was king, and prepared to oust his brother, just as if there were no enemies in the land. The result of this foolish confidence was soon seen. The local governors and chiefs were still loyal to Bahadur, and he had purchased the support of the Portuguese by allowing them to build a fort at Diu. Finding his invaders fast asleep, the king advanced, and was everywhere welcomed with enthusiasm. Askari retired, and Gujarat reverted to its old ruler. Nor was this all. Humayun's fatal weakness in Bihar was working its inevitable punishment. Sher Khan had become supreme on the borders of Bengal, and Mohammad Sultan was already proclaimed king at Kanauj. What ought to have been done before had to be done now, and Humayun marched north to recover what his own folly had lost. No sooner was he gone than Malwa threw off the Moghul authority and was joined again to Gujarat. One year had seen the rapid conquest of the two great provinces; the next saw them as quickly lost.

The only justification for the abandonment of so rich a prize would be the paramount necessity of suppressing the growing revolt in the eastern provinces. Yet the feckless emperor wasted a whole year at Agra in merrymaking and opiated idleness before he moved to the scene of rebellion. He even thought of first returning to recover Malwa and Gujarat before grappling with the very danger that had caused their abandonment. Nothing could more clearly show the incurable vacillation and military incompetence of this amiable prince. When at last he set out in July, 1537, with every man he could muster, he carried all before him. The Rumi Khan, who, being an adventurer, had deserted to the winning side on the flight of the king of Gujarat, now plied his guns for Humayun, and his science compelled the surrender of Sher Khan's fortress of Chunar, in the absence of its lord, who was then busily engaged in reducing the whole of Bengal to his sway.

This indomitable Afghan, whose bold career deserves a volume to itself, had long fixed his eyes on the decaying power of the Bengal kings and dreamed of a restoration of the Afghan ascendancy. Descended from the royal house of Sur, kings of Ghor, he had risen from the rank of a mere administrator of a small district near Rohtas to be prime minister of one of the Lohani Afghans who styled themselves kings of Bihar in the time of Babar. On that emperor's advance, Sher Khan — 'Tiger-lord,' so called because he killed a tiger that lept suddenly upon the king of Bihar — at first nominally sided with the conqueror, but this did not prevent his joining in Mahmud Lodi's attempt to recover the throne, nor his treacherously deserting the pretender at the battle with Humayun near Lucknow which dispelled the Lodi's hopes. Though then again nominally reconciled with the Moghuls, and making his submission to Humayun when Chunar was besieged in 1532, the Afghan chief never abandoned his dream of sovereignty. During Humayun's long absence in the west, he skilfully enlarged his territories and strengthened his army, and while the emperor was busy for six months in a second siege of Chunar its master was conquering Gaur, the capital of Bengal.

With unusual energy Humayun immediately pressed on to eject him before conquest had been consolidated into permanent rule in the wealthiest agricultural province of Hindustan. Sher Khan would listen to no overtures, though the emperor offered him pardon and the government of Jaunpur if he would submit. Leaving his son Jalal Khan to hold the pass which leads from Bihar into Bengal at the foot of the Rajmahall hills, the Afghan hurriedly conveyed his booty, treasure, artillery, and family into the impregnable fort of Rohtas, which he captured from its Hindu chief by the familiar strata-gem of introducing armed men in women's litters. As soon as this manœuvre was accomplished and all was safe in Rohtas, Jalal, who had held the pass as long as was needed and had inflicted considerable loss on the imperial advance guard, joined his father, and Humayun was allowed to march into Bengal (1538). He entered a devastated and ruined country, and found a capital strewn with corpses. Neverthe-less here he enjoyed himself and feasted six precious months away, admiring the sights of the fertile pro-vince, and indulging with all his court and all his army in 'jollity and sensual pursuits.'

During this interval of periodical eclipse the em-peror seems never to have realized that he was cut off. Sher Khan, a master of strategy, had let

Humayun into Bengal only to seize the approaches
and sever his communications. He had the less difficulty inasmuch as the emperor, with his usual im-
providence, had taken no steps to keep them
open; whilst in the west his brothers were quite
satisfied to leave him to his fate. Hindal, who had
taken part in the Bengal campaign, and had been
allowed to go to Tirhut to bring up stores, seized the
opportunity to return to Agra, where he was soon
persuaded by interested counsellors to proclaim himself emperor; and the pious shaikh, whom Humayun
sent to bring him gently to reason, was murdered by
the inflated usurper. Loyal officers, anxious to preserve Delhi for the lawful sovereign, called in the
help of Kamran, who quickly reduced the preten-
sions of his younger brother. But Kamran was as
unwilling as Hindal to go to the rescue of the
emperor, whose critical position was perfectly known
to all. They went a few marches together, and
then turned back. Their plan was to let Humayun
be worsted by Sher Khan and then to engage the
Afghan in their own behoof. They did not know the
man they had to deal with. Sher Khan had seized
every road leading from Bengal, he was laying siege
to Chunar and Jaunpur, held all the country as far
west as Kanauj, and had proclaimed himself king at
Rohtas with the title of Sultan Sher Shah.

These disastrous tidings, filtering through the
bazar gossip, gradually roused Humayun from his
torpor. With mutiny open or concealed at Agra,
with a rival king standing across his communications
and besieging his cities, with no hope of succour from

any side, it was certainly time to act. Six months had he trifled in Bengal, and now the question was how to get out. His troops were demoralized by dissipation, disheartened by inaction, and reduced by sickness. They had to be bribed to advance. When they did at last march, they met with no opposition. Sher Shah was known to be on the watch, but he did not attempt to stop them. His design was apparently to avoid a pitched battle and rather to harass and if possible surprise the imperial army than to attempt its destruction in the field. Humayun accordingly was suffered to march along the left bank of the Ganges as far as Manghir, where he de-

SILVER COIN OF SHER SHAH STRUCK AT DELHI, A.H. 947 (A.D. 1540–1).

liberately crossed over to the right or south bank—the side on which Sher Shah lay—in order apparently to show that he was not afraid of him.

Thus he proceeded past Patna till he reached a spot close to where the battle of Buxar two hundred and thirty years later once more decided the fate of the same Moghul empire. Here, at Chaunsa, the army was suddenly checked by Sher Shah, who, tempted by the dispirited state of the imperialists, abandoned his watching attitude and rode in hot haste to stop their advance. The two forces camped opposite one another, and as neither seemed strong enough to warrant an attack, there they remained confronted for two months. The imperial troops were suffering grievously. The cattle and many of the horses were dead, troopers were dismounted, the country in front was in the enemy's hands, supplies were scarce, and of any help from Agra there was no hope. The situation was desperate and Humayun opened negotiations. A treaty was arranged by which Sher Shah was to retain Bengal and part of Bihar, on condition of due and public recognition of the emperor as his suzerain. Everything seemed settled or on the point of settlement, and the two armies began to fraternize whilst preparing to break up their camp. Suddenly, in the midst of the confusion of the removal, at break of dawn, the Afghans fell upon the unsuspecting Moghuls from all sides. The surprise was complete. Many were slain asleep. Few had time to mount. Humayun himself was only saved by a water-carrier who supported him on his water-skin across the Ganges, into which he had recklessly plunged. Most of his army was drowned or captured, and the unlucky emperor arrived at Agra almost alone (May, 1539).

For nearly a year both sides gathered their forces for the final struggle: Sher Shah consolidating his power in Bengal; Humayun vacillating and wasting time, yet striving to unite his brothers in the common cause. On May 17, 1540, the armies met again opposite Kanauj, and the ' battle of the Ganges' for a time put an end to the Moghul empire. Humayuns' army, though at first 100,000 strong, was half-hearted, badly officered, weakened by constant desertions, and hampered with crowds of panic-stricken camp-followers; and the fight was over almost as soon as begun. 'Before the enemy had discharged an arrow,' says the historian Mirza Haidar, who was present, 'the whole army was scattered and defeated' by mere panic and crowding; 'not a gun was fired.' All fled to the Ganges, where the bridge broke down and many were drowned in their heavy armour. Humayun again escaped by the skin of his teeth. India had cast him off.

From that day for fifteen years he led a life of wandering. He was in the deserts of Rajputana and Sind for three years, in great straits and hardships, trying to beat up recruits; here he fell in love with the daughter of his brother Hindal's shaikh, a sayyid of the Prophet's race; and here at Amarkot his son Akbar was born, October 15, 1542. Then he fled to Persia, where he became the not very welcome guest of Shah Tahmasp. Aided by the shah he conquered Kandahar from his own brother Askari in 1545, and took Kabul from Kamran in 1547. He was now in much the same position that Babar had occupied before his invasion of India twenty-five years earlier.

The next nine years were spent in varying fortunes, sometimes in conquest, sometimes in loss, and it was not till his brothers were dead or exiled that Humayun had peace in his little Afghan realm. Hindal fell in battle; Askari died on pilgrimage to Mekka; and the irreconcilable Kamran, after repeated forgivings, had to be blinded and sent to Mekka where he too died. Humayun owed much of his misfortunes to this unnatural brother, and cannot be charged with anything but long-suffering patience of his misdeeds.

Meanwhile Sher Shah had reduced the greater part of Hindustan to submission, and among the Muslims at least there was every disposition to hail the accession of an Afghan king, born in India, and gifted with unusual administrative as well as military talents. His ability and wisdom are unquestioned, and in his fiscal and other reforms we see the true origin of many of Akbar's most famous measures. ' The whole of his brief administration,' says Mr. Keene,[1] 'was based on the principle of union. A devout Muslim, he never oppressed his Hindu subjects. The disputes of his own people he suppressed with all the energy of his nature. He laboured day and night, for he said " It behooves the great to be always active." He divided his territory into hundreds, in each of which were local officers whose place it was to mediate between the people and the officers of the crown. Not content with the administrative side of social reform, he went beyond most Muslim rulers and attempted a certain crude legislation. The nature of the attempts attributed to him shows that a critical moment was passing in mediæval India. His ordinances touched on almost all the primary parts of administration, and evinced real care for the people's welfare. . . . All this has an importance beyond the immediate time. After the Moghul

[1] *History of Hindustan*, 79–81.

restoration Sher Shah's officials passed into Akbar's service; the faults imputed by the shah to what he called Moghul administration—but which are common to all Turks—were prevented; and this far-sighted man, even after his death and the subversion of his dynasty, remained the originator of all that was done by mediæval Indian rulers for the good of the people.'

It must not be imagined that all this was accomplished by mildness. 'Sher Shah's authority,' says his historian, Abbas Khan, 'whether he was absent or present, was completely established over the race of Afghans. From the fear either of personal punishment or of deprivation of office there was not a creature who dared to act in opposition to his regulations; and if a son of his own, or a brother, or any of his relations and kin, or any chief or minister, did a thing displeasing to Sher Shah, and it got to his knowledge, he would order him to be bound and put to death. All, laying aside every bond of friendship or regard, for the sake of the honour of the Afghan name, obeyed unhesitatingly his irresistible decrees. . . . From the day that Sher Shah was established on the throne no man dared to breathe in opposition to him; nor did anyone raise the standard of contumacy or rebellion against him; nor was any heart-tormenting thorn grown in the garden of his kingdom; nor was there any of his nobles or soldiery, or a thief or a robber, who dared to turn the eye of dishonesty upon another's goods, nor did any robbery or stealing ever occur in his dominions. Travellers and wayfarers in Sher Shah's reign had

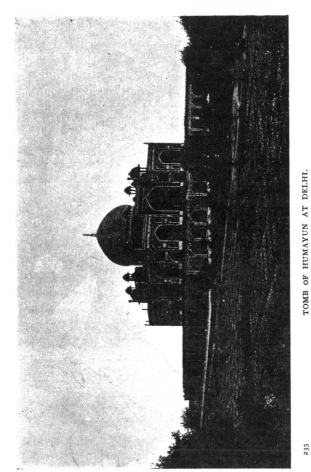

TOMB OF HUMAYUN AT DELHI.

235

no need to keep watch, nor feared to halt in the midst of a desert. They camped at night at every place, desert or inhabited, without fear; they set their goods and provisions upon the plain and turned out their mules to graze, and themselves slept with easy mind and free from care as if at home, and the mansabdars (for fear that they should suffer and be arrested for any mischief that might befall the travellers) kept watch over them. " Such a protection o'ershadowed the world that a cripple was not afraid of a Rustam." [1]

His brief but beneficent rule came to an end in 1545 when he was killed at the siege of Kalinjar during a vigorous attempt to subdue the indomitable Rajputs. He left no fit successor to carry on his wise schemes, on which he was still meditating as he lay wounded in his tent. Under his son Islam Shah the ancient rivalries of the Afghans revived, and when Islam Shah died nine years later everything was in confusion. His son, a boy of twelve, was murdered by his uncle Adil Shah (or Adali), a debauched brute, who left all real power in the hands of his Hindu vezir Himu. Naturally rebellions arose. Ibrahim Sur seized Delhi and Agra, and Sikandar Sur, another nephew of Sher Shah, took possession of the Panjab, and then drove Ibrahim out of his new sovereignty.

In the midst of this turmoil Humayun, for once, grasped his opportunity. Descending from Kabul with only 15,000 horse in 1555, and seizing the Panjab, he routed Sikandar at Sirhind, drove him

[1] *Tarikh-i-Sher-Shahi*, E. and D., iv, 427, 433.

to the Himalayas, and took possession of Delhi and Agra. Prince Akbar was sent in pursuit of the fugitive Afghans, whilst Humayun set about organizing his recovered kingdom. It seemed as if his luck had turned at last. But nothing ever went well for long with this unfortunate monarch. Scarcely had he enjoyed his throne at Delhi for six months when he slipped down the polished steps of his palace, and died in his forty-ninth year (Jan. 24, 1556). His end was of a piece with his character. If there was a possibility of falling, Humayun was not the man to miss it. He tumbled through life, and he tumbled out of it. At his tomb, three centuries later, the last of the Moghul emperors, the feeble and aged Shah Alam, surrendered to Hodson of Hodson's Horse, and the old man's savage and worthless sons paid the penalty of their treachery. It was perhaps fitting that the grave of the humane and chivalrous son of Babar should be the silent witness of a righteous vengeance.

CHAPTER X

THE UNITED EMPIRE

AKBAR

1556–1605

THE long reign of Akbar, which lasted from 1556 to 1605, has been represented as the golden age of the Moghul empire. It was in reality but the beginning of the period of splendour which ended with the disastrous wars of Aurangzib. Akbar was the true founder and organizer of the empire, but it is too often forgotten that it took him twenty years of hard fighting to bring Hindustan under subjection, and that even at his death the process was incomplete. There was no sudden and miraculous submission to the boy of thirteen who found himself called to an as yet unconquered throne by the accident that ended his father's ineffectual life in the beginning of 1556. A hard struggle was before him ere he could call himself king even of Delhi. He was fortunate, no doubt, in the divisions of his adversaries, and after the crushing defeat of Himu at Panipat he was never called upon to meet a general muster of Indian troops; but the process of reducing usurper after usurper, and suppressing one rebellion after another, was tedious and harassing, and in spite of a wise statesmanship matured by experience, and a clemency and toleration which grew with advancing years, to the day of his death Akbar seldom knew what it was to enjoy a year's freedom from war.

At the time of his accession the only parts of India that he possessed were the Panjab and Delhi in the north, which were the fruits of the victory at Sirhind in 1555. The Afghan dynasty still held Bengal and the Ganges valley; the Rajputs were independent in western Hindustan, and there were innumerable chiefs in possession of separate principalities all over the country. It was not till the third year of his reign that Akbar was able to occupy Ajmir. Gwaliar fell in 1558, and by 1561 he had driven the Afghans back from Lucknow and Jaunpur. The Moghul empire so far was almost restricted to the Panjab and the North-West Provinces, though Malwa was partly overrun in 1561, and Burhanpur in Khandesh captured a year later. The storming of Chitor in 1567 was a conspicuous landmark in the history, but it was not till 1572 that the Rajputs were finally brought into the empire. Bengal was not conquered before 1575, and Gujarat, though occupied in 1572, had to be retaken in 1584 and gave trouble for several years more. Kabul, under his brother Hakim, was almost a separate kingdom and frequently aggressive. Among the outlying provinces, Orisa became part of the empire as late as 1590, Kashmir in 1587, Sind in 1592, Kandahar in 1594, and only a small portion of the Deccan was annexed in Akbar's life.

The reign was thus a perpetual series of efforts towards the expansion of an originally small territory. So doubtful indeed seemed Akbar's prospects of Indian sovereignty at the moment when his father's unexpected death placed him in command, that in the first council of war the generals strongly urged an immediate retreat upon Kabul, and their advice was only overruled by the firm decision of the regent Bairam, an old Turkman officer who had followed Babar and Humayun, and realized better than the others the divided and leaderless state of the enemy. Matters were certainly in an alarming position. Sikandar of Delhi had been driven to the mountains, where he held Mankot against all attacks; but a far more formidable army was marching to take vengeance. Himu, the general of the Bengal kingdom, a Hindu who from a mere shopkeeper had rapidly advanced to practically supreme power, entered Agra unopposed, defeated Tardi Beg at Delhi, occupied the capital, assumed the historic title of Raja Vikramajit, and then advanced to crush the Moghul forces.

When the dispirited remnant of the garrison of Delhi reached Akbar's headquarters at Sirhind, news had just arrived of another blow, the revolt of Kabul. Fortunately the young emperor had a great soldier at his side to meet the crisis. Bairam, the atalik or regent, was a consummate general, and a man of iron resolution. He instantly made an example of Tardi Beg, for the loss of Delhi, and placed the other disgraced officers under arrest. Then he sent on the advance - guard, which was lucky enough to intercept the entire park of Ottoman artillery which Himu had incautiously sent adrift; and on Friday the 5th of November, 1556, the two armies confronted each other on the field of Panipat, where thirty years before Babar had overthrown the Afghan power, and where two centuries later another battle swept away the Maratha hordes and prepared the way for England.

In spite of the loss of his guns, Himu commanded a force sufficient to dismay the Moghul leaders. He had three divisions, of which the centre was composed of 20,000 horse (Afghans and Rajputs) supported by 500 elephants, and the whole force of elephantry numbered at least 1500. Himu led the advance, 'scowling on his elephant Hawa, "the Wind."' His charge upon the Moghul left was successful; he then turned to crush their centre. But here the archers stood firm, the enemy were harassed by showers of arrows, and one fortunate shaft pierced the eye of the Hindu leader. There was no one in authority to take up the command, and the masterless crowd broke up like a herd of stampeded horses. Himu on his elephant was driven straight into the presence of Akbar, and Bairam bade the boy flesh his sword on the dying 'infidel.' The honourable chivalry which distinguished Akbar above all his line at once burst forth: 'How can I strike a man who is as good as dead?' he cried. Bairam

16

had no such fine scruples, and immediately dispatched the wounded man.

The crisis had been bravely met, and Akbar had never again to confront so dangerous an enemy. Henceforward, though constantly fighting, he had the advantage — incalculable in oriental warfare — of being in the position of the attacker, not the attacked. Delhi again opened its gates and received him with effusive loyalty. Agra followed the example of the capital, and after an eight months' siege Sikandar surrendered Mankot and retired to Bengal. The young prince was now king at least in the north-west corner of India. The process of settling this comparatively small territory and dealing with the revenues and the status of the military vassals occupied the next few years, and, except for the reduction of the great fortress of Gwaliar and the conquest of the Ganges valley as far as Jaunpur and Benares, the limits of the kingdom were not greatly extended.

In 1560 Akbar took the reins into his own hands. He had chafed under the masterful management of Bairam, whose severity and jealousy had been shown in several high-handed executions and had roused general discontent. Palace intrigue set Akbar's mind against his old tutor, who was doubtless slow to realize that his pupil was no longer a child to be held on a leading string. In an eastern harim there are powerful influences against which few ministers can prevail, and Akbar's foster-mother, Maham Anaga, ruled the palace in those early years. She used her power to undermine the emperor's esteem

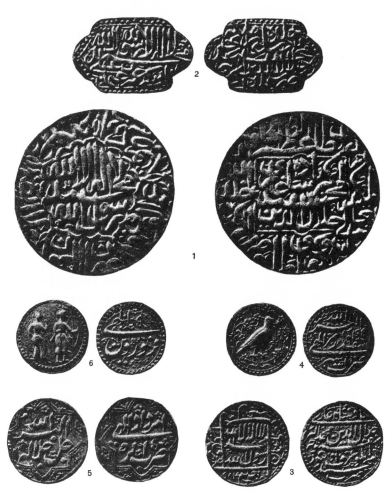

GOLD COINS OF AKBAR.

1. Agra, A. H. 971.
2. Agra, 981.
3. Mohammadabad (Udaipur). 984.
4. Asir, 1008.
5. Agra, 1013.
6. 1013.

for Bairam.   Taking advantage of a visit to Delhi, where he was free from the regent's domination, she worked upon his natural impatience of the khan-khanan's arrogance, and induced him to break his cords.   Akbar publicly announced that he had taken the government into his own hands, and sent orders to the deposed minister to go on pilgrimage to Mekka — a courteous form of temporary banishment. The young emperor might perhaps have dealt more gently with the honoured servant of his father and grandfather,— one, too, who had so strenuously served him in his hour of peril,— but the change had to be made, and it could not be easy in any way. Bairam left for Gujarat, to take boat for Arabia, but on his way he fell among evil counsellors who tempted him to revolt.   He was defeated, and made humble submission, when Akbar instantly pardoned him with all his old kindness.   But there could be no place for Bairam now in the government, and he sadly set forth on his pilgrimage, once the chief desire of the staunch Muslim but now a mark of his downfall.   Before he could embark he was assassinated by an Afghan in quittance of a blood-feud.

The nurse's triumph was not for long.   For a time she acted almost as a prime minister, and her quick intelligence as well as her devotion to her foster-son made her invaluable to him.   Unhappily her hopes were wrapped up in her son, Adham Khan.   She pushed him forward to high command, which he filled with more arrogance and conceit than loyalty; he fell into disgrace, and when finally out of envy and chagrin, in 1563, he murdered Akbar's foster-father the prime minister Shams-ad-din, and then stood at the door of the harim as if in sanctuary, his cup was full. The emperor rushed out, sword in hand, felled the assassin with a blow of his fist, and foster-brother though he was Adham was instantly thrown over the battlements of the palace. It broke his mother's heart, and she survived him but forty days.

It was time that Akbar freed himself from this harim influence. Adham had already tarnished the emperor's name in Malwa, where after expelling the pleasure-loving cultured Afghan governor Baz Bahadur, he behaved grossly towards the vanquished. 'Baz Bahadur had a Hindu mistress who is said to have been one of the most beautiful women ever seen in India. She was as accomplished as she was fair, and was celebrated for her verses in the Hindi language. She fell into the hands of Adham Khan on the flight of Baz Bahadur, and, finding herself unable to resist his importunities and threatened violence, she appointed an hour to receive him, put on her most splendid dress, on which she sprinkled the richest perfumes, and lay down on a couch with her mantle drawn over her face. Her attendants thought that she had fallen asleep, but on endeavouring to awake her on the approach of the khan, they found she had taken poison, and was already dead.' Nor was this all. Other ladies of Baz Bahadur's harim were in Adham's possession, and when Akbar himself rode to Malwa in hot haste and bitter shame to stop his lieutenant's atrocities, Maham Anaga had

[1] KHAFI KHAN; ELPHINSTONE, 501, note.

these innocent women killed, lest they should tell tales to the emperor. Akbar was well quit of both mother and son.

Although the young emperor was still immature, and it was many years before he entered upon that stage of philosophic enlightenment which has made his name a household word for wisdom and toleration, he had already shown something of his character and self-reliance. His refusal to strike the dying Himu, his firm and yet not unkind treatment of his revolted regent, his honest indignation at Adham's iniquities, show that Akbar possessed the right spirit. Physically he is described by his son Jahangir, in later life, as of middle stature, long in the arms and sturdy of figure, rather sallow in face, with black eyes and eyebrows and an open forehead. A wart on the left side of his nose was regarded as not only auspicious but exceedingly beautiful. His voice was ringing, and in spite of little culture his conversation had a charm of its own. ' His manners and habits,' adds the son, ' were quite different from those of other people, and his countenance was full of godlike dignity.' His mode of life was regular and abstemious. His time was carefully filled, and he slept little; 'his sleep looked more like waking.' He ate but one meal a day, and that in moderation, never approaching satiety. Ganges water, 'cooled with saltpetre,' was his drink, and it was kept sealed for fear of poison. He took meat but twice a week, and even then with repugnance, for he disliked making his body a ' tomb for beasts '; but some meat he found

necessary to support his fatigues. He was a man
of great energy and constant occupation, capable of
immense and prolonged effort, and fond of all manly
exercises. He was a fine polo player, and so devoted to the game that he used even to play it
by night, using fireballs. The chase was his keenest
delight, and he would break the tedium of the long
marches of his many campaigns by hunting elephants or tigers on the way. We read of 350
elephants taken in a single day; at another time he
stalked wild asses for thirty-five miles, and shot sixteen. He had names for his guns, and kept records
of their performances. There were vast battues
(*kamurgha*), when thousands of deer, nilgao, jackals,
and foxes, were driven by the beaters in a circle
of forty miles, and the lines drawn closer and closer,
till Akbar could enjoy at his ease several days
shooting and hawking with plenty of sport, and still
leave a few thousand head for his followers to practise on. These battues sometimes took place by
night, and there is a curious painting of the period
showing one of these nocturnal hunts, with the emperor on horseback, and the game, startled by the
bright flashing of a lantern, leaping as the chief shikar
draws his bow. Akbar had mechanical genius. He
devised a new method of making gun-barrels of
spirally rolled iron, which could not burst; he invented a machine which cleaned sixteen barrels at
once, and another by which seventeen guns could
be fired simultaneously with one match. There
were many other things that he improved by his
talent for mechanical invention.

Nothing seemed to fatigue Akbar. He is said to
have ridden from Ajmir to Agra, a distance of 240
miles, in a day and a night, and even if (with some
authorities) we double the time, it is still wonderful
travelling, and one is not surprised to read that he
often knocked up his horses when pushing on night
and day at break-neck speed. He liked to see a
good fight, too, and one day at Thanesar he chanced
upon a curious spectacle. It was the annual festival,
and there was a vast crowd beside the sacred lake;
the holy men were gathering a rich harvest in charity, when the customary struggle arose between two
sects of fanatics for the possession of the bathing
place. They came to the emperor and begged to
be allowed to fight it out according to their habit.
He consented, and allowed some of his soldiers to
smear their bodies with ashes and go in to support the weaker side. There was a splendid fight;
many were killed, we are told; and 'the emperor
greatly enjoyed the sight.'

On a campaign Akbar was indefatigable. In one
of his pursuits of Ali Kuli Khan-zaman, an Uzbeg
officer who repeatedly revolted in the name of
Akbar's jealous brother Hakim, and was as often
pardoned by his too-forgiving sovereign, he pushed
on so rapidly that of his army only 500 men and
elephants succeeded in being in at the finish. In
spite of his reduced force Akbar rode straight for
the enemy, and took his own share of the fighting.
'As the battle grew hot, the emperor alighted from
his elephant, Balsundar, and mounted a horse.
Then he gave orders for the elephants to be driven

against the lines of Ali Kuli Khan. There was
among them an elephant named Hiranand, and
when he approached the ranks of the enemy they
let loose against him an elephant called Diyana;
but Hiranand gave him such a butt that he fell upon
the spot. Ali Kuli received a wound from an
arrow, and while he was drawing it out another
struck his horse. The animal became restive and Ali
Kuli was thrown. An elephant named Narsing now
came up and was about to crush him, when Ali
Kuli cried out to the driver, " I am a great man;
if you take me alive to the emperor he will reward
you." The driver paid no heed to his words but
drove the animal over him and crushed him under
foot.' Many prisoners were cast to the elephants to
be trampled to death, a common mode of execution
in India, in which Akbar showed no scruple. After
refusing, in his chivalrous way, to attack an un-
prepared enemy till the trumpets had announced
his approach, he had no qualms about making a
pyramid of two thousand rebels' heads after the
fashion of his ancestor Timur. He could be terribly
stern, and was subject to paroxysms of rage, in one
of which he threw a servant from the battlements
for falling asleep in the palace; but his natural in-
clination was ever towards mercy, and his forgiveness often cost him dear.

As an example of personal courage his attack on
his rebellious cousins, the Mirzas, at Surat in 1572
may be instanced. Pressing on at his usual speed
he found himself on the bank of the Mahindri river
in face of the enemy, with only forty men to his

back. Sixty more soon joined him, and with this handful he forthwith swam the river, stormed the town, and rushing through discovered the enemy in a plain on the other side. The emperor's force was outmatched by ten to one, and the fighting was desperate. 'The royal forces were in a narrow place, hedged in with thorns, where three horsemen could not pass abreast. The emperor with much courage was at the front, with Raja Bhagwan Das beside him. Three of the enemy's horsemen now charged them. One attacked the raja, who hurled his spear at him and wounded him as he was entangled in the thorns, so that he fled; the other two attacked his majesty, who received them so stoutiy that they were forced to make off.' Two officers now joined Akbar, who, refusing their escort, sent them after his assailants; and the little force, roused by their emperor's danger, utterly routed the enemy. The courage of Akbar had put every man on his mettle, and the victors returned to Baroda the heroes of the hour. In the campaign of 1572–3 Akbar not only retook Ahmadabad and entered Cambay and Baroda, but captured the strong fort of Surat, which had been built with extraordinary care and skill to keep out the Portuguese, and contained mortars bearing the name of Suleyman the Great of Turkey. When Akbar took the fort of Junagarh in Kathiawar in 1591 he found there a gun of the same sultan, whose fleet had vainly attacked the coast castles and was forced to abandon the guns.

The presence of the Raja Bhagwan Das at Akbar's

side in the skirmish just described is significant. If he had not been altogether successful in managing his Mohammedan followers—a turbulent body of adventurers—the emperor more than redeemed his over-indulgence to rebellious Muslims by his wise conciliation of Hindus. It may be that the very truculence and insubordination which he found so hard to check among his Turkish officers threw him perforce into the arms of the Rajputs; for we can hardly believe that a mere lad, brought up in an atmosphere of despotic rule, could as yet have imagined the ideal of a government resting upon the loyalty of the native population. As early as 1562 Bhagwan's father, Raja Bihari Mal, the lord of Amber and ancestor of the present maharajas of Jaipur, had come to pay his homage to the new sovereign. 'He was received with great honour and consideration, and his daughter, an honourable lady, was accepted by his majesty, and took her place among the ladies of the court.'[1] Akbar had already married his cousins Rukayya and Salima, but this union with a Rajput princess marked a new policy. Her father was decorated with the highest rank of the official aristocracy, as a mansabdar or general of 5000 horse, and the bride, freely exercising the rites of her own faith and performing the usual Hindu sacrifices, encouraged her husband's tendency towards religious toleration. Later on he took other women, Hindu, Persian, Moghul, and even an

---

[1] *Tabakat-i-Akbari*, E. and D., v., 274. This history by the contemporary writer Nizam-ad-din, who was often in Akbar's suite, is one of our best authorities for the greater part of the reign.

Armenian, until his harim formed a parliament of religions, though no rumour of their probable debates ever reached the outside world. Abu-l-Fazl says there were more than five thousand women, in various capacities, in the harim, and sagely remarks that 'the large number of women—a vexatious question even for great statesmen—furnished his majesty with an opportunity to display his wisdom.'

An almost immediate result of this alliance with the Rajput princess was the abolition (in 1562) of the *jizya* or poll-tax which Mohammedan conquerors levied upon unbelievers in accordance with the law of Islam. His next act was to discontinue the tax upon Hindu pilgrims, on the ground that, however superstitious the rites of pilgrimage might be, it was wrong to place any obstacle in the way of a man's service to God. No more popular measures could have been enacted. The jizya was an insult as well as a burden, and both taxes bore heavily on the poor and were bitterly resented. It was the re-imposition of the tax on religion in the time of Aurangzib that, more than anything else, uprooted the wise system established by his ancestor. But whilst conciliating the Hindus by just and equal government, Akbar did not hesitate to interfere with some of their most cherished practices when they offended his sense of humanity. He forbade child-marriage, trial by ordeal, animal sacrifice; he permitted widows to marry again, and set his face resolutely against the burning of widows on their husband's pyres: wholly to abolish *suttee* was beyond his power, but he ordained that the sacrifice

must be voluntary, and he took personal pains to
see that no compulsion should be used. He also
insisted that 'the consent of the bride and bride-
groom and the permission of the parents are absolutely necessary in marriage contracts'—a new

AGRA GATE, FATHPUR-SIKRI.

idea in a country where girls were married without
option.

Akbar was too shrewd a man to suppose that the
hereditary pride of the Rajputs was to be conquered
merely by kind words and mild measures. He knew
that often the best way to make friends with a man

is to knock him down. Udai Singh, the great rana of Mewar (son of Sanga, Babar's adversary), left him in no doubt as to his hostility. He sheltered Baz Bahadur when driven out of Malwa by the imperial army, and when other rajas came in and tendered their allegiance to the Moghul, Udai Singh stood aloof, apparently secure in his rocky fortresses and numerous array of troops and elephants. Akbar, he thought, could never take his strong castle of Chitor, standing on an isolated crag, four hundred feet high, and with almost perpendicular sides towards the top. The summit was occupied by an immense fortress, well supplied with provisions, wells, and water-tanks, and garrisoned by 8000 veterans of the Rajput race under a famous leader, Jai Mal, the rana himself having prudently retreated to the Aravali hills on Akbar's approach in 1567.

Mulla Ahmad described Chitor in Akbar's time [1]: 'The castle is situated in the midst of a level plain which has no other hills. The mountain is twelve miles round at the base, and nearly six at the summit. On the east and north it is faced with hard stone, and the garrison had no fears on those sides, nor could guns, swivels, stone-slings or mangonels do much damage on the other sides, if they managed to reach them. Travellers do not mention any fortress like this in all the world. The whole summit was crowded with buildings, some several storeys high, and the battlements were strongly guarded and the magazines full.' The garrison laughed at the slender forces—3000 or 4000—which

[1] *Tarikh-i-Alfi*, E. and D., v, 170-4.

the emperor had brought against a fortress twelve miles in girth, and well they might.

They had to deal with a skilful engineer, however, and Akbar made his dispositions with great care. Batteries were set up all around the fort, and a strict blockade was established. Meanwhile generals were sent to seize Rampur and Udaipur and lay the surrounding country waste. 'From day to day,' says Mulla Ahmad, 'the gallant assailants brought their attacks closer to the fort on every side, though many fell under the resolute fire of the defenders. Orders were given for digging trenches and making *sabats*, and nearly 5000 builders, carpenters, masons, smiths, and sappers were mustered from all parts. Sabats are contrivances peculiar to Hindustan, for the strong forts of that land are full of guns, muskets, and defensive machines, and can only be taken by this means. A sabat is a broad covered way, under the shelter of which the besiegers approach a fortress protected from gun and musket fire. Two sabats were accordingly begun; one, opposite the royal quarters, was so broad and high that two elephants and two horses could easily pass abreast, with raised spears. The sabats were begun from the brow of the hill (*i. e.* half-way up, below the perpendicular scarp), which is a fortress upon a fortress.' Seven or eight thousand horsemen and gunners strove to stop the work, and in spite of the bull-hide roofs over the labourers a hundred or so were killed every day, and their corpses were used as building materials. There was no forced labour, by Akbar's order, but the volunteers were stimulated by showers of money. Soon one of the sabats overtopped the wall of the castle, and on the roof of it a gallery was made whence the emperor could watch the fight.

Meanwhile the sappers had not been idle. Two bastions were mined with gunpowder, and a storming party was drawn up. The first mine blew a bastion into the air, and the stormers rushed into the breach, shouting their war-cry, and were at once at hand-grip with the garrison. At that moment the second mine, owing to a miscalculation, exploded and sent the struggling crowd in the breach in fragments into the air. The charge was so heavy that stones and corpses were hurled 'miles' away, according to the historian, and the royal army was half blinded by the dust and smoke and hail of stones and bodies.

The first approach had failed: Akbar now ordered the other sabat to be pushed forward. He was more resolved than ever to take the fort by storm 'so that in future no other fortress should dare to withstand him.' He took up his position in the gallery on the top of the sabat, as before, armed with his musket, 'deadly as the darts of fate, with which he killed every moving thing that caught his eye.' At last the walls were breached, and the assault was ordered. Jai Mal, the commandant, 'an infidel yet valiant,' struggled bravely in every part and all day long, encouraging his men to beat off the enemy. At the hour of evening prayer he came in front of the royal battery, where Akbar sat discharging his gun 'Sangram' as often as light flashed forth in the bastion. Jai Mal happened to be standing in the tower heartening his men just when a blaze of light revealed his face to Akbar, who fired and killed him on the spot. Then the garrison gave up hope, and after burning the body of their leader, they performed their dismal rite of *jauhar*,— burned all their families and goods in huge bonfires, and then rushed upon death. The besiegers saw the flare of the pyres, and poured through the breaches, whilst Akbar looked on from the top of the sabat. Three elephants he sent into the castle to aid in the general massacre of the devoted garrison. The Rajputs fought every step; each lane and street and bazar was sternly disputed; they fought up to the very temple. Two thousand were killed by midday; the total death-roll of the Hindus was at least 8000 men, besides their families; the rest were made prisoners.[1] The heroism of the defence was long commemorated in popular tradition by the two statues, supposed to represent Jai Mal and his brother, mounted on stone elephants, which flanked the gate of the fortress at Delhi. 'These two elephants,' says Bernier, 'mounted by the two heroes, have an air of grandeur and inspire me with an awe and respect which I cannot describe.'

The fall of Chitor, followed by two other famous fortresses, Rantambhor and Kalinjar, a few months later, secured the allegiance of the Rajputs. The rajas agreed to acclaim a power which they found as irresistible as it was just and tolerant. Akbar cemented the good feeling by marrying another

---

[1] This account is practically identical in the *Tarikh-i-Alfi* and the *Tabakat-i-Akbari;* the author of the latter work was present in one of the batteries.

princess, daughter of the raja of Bikanir, and henceforward he could rely on the loyalty of the most splendid soldiery in India.[1] In his future campaigns, as in those of his son and grandson, there were always brave Hindus to the fore, and the names of Bhagwan Das, Man Singh, and Todar Mal are famous in the annals of Moghul warfare and administration. Bhagwan Das and Man Singh not only distinguished themselves in the wearisome and re-iterated campaigns which the unsettled state of Gujarat compelled Akbar to undertake for a space of twenty years, but were even trusted by him in 1578 to wage war upon the ever hostile rana of Udaipur, Rajput against Rajput. They justified his confidence, drove the rana to the Indus, and captured his strongholds of Goganda and Kunbhalmir.

[1] The rana of Udaipur, however, though he had lost Chitor, retained his pride. He never submitted ; and his family, alone among the Rajput princely houses, for ever disdained to marry its daughters with the Great Moghuls. The present lord of Udaipur still boasts unpolluted Rajput blood.

CHAPTER XI

AKBAR'S REFORMS

THE DIVINE FAITH

1566–1605

THIS assimilation of the Hindu chiefs was the most conspicuous feature of Akbar's reign. His wars were like other Indian wars, only mitigated by his sovereign quality of mercy to those who submitted, and his scrupulous care that the peasants should not suffer by the passage of his troops. The empire was gradually extended till it stretched from Kandahar to the bay of Bengal, and included the whole of Hindustan down to the Narbada. But the remarkable points about this expansion to the old limits of Ala-ad-din's realm were, first, that it was done with the willing help of the Hindu princes, and, secondly, that expansion went hand in hand with orderly administration. This was a new thing in Indian government, for hitherto the local officials had done pretty much as it pleased them, and the central authority had seldom interfered so long as the revenue did not suffer. Akbar allowed no oppression — if he

knew of it — by his lieutenants, and not a few of his
campaigns were undertaken mainly for the purpose
of punishing governors who had been guilty of self-
seeking and peculation.   Much of the improvement
was due to his employment of Hindus, who at that

THE DIWAN-I-KHAS, FATHPUR-SIKRI.

time were better men of business than the unedu-
cated and mercenary adventurers who formed a large
proportion of the Mohammedan invaders.

No Muslim served Akbar more zealously or with
further reaching results than the great financier, Raja
Todar Mal, a Khatri Rajput, who had served in his

youth under the able administration of Sher Shah, and had thus gained priceless experience in the management of lands and revenues. He assisted Akbar's first chancellor of the exchequer, Muzaffar Khan, in settling the newly acquired kingdom, and in 1566 took a leading part in suppressing the revolt of Ali Kuli. It was the first time, in Moghul rule, that a Hindu had been sent against a Muslim enemy, and his employment was doubtless due to Akbar's suspicion that the Mohammedan generals might act in collusion with their old comrade, the rebel. After this he was employed in settling the revenue system of Gujarat, and then again took military command in the conquest of Bengal in 1574–7 and its reduction in 1581, when he distinguished himself by his firm courage. He was rewarded soon afterwards with the office of vezir; and in 1582 he became chief finance minister, and introduced the famous reforms and the new assessment known as Todar Mal's rent-roll, the Domesday Book of the Moghul empire. He died in 1589. 'Careful to keep himself from selfish ambition,' writes Abu-l-Fazl, 'he devoted himself to the service of the state, and earned an everlasting fame.'

There is no name in mediæval history more renowned in India to the present day than that of Todar Mal, and the reason is that nothing in Akbar's reforms more nearly touched the welfare of the people than the great financier's reconstruction of the revenue system. The land-tax was always the main source of revenue in India, and it had become almost the sole universal burden since Akbar had abolished not only the poll-tax and pilgrims' dues but over fifty minor duties.[1] The object was now to levy a fair rent on the land, which should support the administration without unduly burdening the cultivators. An able modern Indian administrator thus describes the system.[2] 'The basis of the land-revenue was the recognition that the agriculturist was the owner of the soil, the state being entitled to the surplus produce. Sometimes an official or a court favourite obtains an alienation of the state's demands on a township or group of townships; but the grant, even if declared to be perpetual, is usually treated as temporary, in the sense that it is liable to be resumed at the death of the grantee or at the demise of the crown. That being the normal conception in systems like that of the Muslims in Hindustan, the agriculturists—especially if they were Hindus—were *taillables et corvéables à merci*. It was Sher Shah who, first among these rulers, perceived the benefit that might be expected from leaving a definite margin between the state's demand and the

---

[1] The increasing land revenue of the Moghul emperors is shown in the following table :

Akbar............	1594............	£18,650,000
"	1605............	19,430,000
Jahangir.........	1628............	19,680,000
Shah-Jahan.......	1648............	24,750,000
"	1655............	30,000,000
Aurangzib........	1667............	30,850,000
"	1697............	43,500,000

(See my remarks in Sir W. W. HUNTER's *Indian Empire*, 3d ed., 354–356.)

[2] H. G. KEENE, *Sketch of the History of Hindustan*, 160–162, etc.

expenses of cultivation. The determination of this margin, and the recognition of the person who should be secured in its enjoyment, formed the basis of the system which, under the name of "settlement," still prevails in most parts of India.

'A fixed standard of mensuration having been adopted, the land was surveyed. It was then classified, according as it was waste, fallow, or under crop. The last class was taken as the basis of assessment, that which produced cereals, vetches, or oil-seeds being assessed to pay one-third of the average gross produce to the state, the other two-thirds being left to the cultivators. . . . This was a complete departure from the law of Islam, for it made no difference between the revenue raised from Muslims and that raised from unbelievers. Sher Shah's demand was in no case to be exceeded. It is very noticeable that Akbar added to his policy of union the equally important policy of continuity of system. He aimed at securing to the peasant the power of enjoying his property and profiting by the fruit of his labours. The needy husbandman was furnished with advances, repayable on easy terms. The assessments when once made were assessed for nineteen years; and after the 24th year of the reign, the aggregate collections of the past ten years having been added together and divided by ten, the future collections were made on the basis of this decennial average.

'Care was taken to provide easy means of complaint when undue collections were exacted and to punish severely the guilty exactors. The number of minor officials employed in realizing the recorded dues was diminished by one-half. The cultivators were to be made responsible, jointly as well as severally; the cultivators of fallow land were to be favoured for two years; advances of seed and money were to be made when necessary, arrears being remitted in the case of small holdings. Collectors were to make yearly reports on the conduct of their subordinates. Monthly returns were to be transmitted to the imperial exchequer. Special reports were to be sent up of any special calamities, hail, flood, or drought. The collectors were to see that the farmers got receipts for their payments, which were to be remitted four times in the year; at the end of that period no balance should be outstanding. Payments were if possible to be voluntary, but the standing crops were theoretically hypothecated, and where needful were to be attached. Above all, there was to be an accurate and minute record of each man's holding and liabilities. The very successful land-revenue system of British India is little more than a modification of these principles.'

One special feature of Todar Mal's system was the enactment that all government accounts should be kept in Persian instead of in Hindi, as heretofore. ' He thus forced his co-religionists to learn the court language of their rulers—a circumstance that may be compared with the introduction of the English language in the courts of India. The study of Persian therefore became necessary for its pecuniary advantage. Todar Mal's order, and Akbar's generous policy of allowing Hindus to compete for the highest honours,—Man Singh was the first "Commander of 7000,"—explain two facts: first, that

THE CENTRAL COLUMN IN THE DIWAN-I-KHAS, FATHPUR-SIKRI.

before the end of the 18th century the Hindus had almost become the Persian teachers of the Mohammedans; secondly, that a new dialect could arise in

Upper India, the *Urdu*, which, without the Hindus as receiving medium, could never have been called into existence. Whether we attach more importance to Todar Mal's order or to Akbar's policy, which when once initiated his successors, willing or not, had to follow, one fact should be borne in mind,— that before the time of Akbar the Hindus as a rule did not study Persian and stood therefore politically below their Mohammedan rulers.' [1]

Such changes, which put the subdued Hindu absolutely on a level with the conquering Muslim, were naturally repugnant to Akbar's more bigoted followers. The contemporary historian Badauni writes bitterly on the subject, and his cynicism is a useful corrective to the enthusiastic panegyrics of other writers of the time. Yet even when he wishes to make things appear in the worst light, he really shows the excellence of the intentions, at least, of the new measures, whilst exposing some of their defects. For instance, referring to one of the early attempts at land assessment, in 1574, he says [2]:

'In this year an order was promulgated for improving the cultivation of the country and for bettering the condition of the rayats (peasants). All the *parganas* (fiscal unions) of the country, whether dry or irrigated, in towns or hills, deserts or jungles, by rivers or reservoirs or wells, were to be measured, and every piece of land large enough to produce when cultivated one cror of tankas was

---

[1] H. BLOCHMANN, *Ain-i-Akbari*, i, 352.
[2] BADAUNI, ii, 189; E. and D., v, 513–516.

to be divided off and placed under the charge of an officer called the *crori*, selected for his trustworthiness and without regard to his acquaintance with the revenue officials: so that in three years' time all the uncultivated land might be brought under crops, and the treasury be replenished. The measurement was begun near Fathpur, and one cror was named Adampur, another Sethpur, and so on after prophets and patriarchs. Rules were laid down, but were not properly observed, and much of the land was laid waste through the rapacity of the croris; the peasants' wives and children were sold and dispersed, and everything went to confusion. But the croris were brought to account by Raja Todar Mal, and many pious men died from severe beatings and the torture of rack and pincers. Indeed so many died after long imprisonment by the revenue officers that the executioner or headsman was forestalled.'

All this is intended by the writer to cast ridicule on the reforms, but it really shows that they were good and moreover were strictly enforced. The same cynic can see no advantage in Akbar's system of territorial commands. The Moghul officers — Hindus and Muslims — were spread over the land, and the state taxes were granted to them in certain districts—except the *Khalisa* or exchequer lands—in return for military service. They had to bring a fixed number of men-at-arms, horses, and elephants, into the field, and were rated, according to the number they brought, as mansabdars of ten, twenty, a hundred, a thousand, etc. It was no invention of Akbar's, for we have seen it at work in much earlier times, and of course it was liable to abuse, though Akbar did much to remove the old dangers and corruptions of the system. Badauni said that the laziness, licence, extravagance, and greed of the mansabdars ate up all the grant, and no money was left to pay the soldiers, so the amirs dressed up their grooms and servants as men-at-arms and passed them off at the muster, and then sent them back to their duties. 'The treasure, tax-gathering, and expenditure of the mansabdars remained unchanged, but in every way dirt fell into the plate of the poor soldier, and he could not gird up his loins. Weavers, cotton-dressers, carpenters, and Hindu and Muslim chandlers would hire a charger, bring it to the muster, obtain a mansab [or order on the land-revenue], and become a crori, trooper, or substitute for someone : a few days later not a trace would be found of the hired horse, and they became footmen again. . . . This sort of trade was carried on to a great extent [and Akbar knew it]; nevertheless the emperor's good luck was such that his foes were everywhere crushed, and soldiers were not so much wanted.' As the enemies could not be crushed without soldiers, the system, though abused, appears to have answered its purpose.

There were doubtless many imperfections and many cases of malversation in spite of Akbar's efforts; but this is only to say that the best system in the world is open to abuse, especially in an oriental country where to cheat the government is a virtue and to grind the faces of the poor a venial fault. The real reason that Badauni is so severe upon these reforms is that they were but a part of a general tendency to lax views on the part of the emperor. It was not merely in his just and equable treatment of the Hindus that Akbar showed his broad and open mind. There were other influences at work besides those of his Hindu wives and friends, and they all made for what the orthodox Badauni denounced as latitudinarian. A king who was constitutionally unable to see why a Hindu should pay more taxes than a Muslim was also liable to equally deplorable liberality in matters of faith, and Akbar had been deeply moved by the mystical doctrines of the Persian Sufis as revealed to him by two brilliant brothers. From the time when Faizi, the mystic poet, joined the emperor's suite at the siege of Chitor in 1568, and still more when seven years later he introduced his young brother, the gentle and enthusiastic scholar Abu-l-Fazl, Akbar's mind had been unsettled in religion. He was essentially eclectic, and saw good in almost every form of worship. From his youth he had delighted in the conversation of scholars and philosophers and shown the greatest deference to real learning; he had books read aloud to him daily from his rich library, and would go through them again and again; and now under the influence of the speculative mind of Abu-l-Fazl,— a man of wide culture and pure spiritual ideals, who recognized his hero in his king, and devoted himself to him with his whole heart,— he began to encourage debates on doctrinal and philosophical questions and displayed an eager curiosity in the discussions.

These debates took place in a hall called the

Hall of Worship (Ibadat-Khana,— supposed to be identical with that now known as the Diwan-i-Khas) founded in 1574 at the city of Fathpur, which had become the emperor's favourite residence.[1] The city itself was the offspring of faith. Akbar, at least in

THE GREAT GATEWAY, BALAND DARWAZA, FATHPUR-SIKRI.

the earlier part of his reign, was a devout visitor of holy places, and frequented the tombs of Muslim saints. We read again and again how he made

---

[1] He had already built the famous Red Fort at Agra, where the court had usually resided. Later, Delhi and Lahore also became favourite cities where Akbar often held his court.

solemn pilgrimages to famous shrines; and one of his objects was to secure an heir, for up to the fourteenth year of his reign none of the sons born to him had lived. He repaired to a holy man dwelling in a cave at the village of Sikri, not far from Agra; the hermit promised him a son; and Akbar placed his wife, the princess of Amber, under the care of the saint till her time should be accomplished. Sikri, as well as its local prophet, waxed rich and populous by the numerous visits of the anxious king. Palaces began to rise (1569), and the prophet, Salim Chishti, set up a new monastery and a noble mosque. The aristocrats built them mansions near the palace. Sikri knew itself no more, and its name was changed to Fathpur, 'the town of victory.' Happily the seer was justified in the event, and Akbar's son, named after the holy man Salim, but better known afterwards as the emperor Jahangir, was safely ushered into the world. Fathpur derived fresh lustre from this auspicious event, and Akbar lavished all the taste and art of the age upon its adornment.

Nothing sadder or more beautiful exists in India than this deserted city — the silent witness of a vanished dream. It still stands, with its circuit of seven miles, its seven bastioned gates, its wonderful palaces, peerless in all India for noble design and delicate adornment; its splendid mosque and pure marble shrine of the hermit saint; its carvings and paintings — stands as it stood in Akbar's time, but now a body without a soul. Reared with infinite thought and curious care, it was deserted fourteen years later. When William Finch visited it five years after its founder's death he found it 'ruinate, lying like a waste district, and very dangerous to pass through at night.' Ruinate it has remained ever since, desolate and abandoned. No later ruler of India has ever aspired to dwell in Akbar's Versailles, just as none ever rose to the height of Akbar's ideals. In the empty palaces, the glorious mosque, the pure white tomb, the baths, the lake, at every turn we recognize some memory of the greatest of Indian emperors. We may even enter his bedroom, the Khwabgah or 'home of dreams,' and see the very screens of beautiful stone tracery, the same Persian couplets, the identic ornament in gold and ultramarine on which Akbar feasted his eyes in the long sultry afternoons of the Indian plains. We may walk into the houses of Faizi and Abu-l-Fazl, the laureate and the premier of his empire, who sang his glory and chronicled his reign. We may stand in the audience hall, with its pillar throne and galleries, where the keenest dialectic of Muslim schoolmen, Catholic priests, Pantheists, Fireworshippers, Brahmans, and Buddhists, rose in heated battle for their creeds, till quarrels and coarse vituperation called up the bitter sneer of the puritanic Badauni and the regretful contempt of the royal seeker after truth.

Fathpur, with its beauty in desolation, has stirred the poet's vision of a Heber, and compelled the homage of the wisest critic of Indian art. Fergusson wrote of the 'Turkish Sultana's House,' which still overlooks the Pachisi Court, where Akbar is said to have played his games of living chess with slave-girls as pieces moving on the chequered pavement, that nothing can be conceived so picturesque in outline, so richly and marvellously carved, without one touch of extravagance or false taste. The five-storeyed Panch Mahall, a kind of Buddhist Vihara, and the house of Akbar's witty Hindu favourite, Raja Birbal, have their individual charm; and the frescoes in 'Miraim's Kothi' are curious documents in the history of Indian painting, of which we obtain some glimpses in the albums of Moghul portraits, drawn by artists of the Panjab, now preserved in the British Museum and a few private collections. The presence of Jesuit Fathers at Agra, attracted by the benevolent catholicism of Akbar, accounts for some of the characteristics of these curious paintings.[1] Aureoles and angels appear; a little later we find the Blessed Virgin represented in a kiosk of Jahangir; and scenes of Christian hagiography were favourite subjects with Moghul artists. The Annunciation is

---

[1] ' In 986 (1578) the missionaries of Europe, who are called Padres, and whose chief pontiff called Papa promulgates his interpretations for the use of the people, and who issues mandates that even kings dare not disobey, brought their Gospel to the emperor's notice, advanced proofs of the Trinity, and affirmed the truth and spread abroad the knowledge of the religion of Jesus. The emperor ordered Prince Murad to learn a few lessons from the Gospel and to treat it with all due respect, and Shaikh Abu-l-Fazl was ordered to translate it. Instead of the prefatory *Bismillah*, the following ejaculation was enjoined: "O thou whose name is Jesus Christ." ' —BADAUNI, ii, 260, but he translates *Ay nam-i-way Zhezhu Kiristu* (which is obscurely written) as ' O thou whose name is merciful and bountiful ': E. and D., v, 529 ; *Ain*, i, 183, where the better form *Ay nam-i-tu Dezuz o Kiristo* (from the *Dabistan*) is given.

18

believed to be depicted in a fresco at Fathpur-Sikri, whilst another strongly resembles the fall of Adam. There are even traces of the work of Chinese artists in the Buddhist paintings in the ' Home of Dreams.' Indeed this Indian Pompeii, with its unique and never iterative designs, is a museum of exquisite æsthetic genius.' Akbar's views on art were characteristic. One day he remarked to some friends : ' There are many that hate painting, but such men I dislike. It appears to me as if a painter had quite peculiar means of recognizing God ; for a painter, in sketching anything that has life, and in devising its limbs one after the other, must come to feel that he cannot bestow personality upon his work, and is thus forced to think of God, the giver of life, and will thus increase in knowledge.' [2] He had always been fond of painting, and kept a number of painters at court, whose work was displayed before him every week. ' Hence the art flourishes,' says Abu-l-Fazl, ' and many painters have obtained great reputations .   .
.   . and masterpieces worthy of [the famous Persian court painter] Bihzad may be placed at the side of the wonderful works of the European painters who have attained world-wide fame. The minuteness in detail, the general finish, the boldness of execution, etc., now observed in pictures, are incomparble.' This was written in Akbar's lifetime, and it is noteworthy that the historian distinguishes the

[1] It has been admirably surveyed, described, and illustrated, by Mr. E. W. SMITH, of the Archæological Survey of India: *The Moghul Architecture of Fathpur-Sikri*, 4 vols., 1894 ff.
[2] *Ain*, i, 107, 108.

Hindu painters as the best among the hundred famous masters of the age, though he mentions some great artists from Persia.

In this fairy city Akbar's dream of a universal religion grew into definite shape. It was in the Hall of Worship that he sought wearily to elicit truth from the debates of professors. 'The unity that had existed among the learned disappeared in the very beginning; abuse took the place of argument, and the plainest rules of etiquette were, even in the presence of the emperor, forgotten. Akbar's doubts instead of being cleared up only increased; certain points of the Hanafi law, to which most Sunnis cling, were found to be better established by the dicta of lawyers belonging to the other three sects; and the moral character of the Prophet was next scrutinized and found wanting. Makhdum-al-mulk [the head of the ultra-bigoted orthodox party] wrote a spiteful pamphlet against Shaikh Abd-an-Nabi, the Sadr [or chancellor] of the empire, and the latter retorted by calling Makhdum a fool and cursing him. Abu-l-Fazl, upon whom Akbar from the beginning had fixed as the leader of his party, fanned the quarrels by skilfully shifting the disputes from one point to another.'[1] The heated discussions of the learned men whom he gathered together on Thursday nights to defend the dogmas of their creeds only inspired him with compassion for the futility of their reasoning and contempt for the narrowness of their grasp. To Akbar's open eyes there was truth in all faiths, but no one creed could hold

[1] BLOCHMANN, *Ain*, i, p. xiii.

'THE TURKISH SULTANA'S HOUSE,' FATHPUR-SIKRI.

276

the master-key of the infinite.   In Abu-l-Fazl's
words,—

O God, in every temple I see those who see thee, and in
    every tongue that is spoken, thou art praised.
Polytheism and Islam grope after thee.
Each religion says, 'Thou art one, without equal.'
Be it mosque, men murmur holy prayer; or church, the
    bells ring, for love of thee.
Awhile I frequent the Christian cloister, anon the mosque:
But thee only I seek from fane to fane.
Thine elect know naught of heresy or orthodoxy, whereof
    neither stands behind the screen of thy truth.
Heresy to the heretic,—dogma to the orthodox,—
But the dust of the rose-petal belongs to the heart of the
    perfume-seller.

Tennyson has finely expressed Akbar's dream
of a pure and universal faith :

> I can but lift the torch
> Of reason in the dusky cave of Life,
> And gaze on this great miracle, the World,
> Adoring That who made, and makes, and is,
> And is not, what I gaze on — all else Form,
> Ritual, varying with the tribes of men.

It had taken many years to develop this new
religion of catholic comprehension.   Akbar would
often sit, in the first hour of dawn, on a stone in his
palace court, watching the rising of the day-god and
meditating on the mystery of life.   He was passing
through a stage of earnest doubt.   He listened
eagerly to the words of the Christian fathers, to the

Vedanta philosophy of ascetic yogis; he had Sanskrit classics translated for him, and ordered a translation of the Gospels; he must have known the
Buddhist doctrine and the profound metaphysic
of India. Islam no longer satisfied him, though his
instinctive devoutness still took him on pilgrimages
to Muslim shrines, and as late as the twenty-first
year of his reign he was contemplating a journey to
Mekka. But Islam was too bounded for his ex-
panding soul. The outward symbols went: the Muslim shibboleth vanished from the coinage, and the
ambiguous formula 'Allahu Akbar,' 'God is most
great' (or, as detractors construed it, 'Akbar is
God'), took its place. When Muslims met, instead
of the customary *salam*, they were to say 'Allahu
Akbar,' and the reply, 'Jalla Jalaluh,' 'May his
glory shine!' contained another suspicious reference
to Akbar's surname Jalal-ad-din. Whilst plainly de-
claring that he pretended to no divine incarnation,
such as the Shi'a avow, the emperor assumed a
wholly new position in relation to matters of faith.
He found that the rigid Muslims of the court were
always casting in his teeth some absolute authority,
a book, a tradition, a decision of a canonical divine,
and like Henry VIII he resolved to cut the ground
from under them : he would himself be the head of
the church, and there should be no pope in India but
Akbar.

His first assumption of the rôle of priest-king was
unintentionally dramatic. Following the precedents
of the caliphs of old, he stood before the people in
the great mosque of Fathpur one Friday in 1580,

and began to read the bidding-prayer (*khutba*), into which Faizi had introduced these lines:

> The Lord to me the Kingdom gave,
> He made me prudent, strong and brave,
> He guided me with right and ruth,
> Filling my heart with love of truth ;
> No tongue of man can sum His State—
> Allahu Akbar ! God is great.[1]

But the emotion of the scene, the sight of the multitude, the thought of his high office, were too much for him. Akbar faltered and broke down, and the court preacher had to finish the prayer.

Soon afterwards Akbar promulgated a document unique in the history of the Mohammedan world. It was drawn up by the father of Faizi and Abu-l-Fazl, himself a Shi'a pantheist, and it was signed, sorely against their will, by the orthodox divines and lawyers of the court. It set forth in unmistakable terms that the authority of the just king is higher than that of a Mujtahid (or sublime doctor of the faith), and therefore that, should a religious question come up regarding which the Mujtahids are at variance, the emperor's decision should be binding on the Muslims of India, and any opposition to the imperial decrees should involve the loss of goods and religion in this world and insure damnation in the world to come.[2] In other words Akbar's judgment was set above every legal and religious authority

---

[1] Mr. H. G. KEENE's rendering.
[2] BADAUNI, ii, 272 ; BLOCHMANN, *Ain*, i, 186–187.

except the plain letter of the Koran. It was a promulgation of a doctrine of imperial infallibility.

After thus breaking sharply with the principles of
Mohammedan tradition, Akbar went as of old on
pilgrimage to a saint's tomb. Badauni grimly smiled
and said 'it was strange that his majesty should
have such faith in the good man of Ajmir whilst
rejecting the foundation of everything, our Prophet,
from whose skirt hundreds of thousands of first-class
saints had sprung.' With the same superstitious
bent, oddly contrasting with his philosophic theory,
Akbar is said to have varied the colours of his
clothes in accordance with the regent planet of the
day, to have muttered spells at night to subdue the
sun to his desires, prostrated himself publicly before
the sun and the sacred fire, and made the whole
court rise respectfully when the lamps were lighted.
On the festival of the eighth day after the sun
entered Virgo, the emperor came forth to the
audience chamber with his brow marked in Hindu
fashion and with jewelled strings tied by Brahmans
on his wrist to represent the sacred thread. He
was not above charms and sortileges. He studied
alchemy as well as astronomy, and is reported to have
exhibited the gold he had professedly transmuted,
and he took boundless interest in the tricks and
miracles of the Hindu ascetics or yogis, as well as
of the Muslim fakirs.

The truth is that Akbar was singularly sensitive
to religious impressions of every kind, and that his
new religion, the *Din-i-Ilahi*, 'divine faith,' an eclectic pantheism, contained elements taken from very

diverse faiths. Whilst overthrowing most of the ceremonial rules, whether of Islam or of Hinduism, and making almost all things lawful save excess,[1] he took ideas from learned Brahmans as well as Portuguese missionaries; he adopted the worship of the

DARUGHA PERSHAD'S HOUSE, FATHPUR-SIKRI.

sun, as the symbol of the Creator, and in gratitude for the blessings of light and fertilizing warmth;

[1] For example wine was allowed to be publicly sold, but intoxication was punished; the women of the town were registered and limited to the quarter known as Shaitanpur or Devilsbury, where their commerce was legalized and taxed; but the seduction of virgins was severely reprobated.

and himself daily set the example of 'adoring Him the Timeless in the flame that measures Time'; he introduced the solar year beginning at the vernal equinox as the starting point of his new Ilahi era; forbade cow eating, in deference to Indians, and had himself ceremonially weighed in Hindu fashion on both his solar and lunar birthday; instituted the sacred fire adored of the Parsis, and encouraged the *hom* sacrifice of the Hindus in his palace. The new cult was cordially professed only by a small band of courtiers calling themselves 'the elect,' and including Faizi, Abu-l-Fazl, and other Persians, chiefly poets, and one Hindu, Birbal, but the rest even of the court remained indifferent when not hostile. Some boldly refused to join the new faith, but the most part temporized for fear of losing favour. Of course an eclectic religion never takes hold of a people, and Akbar's curiously interesting hotchpotch of philosophy, mysticism, and nature worship practically died with him. But the broad-minded sympathy which inspired such a vision of catholicity left a lasting impress upon a land of warring creeds and tribes, and for a brief while created a nation where before there had been only factions.

With the promulgation of the emperor's infallibility the debates in the Hall of Worship came to an end; the leading bigots Makhdum and Abd-an-Nabi were sent to refresh their fanaticism at Mekka; and the pantheists under Abu-l-Fazl and his brother had their brief triumph. Both held high rank, but Faizi prized his office of poet laureate above any political power, whilst Abu-l-Fazl became

Diwan or Treasurer of the Province of Delhi. These two brilliant and sympathetic brothers were now Akbar's chief intimates, and he found in their devotion more than compensation for the solitary elevation that is the inevitable fate of a reforming sovereign born centuries before the acceptable time. Probably they encouraged him in the fancies and extravagances which somewhat marred his later life. One of these fancies was a belief that the religion of Islam would not survive its millennium, and that its collapse would be accompanied by the advent of the Mahdi, the Lord of the Age, in whom Akbar was easily induced to recognize himself. He ordered a 'History of the Millennium' (*Tarikh-i-Alfi*) to be compiled by a company of scholars, including the reluctant Badauni, to put a seal, as it were, upon an extinct religion. The events of the thousand years of doomed Islam were related from a Shi'a point of view, and to add to the confusion the chronology was reckoned from the death instead of from the flight (Hijra) of the Prophet.

This was an example of Akbar's love of innovation, and it is impossible to deny that he was fond of experiment and novelty for their own sake. 'All good things must once have been new,' he remarked, and accordingly he tested the novel habit of smoking tobacco, which was first introduced in India in his reign: but soon he gave it up. As Dr. Holden said, 'He experimented in all departments, from religion to metallurgy,' and some of his changes appear to be dictated by mere whim, or restless curiosity, rather than reason and judgment. His experimental spirit was displayed in the way he endeavoured to ascertain the natural religion of the untaught child. He separated a score of hapless babies from their mothers, and shut them up in a house where none might speak to them, in order to see what faith they would evolve. After three or four years the children were let out, and they came forth—dumb! The emperor's experiments were not always wise.

Nevertheless he had wise counsellors, and it was an age of great literary abounding. Faizi was one of the most exquisite poets India has ever produced, and Abu-l-Fazl's 'Book of Akbar' (*Akbarnama*, the third volume of which forms the celebrated *Ain-i-Akbari* or 'Acts of Akbar'), published in 1597, will always retain its fascination as a minute record of the customs and institutions of the greatest age of the Moghul empire. As one of its translators has said,[1] 'it crystallizes and records in brief for all time the state of Hindu learning, and, besides its statistical utility, serves as an admirable treatise of reference on numerous branches of Brahmanical science and on the manners, beliefs, traditions, and indigenous lore, which for the most part still retain and will long continue their hold on the popular mind. Above all as a register of the fiscal areas, the revenue settlements, and changes introduced at various periods, the harvest returns, valuations and imposts throughout the provinces of the empire, its originality is as indisputable as its surpassing historical importance.'

Whilst Akbar was busy in enlarging the bound-

[1] Col. H. S. JARRETT, *Ain*, iii, p. vii.

aries of faith, his material empire had not stood still. The conquests of Gujarat and Bengal, though requiring more than one repetition, had brought the empire to the normal limits of Hindustan. Kabul and the Afghan country, ruled by his disloyal brother Hakim, had repeatedly revolted ; Badakhshan was finally lost in 1585, and the merry Raja Birbal fell in a disastrous attempt to coerce the wild Yusufzais in 1586. But after Hakim's death Kabul was pacified, and Kashmir annexed (1587) ; and in 1594 Kandahar was included in the empire. These were small changes ; but more important conquests were attempted in the south. Again and again in Indian history we find in the Deccan the bane of Delhi kings. Nature never intended the same ruler to govern both sides of the Vindhya mountains, for people, character, and geographical conditions are dissimilar. Nevertheless to conquer the Deccan has been the ambition of every great king of Delhi, and the attempt has always brought disaster. Akbar was not immune from the Deccan fever, but it seized him late in life. Up to the last decade of his reign his power had hardly been felt south of the Satpura range. As early as 1562 indeed he had taken Burhanpur and made the rajas of Khandesh and Berar his tributaries, but their tribute was intermittent and their fealty barely nominal.

A viceroy of the Deccan was eventually appointed to consolidate authority, but in the hands of the emperor's son Murad and his successor Prince Daniyal— both of whom died of drink — the office became contemptible. Murad's incompetence to subdue open rebellion in Berar led to his recall and the appointment of Abu-l-Fazl to the command of the army which in 1599 resolutely set about the reconquest of the Deccan. Akbar himself arrived at the seat of war, and success soon followed. Ahmadnagar, formerly strenuously defended by the princess Chand Bibi, had again fallen after six months' siege, and Asirgarh, the strongest fortress in Khandesh, opened its gate in 1600. An inscription on that glorious gateway, the Baland Darwaza at Fathpur, records how ' His Majesty, King of Kings, Heaven of the court, Shadow of God, Jalal-ad-din Mohammad Akbar Padishah conquered the Kingdom of the South and Dandesh, which was heretofore Khandesh, in the Ilahi year 46, which is the year of the Hijra 1010. Having reached Fathpur he went on to Agra. Jesus said (on whom be peace) the world is a bridge; pass over it, but build no house there: he who hopeth for an hour may hope for eternity : the world is but an hour — spend it in devotion : the rest is unseen.'

In these last sad years the great heart of the emperor was weighed down with his grief. He had lost his beloved friend the poet Faizi in 1595, two of his own sons were sinking to their dishonoured deaths; the eldest, Salim, was little better and had shown flagrant insubordination. And now the closest of his friends, the inspirer of many of his best thoughts and acts, was to be sacrificed. Prince Salim, jealous of Abu-l-Fazl's influence and impatient of his censure, caused this upright and faithful servant of his father to be murdered on his way back from the Deccan in 1602.

AKBAR'S TOMB, AT SIKANDRA.

287

It was the last and crowning sorrow, and Akbar never recovered from the shock. The quarrels and intrigues of his worthless family hastened the end. At an elephant fight there was a scene of jealous disputing in his presence; the weary king gave way to ungovernable fury, as he too often did in this stricken period of his decay, and he was led away sick unto death. Round the bed of the dying Akbar the intrigues for the succession went on shamelessly, but at the last he received his only surviving son Salim, and invested him with the sword of state. He died in October, 1605, the noblest king that ever ruled in India.

CHAPTER XII

THE GREAT MOGHUL

AND EUROPEAN TRAVELLERS

1605–1627

TOWARDS the close of the sixteenth century the curious began to listen to rumours, vague indeed, but impossible to be ignored, of a new and singular Power that had arisen in the East. Stories were told of an emperor who had conquered the whole of Hindustan, and was ruling his vast dominions with extraordinary wisdom. Strange tales were bruited about of his toleration. It was said that Christians were sure of a welcome at his court; that he had even taken a Christian to wife. Toleration was sufficiently out of tune with Tudor England, but in the barbarous East it possessed the charm of the wholly unexpected. The name and character of the Great Moghul became the common talk. In a few years Englishmen came to see him face to face as no Indian king had been seen by Europeans since the days when Alexander met Porus on the plains of the Jehlam.

Hitherto India, except in parts of the coasts of the

peninsula, had been practically a *terra incognita.*
What little was known had filtered through Portuguese missionaries, and one has only to turn over a
few pages of the Travels of Europeans in the first
quarter of the seventeenth century to realize how
little these writers were prepared for the sights they
saw. They found a novel and almost undreamt of
civilization, possessing elements of practical statesmanship and sagacity which the most philosophic of
them all, the French physician Bernier, finds worthy
to be commended to the serious consideration of the
minister of Louis XIV. They met with a series of
spectacles, ceremonies, customs, religions, systems
of government, wholly unforeseen; and where they
expected to find at the utmost rude and vacuous
pomp, they encountered literature and learning,
poetry and art, and a reasoned theory of government,
which, in spite of their Western prejudices, fairly
compelled their admiration. With all this they discovered examples enough of superstition and degradation, and witnessed scenes of savage cruelty
contrasted with barbaric splendour; yet the splendour and the degradation were such as belong not to
uncivilized races, but to the exuberance of a great
empire.

The native annalists of the Moghul period are
both numerous and authoritative. No one who has
studied the invaluable series of volumes in which
the late Sir Henry Elliot and Professor Dowson epi-
tomized the 'History of India as told by its own
Historians' will be disposed to depreciate the importance of the Persian chronicles therein extracted with

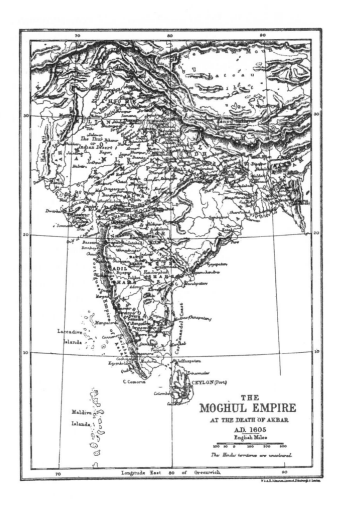

THE
MOGHUL EMPIRE
AT THE DEATH OF AKBAR
A.D. 1605
English Miles

The Hindu territories are uncoloured.

so much skill and erudition. But the native writers
have serious defects. They are prone to panegyric,
and disposed to exaggerate the merits of reigning
sovereigns and contemporary magnates with the traditional obsequiency of the oriental author. They
are apt to suppress facts which tell against their hero,
and it is rare to come across an Indian writer with
the critical or historical faculty. Besides, they naturally assume a familiarity with the every-day customs
and methods of the age in India, which a Western
reader does not possess. They write as Indians to
Indians. Had we to depend entirely upon them,
our insight into life in the Moghul empire in the
seventeenth century would be shallow. Fortunately
we have other witnesses. Europeans of various
nations, qualified in many respects to observe with
penetration and record with accuracy, visited India
in the period of Moghul supremacy, and their observations complete and correct with singular minuteness the narratives of the native chroniclers.

The Fates were unusually propitious when they
ordained that the Saturnian Age of Moghul power
should coincide with a new epoch in European intercourse with the East. Up to the closing years
of the sixteenth century one European nation had
held the monopoly of commerce in the East Indies.
When Vasco da Gama rounded the Cape of Good
Hope and landed at Calicut in 1498, the trade with
India and the Far East passed into a Portuguese
channel. The old routes had been in the hands
of Mohammedan traders, who shipped their goods
by the Persian Gulf and the Red Sea, and so over-

land to Syrian and Egyptian ports, whence the merchandise found its way to Europe in Venetian bottoms. These routes were tapped at their source when Portugal acquired the command of the Indian Ocean. In the hands of such heroes as Pacheco, Almeida, and Albuquerque, the control of Portugal over the whole of the commerce with the East Indies, Spice Islands, and China was assured. The Arab traders and Egyptian navies essayed in vain to oust the invaders of their ancient privileges. From the Cape of Good Hope to China the extended coast-line was armed with a chain of Portuguese fortresses, and no ship could sail without a Portuguese passport.

But the age of heroes for Portuguese India passed away, and there were still no signs of a consolidated Portuguese empire in the East. Albuquerque had dreamed of such an empire, in the spirit of a Dupleix or a Clive, and he had exhausted his little nation by the constant drain of colonization. His policy had not been continued, and an empire on Indian soil was abandoned in favour of fortified trading centres supported by the command of the Eastern seas. The forts remained, but no attempt at any more ambitious settlement was made ; and should the command of the seas be lost, there was nothing to save the commerce of Portugal with the East. The annexation by Spain in 1580 was the deathblow to Portuguese enterprise in the Indies; but the corruption of the fidalgoes themselves, who found their Capua in the tropical verdure of Old Goa, had already paved the way to ruin. In 1597 the Dutch appeared in the Indies, and a few years later they were joined by the English, upon the incorporation of the first East India Company on the 31st of December, 1600. Even so early as Pyrard de Laval's voyage in 1607 the Dutch had almost destroyed the Portuguese monopoly of commerce with the Far East; and as soon as the English founded their factory at Surat, the Indian trade began to be transferred from Portuguese to English bottoms. The naval victories of Best and Downton off Surat and in Swally Roads decided the command of the sea, and the Indian trade of Portugal practically came to an end.

The opening of English trade with India was followed by the arrival in the Moghul empire of European travellers, and the publication of their experiences. Two sea-captains, Hawkins and Herbert; Sir Thomas Roe, the ambassador; two clergymen, Terry and Ovington; Dr. Fryer, and Hedges, the Company's Agent and Governor, form a tolerably representative group of Englishmen, and there were many more, as may be seen in the recently edited correspondence of the East India Company's factors. France sent Pyrard, who did not get beyond the Portuguese settlements in India; but the Travels of Tavernier, Thevenot, and Bernier are among our best authorities. Pietro della Valle was 'a noble Roman,' Mandelslo a gentleman of the court of the Duke of Holstein, Gemelli Careri a Neapolitan doctor, and Manucci a Venetian. In such a cloud of witnesses of varied ranks, professions, and nationalities, truth, divested of insular or continental prejudice, may surely be found. The body of information furnished by their journals, letters, and travels, is indeed of priceless value to the historian of India.

The visit of William Hawkins to the court of the Great Moghul at Agra was a memorable event in the history of British intercourse with India. He was the first Englishman ever received by the emperor of Hindustan as the official representative of the king of England, and he obtained from the Great Moghul the first distinct acknowledgment of the rights of British commerce in India. Hawkins sailed with Sir Francis Drake on his voyage to the South Seas in 1577. Thirty years later, in 1607, he commanded the 'Hector' for the East India Company on a voyage to Surat, charged with letters and presents from James I 'to the princes and governors of Cambaya, on account of his experience and language.' He arrived at the bar of Surat, August 24, 1608, and soon discovered that his credentials would have to be presented to a higher potentate than those of Cambay. After twenty days he obtained leave to land his cargo, and was told he must deliver the king's letter to the Great Moghul in person. Accordingly, he dismissed his vessel to trade with a new cargo to Bantam. The Portuguese, however, were not yet innocuous, and their ships captured the 'Hector' as soon as she sailed. The Portuguese captain-major received Hawkins's remonstrances with contempt, and set to 'vilely abusing his Maiestie, tearming him King of Fishermen, and of an Island of no import, and a

―――― for his Commission.' To these ignominious
expressions a Portuguese naval officer added that
'these seas belonged unto the King of Portugall,
and none ought to come here without his license.'
Such was the reception of the first envoy of England
at the port of the Great Moghul.

Hawkins soon found that his troubles had only
begun. Notwithstanding Akbar's administrative reforms, it is clear that the local authorities in Gujarat
were oppressive and venal, and nothing could be
done without a bribe. The governor pillaged the
seaman's goods, only paying 'such a price as his
owne barbarous conscience afforded. . . . He
came to my house three times, sweeping me cleane
of all things that were good.' Matters came to
such a pass that the traveller had to defend his
house by force of arms, for Padre Pineiro offered
the governor 40,000 'ryals of eight' if he would
deliver up Hawkins to the Portuguese. At last on
February 1, 160$\frac{8}{9}$, he received a pass for his
journey to Agra. At Burhanpur he saw the viceroy
of the Deccan, who received him well, talked to him
in Turkish (a language with which Hawkins was
familiar) for three hours, accepted of course a
present, and invested him with 'two Clokes, one
of fine Woollen and another of Cloth of Gold;
giving mee his most kind letter of favour to the
King which avayled much. This done, he imbraced
me, and so we departed.' A guard of Patans hardly
sufficed to save the traveller from several attempts
at assassination, or what he believed to be such (for
one cannot but suspect that the gallant captain

made the most of his perils); but at length, 'after much labour, toyle, and many dangers,' he arrived at Agra on April 16, 1609.

At this time Akbar had been dead nearly four years, and a very different personage sat on the throne. The emperor Salim, entitled Jahangir, 'World-Grasper,' formed a striking contrast to his father, against whom he had more than once broken

GOLD COINS OF JAHANGIR.

into open insurrection. Born under a superstitious spell, named after a wonder-working saint, petted and spoilt, the boy grew up wilful, indolent, and self-indulgent, too lazy and indifferent to be either actively good or powerfully evil. He had instigated the murder of Akbar's trusted friend and minister, Abu-l-Fazl; he was possessed of a violent and arbitrary temper; and, like his wretched brothers Murad and Daniyal, he was a notorious and habitual drunkard, but unlike them he could control himself when necessary. His image may be seen depicted on his coins, wine-cup in hand, with unblushing effrontery: it is of a piece with the astonishingly simple candour of his own Memoirs. As he grew older he toned down somewhat, partly, he says, from a conviction that he was injuring his health, but chiefly, no doubt, under the influence of his beautiful and talented wife Nur-Jahan, the ' Light of the World.'

When he ascended the throne in 1605, at the age of thirty-seven, his character, never wanting in a certain indolent good-nature, had mellowed. He had become less savage and more sober; by day he was the picture of temperance, at night he became exceeding 'glorious.' But what was done in the evening was entirely ignored in the morning, and any noble who ventured to approach the daily levees with the least odour of wine upon him was destined to certain and severe punishment. Jahangir carried his daylight sobriety so far as even to publish an edict against intemperance, and emulated his far more contemptible 'brother' James of Great Britain by writing a Persian counterblast against tobacco. In spite of his vices, which his fine constitution supported with little apparent injury almost to his sixtieth year, he was no fool; he possessed a shrewd intelligence, and he showed his good sense in carrying on the system of government and principle of toleration inaugurated by Akbar. He was not deficient in energy when war was afoot; he was essentially just when his passions were not thwarted; and he cultivated religious toleration with the easy-

going indifference which was the keynote of his
character. The son of an eclectic philosopher and a
Rajput princess, he professed himself a Muslim,
restored the Mohammedan formulas of faith which
Akbar had abandoned on the coinage, and revived
the Hijra chronology, whilst preserving for regnal
years and months the more convenient solar system.
But he followed his father in his policy towards the
Hindus, and was equally tolerant towards Christians.
He allowed no persecution or badges of heresy, but
welcomed the Jesuit father Corsi to his court, encouraged artists to adorn the imperial palaces with
pictures and statues of Christian saints, and had
two of his nephews baptized, doubtless for his own
purposes. He could be magnanimous and forgiving,
when he was not angry. He even bestirred himself
to redress the grievances of the people,—witness his
specious 'Institutes,' and had a chain and bell
attached to his room at the palace, so that all who
would appeal to him could ring him up without running the gauntlet of the officials. But it is not
on record that anybody was hardy enough to pull
the bell.

William Hawkins was the first to set on record a
portrait of this 'talented drunkard,' and very curious
it is. It was a singular situation for a bluff sea-
captain to find himself, in an unknown land, called
upon to meet a great emperor about whom absolutely
nothing was known in England. There was nothing to suggest the most distant dream that in two
centuries and a half the slight introduction Hawkins
was then effecting between England and India would

culminate in the sovereignty of a British Queen over the whole empire where the 'Light of the World' and her imperial husband then reigned. The gift of prophecy would have considerably added to the sailor's feeling of responsibility. As it was, he was quickly put at his ease by the complaisant emperor. Jahangir was so eager to see this messenger from a new country that he scarcely gave him time to put on his 'best attyre'; and so far from seeming annoyed at the poverty of his offering,—for the governor of Surat had left him nothing but cloth for a present,—the emperor 'with a most kind and smiling countenance bade me most heartily welcome,' reached down from the throne to receive his letter, and having read it by the aid of an old Portuguese Jesuit (who did his best to prejudice him) promised 'by God, that all what the King had there written he would grant and allow with all his heart, and more.' Jahangir then took his visitor into the private audience chamber, where they had a long conversation, and, on leaving, Hawkins was commanded to return every day. The language of the court was Persian, though everyone could speak Hindustani; but Jahangir and several of his ministers were also familiar with Turkish, the native tongue of Babar and his descendants, and this was the language in which the emperor conversed with Hawkins. 'Both night and day, his delight was very much to talk with mee, both of the Affaires of England and other Countries.'

The two evidently suited each other well. Hawkins would have felt constrained in the presence of

Akbar; but it was impossible to regard his son —
at least of an evening — in any other light than as a
jovial and somewhat tipsy boon-fellow. Hawkins
for his part was a simple honest sailor, a little in-
clined to bluster, but just the man to take the

PALACE OF JAHANGIR AT AGRA.

emperor in the right way, and not at all apt to be
shocked at an extra allowance of grog. The result
of the harmony between the two was that Hawkins
acquired a footing in the court more intimate than
was ever afterwards enjoyed by any European, and
held it for years in spite of the strenuous opposition

of the Jesuits. At one time Jahangir granted everything that the Englishman asked, 'swearing by his
Father's soule, that if I would remeyne with him,
he would grant me articles for our Factorie to my
heart's desire, and would never go from his word.'
He talked of sending an ambassador to England,
and tried to induce Hawkins to make India his
home, promising to make him a mansabdar or officer
of 400 horse, with an allowance of £3200 a year.
He even admitted him within the red rails before
the throne, where only the greatest nobles stood,
and saluted him by the lofty title of 'Inglis Khan':
all of which mightily delighted the honest captain.

No wonder 'the Portugalls were like madde
Dogges.' The English khan was universally envied;
but he had to work hard for his glory. Jahangir
gave him little liberty. Half of every twenty-four
hours he served the emperor, by day and night, and
he was obliged to marry an Armenian — a 'white
Mayden out of his Palace',—to cook his meals for
him, for fear of poison being mixed with his food.
His position was moreover extremely precarious.
The commission for an English factory at Surat was
first granted, and then, under pressure from the
Portuguese viceroy, withdrawn. 'Let the English
come no more,' said the emperor, weary of the
squabble. But Hawkins knew the way to mend the
matter, and on his giving Jahangir a fresh present,
this order was rescinded: 'so this time againe I was
afloate.' Then the Portuguese plied the emperor
with bribes, and Hawkins fell out of favour. Nur-
Jahan reversed this state of things for the moment,

but Hawkins found it impossible to pin the emperor to his promises, and retired from court in disgust, Nov. 2, 1611. He sailed for Bantam in the following January in Sir Henry Middleton's fleet, and died a couple of years later on his voyage home.

Hawkins's intimacy with the Great Moghul gave him unrivalled opportunities for observation ; but he was not an educated or penetrating observer. A good deal of his information[1] is obviously based upon hearsay, but there is a large amount of first-hand evidence which no historian of Mohammedan India can afford to neglect. He describes the life-peers, or 'men of Livings or Lordships' as he calls them, in their several ranks, from those ' of the Fame of 12,000 Horsemen' down to those of 20 horse, and says there were altogether 3000 in receipt of such grants. The army raised by these mansabdars amounted to 300,000 horsemen, which were maintained out of the income allowed to their rank. On their death, all their property went to the emperor, and 'all the lands belong to him,' but ' commonly he dealeth well ' with their children. The king's yearly income he places at fifty crors of rupees, or over fifty millions of pounds. The royal treasury contained an infinity of gold plate and jewels, including 500 drinking cups, some of which were made of ' one piece of Ballace Ruby.' The servants, gardeners, grooms, and others, attending upon the court, he estimates at 36,000. There were also 12,000 elephants, of which 300 were reserved

---

[1] *Narrative of Occurrents*, etc., in *The Hawkins Voyages*, ed. Sir Clements Markham (Hakluyt Society, 1878).

exclusively for the emperor's use. The daily expenses of the court were 50,000 rupees, besides 30,000 for the harim; or together, £9000, which comes to three and a quarter millions a year.

He describes the emperor as far from popular with his subjects, 'who stand greatly in fear of him,' and ascribes this partly to his preference for Mohammedans over Rajputs for posts of honour and command, and partly to his innate cruelty. Jahangir took pleasure in seeing men executed or torn to pieces by his elephants, and the dangerous sport of elephant fights was his favourite spectacle on five days in the week. He was said to have killed his secretary with his own hand on mere suspicion, and flogged a man almost to death for breaking a dish. He delighted in combats between men and animals, and made an unarmed man fight with a lion till he was torn to shreds. At last the keepers contrived to tame fifteen young lions, who played before the king, 'frisking betweene men's legs,' and with these animals as opponents the combats became comparatively bloodless. All this cruelty, added to a rapacious and severe government, produced disaffection among his subjects. Thieves and outlaws infested the roads, and many rebellions broke out.

The daily life of the emperor Jahangir was scarcely edifying. 'About the breake of day, he is at his Beades, with his face turned to the westward in a private faire room,' in which is 'the picture of Our Lady and Christ, graven in stone.' Then he shows himself to the people, who flock to bid him good-morrow. Two hours of sleep ensue, then dinner,

after which the emperor retires to his women. At
noon he again holds public levee till three, and
witnesses the elephant fights and other sports. The
nobles at Agra all come and pay him homage, and
he hears all causes and complaints. He then says
his prayers, and has a meal of four or five sorts of
well-dressed meats, of which ' he eateth a bit to stay
his stomach, drinking once of his stronge drinke.
Then he cometh forth into a private roome, where
none can come but such as himself nominateth (for
two yeeres I was one of his attendants here). In
this place he drinketh other five cupfuls, which is
the portion that the Physicians alot him. This done
he eateth opium, and then he ariseth, and being in
the height of his drinke, he layeth him down to
sleep, every man departing to his own home. And
after he hath slept two houres they awake him, and
bring his supper to him, at which time he is not able
to feed himselfe; but it is thrust into his mouth by
others, and this is about one of the clock; and then
he sleepeth the rest of the night.'

Such was Akbar's successor, and such the sovereign
to whom Sir Thomas Roe presented his credentials as
ambassador of the king of England in January, 1615.
Roe had come to complete what Hawkins had only
partly succeeded in effecting. The English agents
and traders were still in a humiliating situation, subject to all kinds of indignities, possessing no recognized or valid rights, and obliged to sue and bribe for
such slight facilities as they could win. Their chiefs,
the agents of the East India Company, had brought
scorn upon their nation by ' kotowing ' to the Moghul

dignitaries, cringing to insult, asserting no trace of dignity; and had even 'suffered blowes of the porters, base Peons, and beene thrust out by them with much scorne by head and shoulders without seeking satisfaction.' Englishmen were flouted, robbed, arrested, even whipped in the streets. It was evident that a different manner of man was needed to retrieve the indignity done to our name and honour. Sir Thomas Roe was invited by the directors, after much consideration and debate, to accept the task, and the choice was approved by King James, whose royal commission duly constituted, appointed, ordained, and deputed 'the said Sir Thomas Rowe our true and undoubted Attorney, Procurator, Legate, and Ambassador' to that 'high and mighty Monarch, the Greate Mogoar, King of the Orientall Indyes, of Condahy, of Chismer, and of Corason.'

Roe was in every way an excellent choice. He combined the business capacity of the great merchant with the urbanity and address of the courtier. His grandfather was lord mayor of London, and the blood of the Greshams ran in his veins; but he was entered at Magdalen College, Oxford, belonged to the Middle Temple, had been esquire of the body to Queen Bess herself, and was on terms of affectionate intimacy with Prince Henry and his sister Elizabeth, the future 'Rose of Bohemia.' Not yet thirty-five, he had led a voyage of discovery to Guiana and explored the Orinoco; he had disputed in Latin with Dutch divines; he had even sat for Tamworth in the 'Addled Parliament.' The East

India directors described him as 'of a pregnant understanding, well spoken, learned, industrious, and of a comelie personage,' and the latest and best editor of his Journal[1] justly adds that 'his commanding presence and dignified bearing were useful qualifications for a mission to an Eastern court, while in the still more important matters of judgment and tact he was equally well equipped. Sprung from a noted City family, he combined the shrewdness, readiness of resource, and business ability which had raised his ancestors to fortune, with the culture and experience obtained by a varied training in most favourable circumstances.'

More than all this, he was a true Elizabethan, with the gallant bravery, the passionate devotion to king and country, the great-hearted fanaticism of his age. It was not the merchant's son, but the Elizabethan gentleman, who faced the Moghul prince as an equal, and told an insulting prime minister that 'if his greatness were no more than his manners he durst not use me soe; that I was an Ambassador from a mighty and free Prince, and in that quality his better.' When the governor of Surat tried slyly to carry out the odious practice, hitherto tamely allowed, of seaching the persons of British subjects, in spite of Roe's claiming the absolute exemption of an ambassador's suite, there was a spirited scene: 'Master Wallis breaking out came up after me and tould me this treachery; whereon

[1] *The Embassy of Sir Thomas Roe to the Court of the Great Moghul*, Edited from contemporary records by W. H. FOSTER (Hakluyt Society, 1899).

I turnd my horse and with all speed rode backe to them, I confess too angry. When I came up, I layd my hand on my sword, and my men breake through and came about me. Then I asked what they entended by soe base treachery: I was free landed, and I would die soe, and if any of them durst touch any belonging to me, I bade him speake and shew himselfe. Then they desired me not to take yt in ill part: it was done in Frendship. I called for a Case of Pistolls, and hanging them at my saddle I replyed those were my Frendes, in them I would trust. . . . It was a Custome to be usd to rouges and theeves and not to free men: I was resolved not to return to my Country with shame; I would rather dye there with Honor.'

Roe was certainly no meek-tempered man. His Journal is full of similar scenes. But he did well to be angry, and his defiant and punctilious assertion of his dignity, as the mirror of his sovereign, his insistence upon every necessary point of courtesy, and his stately refusal to unbend a jot of his proud bearing, had their due effect. When he came to India, the English were very nearly on the point of being driven out of even their slight hold at Surat; the influence of the Portuguese at court threatened to oust the scanty merchant colony which, in deep humiliation, was unconsciously laying the foundations of empire; the Moghul authorities were accustomed to treat the English as beggars to be spurned. All this was changed before he left. Despite the opposition of the prince, afterwards Shah-Jahan, who almost ruled his father, and who, as governor of Surat, had the means of making his enmity felt; in spite of the intrigues of the empress, the prime minister, and the Jesuits, Roe not merely asserted his countrymen's rights, but won a series of important diplomatic victories. He compelled the court favourite to refund his illegal exactions, and 'recovered all bribes, extortions, debts made and taken before my tyme till this day, or at least an honourable composition.' His firmness and courage, combined with wary management, were too much for the cleverness of Father Corsi, and the Portuguese almost lost their influence. The emperor and his son were men fully capable of measuring and admiring Roe's manly qualities; and his independence and dogged persistence, supported by natural dignity and courtliness, won from the Moghul authorities as much advantage as could at that time be expected.

The ambassador tried in vain to obtain a general treaty, embodying articles resembling the capitulations granted in Turkey. Experience taught him that the time was not ripe for any such concession, and the Moghul emperor was too ignorant of foreign kingdoms to measure India with them. 'Neyther will this overgrowne Eliphant,' said Roe, 'descend to Article or bynde himselfe reciprocally to any Prince upon terms of Equality, but only by way of favour admitt our stay.' 'You can never expect to trade here upon Capitulations that shall be permanent. Wee must serve the tyme.' All he could obtain were firmans, or orders to the local authorities, sanctioning the English trade at Surat upon reasonably satisfactory terms. 'You shall be sure of as much priviledge as any stranger,' he promised, and he kept his word. The English factory at Surat was set on a sufficiently stable basis, and recognized officially by emperor and prince-governor.

Indeed Roe was disposed to judge favourably of the Moghul authorities, considering their ignorance and the uncertainty of their official position. 'All the Government dependes upon the present will,' he wrote in 1618, 'whose appetite only governs the lordes of the kingdome; but their Justice is generallie good to strangers; they are not rigorous, except in scearching for thinges to please [*i. c.*, presents and luxuries], and what trouble we have is for hope of them, and by our owne disorders.' He marked the turbulence of the English crews and even of some of the factors, and warned the Company against a policy of aggression: 'A war and trafique are incompatible. By my consent, you shall no way engage yourselves but at sea, wher you are like to gayne as often as to loose. It is the beggering of the Portugall, notwithstanding his many rich residences and territoryes, that hee keepes souldiers that spendes it; yet his garrisons are meane. He never profited by the Indyes since hee defended them. Observe this well. It hath beene also the error of the Dutch, who seeke Plantation heere by the sword. They have a woonderfull stocke, they proule in all Places, they Posses some of the best; yet ther dead Payes consume all the gayne. Lett this bee received as a rule that if you will Profitt, seeke it at Sea, and in quiett trade; for without controversy it is an error to affect Garrisons and Land warrs in India.'

Roe's Journal is perhaps better known than any similar work on India; but it is extremely limited in its scope. It deals almost exclusively with the court and the ambassador's audiences with the emperor, and the political intrigues of the time, but of the state of the country it reveals little.   As a record

TOMB OF NUR-JAHAN'S FATHER AT AGRA.

of court life, however, it forms an admirable complement to Hawkins's narrative. Sir Thomas was admitted to the king's privacy almost with the freedom which the seaman enjoyed. Indeed Jahangir seemed to be unable to distinguish between an ambassador and a buccaneer, and entertained his excellency with a familiar joviality which severely tried the patience of the grave diplomatist. He made him sneeze with his 'strong drink,' to the delight of the assembled court, and then fell asleep in his cups, when the candles were immediately 'popped out,' and Sir Thomas 'groppt' his way out in the dark. Jahangir especially piqued himself on his taste for art; pictures and statues, even of the Madonna, adorned his palace, and in the hall of audience were displayed pictures of 'the King of England, the Queen, the Lady Elizabeth, the Countesse of Somerset and Salisbury, and of a Citizen's wife of London; below them, another of Sir Thomas Smith, Governour of the East-India Companie.' When Roe showed him an English picture, he immediately had it copied by Indian artists, so that the owner could not tell which was the original, whereat the Great Moghul 'was very merry and joyfull, and craked like a Northerne man.' In his usual communicative mood of an evening, 'with many passages of jests, mirth, and bragges concerning the Arts of his Country, hee fell to aske me questions, how often I drank a day, and how much, and what? what Beere was? how made? and whether I could make it here? In all which I satisfied his great demands of State.'

The ambassador must have found the privy council room of an evening anything but a suitable place for business. One night he was summoned thither after he had got to bed, merely to show the Great Moghul a portrait. 'When I came in I found him sitting cross-legd on a little Throne, all clad in Diamonds,

Pearls, and Rubies, before him a table of Gold, in it
about fiftie pieces of Gold plate, set all with stones,
his Nobilitie about him in their best equipage, whom
he commanded to drinke froliquely, several wines
standing by in great flagons. . . . So drinking,
and commanding others, his Majestie and all his
Lords became the finest men I ever saw, of a thousand humours.' At other times Jahangir waxed
solemn and sentimental: 'The good King fell to
dispute of the Lawes of Moses, Jesus and Mahomet,
and in drinke was so kinde, that he turned to me
and said: I am a king, you shall be welcome:
Christians, Moores, Jewes, he medled not with
their faith; they came all in love, and he would
protect them from wrong, they lived under his
safety, and none should oppresse them; and this
often repeated, but in extreame drunkenesse, he fell
to weeping and to divers passions, and so kept us
till midnight.' On another occasion the ambassador
found him sharing the coarse meal of 'a filthy beggar'
— a holy fakir, no doubt — 'taking him up in his
armes, which no cleanly body durst, imbracing him,
and three times laying his hand on his heart, calling
him father': for superstition was a potent factor in
this singular specimen of royalty.

Among the court festivals which Sir Thomas Roe
witnessed none was more curious than the process of
weighing the Great Moghul. 'The first of Septem-
ber was the King's Birth-day, and the solemnitie of
his weighing, to which I went, and was carryed into
a very large and beautiful Garden, the square within
all water, on the sides flowres and trees, in the midst

a Pinacle, where was prepared the scales, being hung in large tressels, and a crosse beame plated on with Gold thinne: the scales of massie Gold, the borders set with small stones, Rubies and Turkeys, the Chaines of Gold large and massie, but strengthened with silke Cords. Here attended the Nobilitie, all sitting about it on Carpets until the King came; who at last appeared clothed or rather loden with Diamonds, Rubies, Pearles, and other precious vanities, so great, so glorious; his Sword, Target, Throne to rest on, correspondent; his head, necke, breast, armes, above the elbows, at the wrists, his fingers every one, with at least two or three Rings; fettered with chaines, or dyalled Diamonds; Rubies as great as Wal-nuts, some greater; and Pearles such as mine eyes were amazed at. Suddenly he entered into the scales, sate like a woman on his legges, and there was put in against him many bagges to fit his weight, which were changed six times, and they say was silver, and that I understood his weight to be nine thousand rupias, which are almost one thousand pounds sterling: after with Gold and Jewels, and precious stones, but I saw none, it being in bagges might be Pibles; then against Cloth of Gold, Silk, Stuffes, Linen, Spices, and all sorts of goods, but I must believe for they were in sardles. Lastly against Meale, Butter, Corne, which is said to be given to the Banian.'

One of the lights thrown by Roe's Journal on the administration of the Moghul Empire is contained in his report of a conversation which he held with the 'Viceroy of Patan,' which shows the profits derived by the mansabdars or life-peers from their appanages: 'As for his Government of Patan onely, he gave the King eleven Lackes of Rupias (the Rupia sterling is two shillings two pence), all other profits were his, wherein he had Regall authoritie to take what he list, which was esteemed at five thousand horse, the pay of every one at two hundred Rupias by the yeare, whereof he kept fifteene hundred, and was allowed the Surplusse as dead pay: besides the King gave him a Pension of one thousand Rupias a day, and some smaller governments. Yet he assured me there were divers had double his entertainment, and about twenty equall.' This being translated means that the governor of Patna was an officer or mansabdar of the rank of 5,000 horsemen, nominal, but was only expected to maintain a force of 1,500, which cost him 300,000 rupees a year. But he drew from the imperial treasury at the rate of 5,000 horse, or 1,000,000 rupees, thus gaining 700,000 profit, besides whatever he could sweat out of the taxes of the province which was farmed out to him, beyond the 1,100,000 rupees he had to pay as rent to the treasury. In other words, this official drew a fixed salary of nearly £80,000 a year, besides what he could make out of the taxes, and without reckoning the pension of 1,000 rupees a day, which is probably a confused repetition of the 300,000 allowed for the troops. It was at any rate four times the pay of a British viceroy of India.

Roe had no easy time, what with the intrigues of the court, the vacillations of the emperor, and the hostility of the Dutch, for whom he always nourished

an inveterate dislike. 'They wrong you in all Parts,
and grow to insuffrable insolencies . . . and vse vs
woorse than any braue enemie would or any other
but vnthanckfull drunckards that wee haue releeued
from Cheese and Cabbage, or rather from a Chayne
with bread and water.' In his solitude and harass-
ments his great consolation was the sense of duty
ungrudgingly performed, and he could write to his
employers proudly, yet without boasting, 'My sincer-
ity toward you in all Actions is without spott; my
Neglect of Priuat Gayne is without example, and my
frugalitye beyond your expectation. I was neuer an
ill husband of my Credit nor any trust committed to
mee. My Patrimoniall vnthriftines only I feele and
repent . . . I will bragg of no industrie nor
successe. Judge mee by my Actions, Not by the
fauour of an Infidell King, with whom yet I stand on
such outward showes of Creditt as Neuer any stranger
did.' His 'frugalitye' was indeed extraordinary.
He kept up the embassy on about £250 a year; his
own salary was only £600; and though the company
received him with twelve coaches at Tower Wharf,
and voted him £1,500 for his services, he returned a
poor man, and was thankful to accept another mission from the king, though it involved a second exile,
to Constantinople. In those days it was an exception for a man in his position to refuse, as unworthy
of his high office, the many opportunities for making
money in India. But Thomas Roe was fashioned in
a refined and exalted ideal of conduct, and his high
principles and noble character stand clearly revealed
in his writings.

We shall obtain no more familiar glimpses of the
jocund court of Jahangir after Sir Thomas Roe's departure in 1618. The ambassador's chaplain, Edward
Terry, in his 'Voyage to the East Indies,' adds
little ; nor is much to be learnt about the court, or
even the country and government, from the Travels
of Pietro della Valle, who visited Surat, Ahmadabad,
and Cambay in 1623, and then turned south to Goa.
He gives an amusing account of the sumptuous way
of life among the English merchants of Surat, but
he has little to tell of the Moghul empire and he did

COIN OF JAHANGIR AND NUR-JAHAN.
Struck at Agra, A. H. 1037 (A.D. 1627-8.)

not see the capital. But of the famous empress, the
' Seal of Womankind ' (Muhr-i-Nisa), Nur-Jahan—or
as she was then called Nur-Mahall, he has this notice :
' He hath one Wife, or Queen, whom he esteems and
favours above all other Women ; and his whole Em-
pire is govern'd at this day by her counsel. . . . She
was born in India, but of Persian Race. . . .
She was formerly Wife in India to another Persian
Captain, who served the Moghul too ; but after her
Husband's death, a fair opportunity being offer'd, as
it falls out many times to some handsome young
Widows I know not how, Sciah Selim had notice

of her, and became in love with her. . . . At
length he determin'd to receive her for his lawful
Wife above all the rest. And as such she commands
and governs at this day in the King's Haram with
supream authority; having cunningly remov'd out
of the Haram, either by marriage, or other handsome ways, all the other Women who might give her
any jealousie; and having also in the Court made
many alterations by deposing and displacing almost
all the old Captains and Officers, and by advancing
to dignities other new ones of her own creatures,
and particularly those of her blood and alliance.
This Queen is call'd at this day Nurmahal, which
signifies Light of the Palace.'

' By degrees,' says Mohammad Hadi, the continuer
of Jahangir's Memoirs, ' she became, in all but name,
undisputed sovereign of the empire, and the king
himself became a tool in her hands. He used to say
that Nur-Jahan Begam has been selected, and is wise
enough, to conduct the matters of state, and that
he wanted only a bottle of wine and a piece of meat
to keep himself merry. Nur-Jahan won golden
opinions from all people. She was liberal and
just to all who begged her support. She was an
asylum for all sufferers, and helpless girls were
married at the expense of her private purse. She
must have portioned above five hundred girls in her
lifetime, and thousands were grateful for her
generosity.'

So great was the influence of this Persian princess
that Jahangir joined her name with his own on the
coinage, a conjunction unparalleled in the history of

ZODIACAL GOLD MOHRS OF JAHANGIR.

Mohammedan money; though the popular story of her having issued the famous Zodiacal Mohrs, when the emperor allowed her the privilege of mint-mistress for a single day, is without foundation. Her un-limited dominion over her husband, who loved her with a supreme devotion, is the more remarkable since she was no longer young when he married her in 1610, and Indian widows of thirty-four are usually widows indeed. This gifted woman aided by her subtle brother, Asaf Khan, practically ruled the empire during the greater part of Jahangir's reign, much to his satisfaction; but although at first her influence kept him straight and benefited the empire, her overweening power, covetousness, and unscru-pulous favouritism aroused bitter jealousies; and to the resulting intrigues were due the troubles that darkened the closing days of that self-indulgent emperor, the weakening of the old martial spirit of the Moghuls, the corruption and cupidity of the court, and the rebellion of Jahangir's son. His reign so far had been successful and curiously little dis-turbed. There had been hostilities with the rana of Udaipur, which were ended in 1614 by the military genius of Prince Khurram, the future Shah-Jahan; and, besides temporary revolts in Bengal and else-where, there was the constant difficulty of maintain-ing a hold upon the Deccan provinces, where there was hard fighting with Malik Amber, the able vezir of the Nizam Shah.[1] The boundaries of the empire remained much where they had been under Akbar, though Kandahar was lost to the Persian Shah in

[1] See below p. 344.

1622 and not recovered till it was betrayed to Shah-Jahan in 1637. On the whole the years had been tranquil until the question of the succession excited rival interests.

Jahangir's eldest son, Prince Khusru, who seems to have been always on bad terms with his father, had openly rebelled in the early days of the reign, and on his defeat was condemned to a lifelong but not severe captivity, whilst many of his followers were impaled by his infuriated father in the presence of the youth whom they had followed to the death. Khusru had by some quality or other acquired extraordinary popularity — as Roe's Journal repeatedly indicates, — and people compassionated his dreary fate, and even rose in open rebellion in his cause, with the like enthusiasm that others in Britain showed for Marie Stuart or Prince Charlie. He was believed to have been blinded by his father, but Della Valle explains that though the eyelids were sewn up the eyes were still uninjured when Jahangir caused them to be unripped, 'so that he was not blinded but saw again and it was only a temporal penance.' Sir Thomas Roe met him and found him an interesting mystery. The second son, Khurram, reckoned him an exceedingly dangerous factor in politics. What actually happened will never be known; but when Prince Khurram went to restore order in the Deccan in 1621 he insisted on taking his elder brother with him, and there the unfortunate Khusru died, — of a fever, as was said, but such fevers sometimes happen very opportunely in the East.

Khurram, or Shah-Jahan as he was already styled, now became more clearly marked out than ever as the future emperor. He was the best general of his time, and had overcome the Rajputs of Udaipur and the many-headed foe in the Deccan. He was an able administrator and a cool calculating statesman. But he was intensely unpopular in those early days, however well he overcame the prejudice afterwards. Sir Thomas Roe found him cold and repellant, though always stately and magnificent. 'I never saw so settled a countenance,' he wrote, 'nor any man keepe so constant a gravitie, never smiling, nor in face shewing any respect or difference of mien.' There was nothing in common between Jahangir and this capable self-contained son whom the father, depressed by his gravity, plaintively exhorted to take a little wine, 'not to excess, but to promote good spirits'; and to Nur-Jahan, who had formerly supported him, he became hateful, perhaps the more so since he had won her brother Asaf's favour by marrying his daughter, the lady of the Taj. Her aim was to induce her husband to name as successor his youngest son (by another wife) Shah-riyar, a handsome fool, who had married her daughter by her first marriage, and so to keep the dreaded Shah-Jahan out of power. Jahangir however favoured his third son Parviz, who could drink level with himself. The result was civil war. Shah-Jahan, no longer impeded by an elder brother's claim, took the field against his father, but was defeated, and after an attempt at independent sovereignty in Bihar and Bengal (1624), and a final resort to the protection of his old enemy Malik Amber in the Deccan, the rebel prince made his submission, surrendered his few remaining forts, and sent two of his sons, Dara and Aurangzib, as hostages to Agra.

Shah-Jahan was now apparently helpless, and the imperious queen next sought to gain the command of the army. The general, Mahabat Khan, however, was not to be won over, and seeing that his own command, even his life, was at stake, he took the bold course of seizing the person of the emperor whilst he was separated from his guard when on the point of crossing the Behat (Hydaspes) on his way to subdue a rising at Kabul (1626). The empress, far from daunted by this unexpected stratagem, lost not a whit of her splendid courage. She secretly escaped to the imperial guard, and marshalled her husband's troops against the division of his captor, riding at the head of the army on her tall elephant, armed with bow and arrows. Mahabat's Rajputs had burned the bridge, but the empress was among the first to cross the ford and engage the enemy on the other side. 'A scene of universal tumult and confusion ensued: the ford was choked with horses and elephants; some fell and were trampled under foot; others sank in the pools and were unable to regain the shore; and numbers plunged into the river and ran the chance of making good their passage or being swept away by the stream. The most furious assault was directed on Nur-Jahan: her elephant was surrounded by a crowd of Rajputs; her guards were overpowered and cut down at its feet; balls and arrows fell thick round her howdah, and one of the latter wounded the infant daughter of Shahriyar, who was seated in her lap. At length her driver was killed; and her elephant, having received a cut on the proboscis, dashed into the river and soon sank in deep water and was carried down the stream. After several plunges he swam out and reached the shore, where Nur-Jahan was surrounded by her women, who came shrieking and lamenting, and found her howdah stained with blood, and herself busy in extracting the arrow and binding up the wound of the infant.[1]

Open war had failed, and the brave woman resorted to other methods. She boldly entered the camp and for months shared her husband's captivity. By degrees her arts lulled to rest the watchful suspicions of the general; she won over some of the leading officers to her side; and finally one day the emperor found himself at liberty with his faithful queen beside him and the army at his command. Mahabat Khan fled to Shah-Jahan. The victory came too late, however, for Jahangir had scarcely restored order at Kabul and paid a visit to the happy vale of Kashmir, his favourite summer resort, when he was seized by his mortal sickness, and died before he had attained his sixtieth year (Oct., 1627). There was little use now in opposing Shah-Jahan, who had Mahabat Khan at his side and the full support of the army. The empress's brother, the minister Asaf Khan, joined the rising power, which he had always favoured, and Prince Shahriyar, who

[1] ELPHINSTONE, _Hist. of India_ (1866 ed.), 570,

TOMB OF JAHANGIR AT LAHORE.

325

never had the smallest title to the throne, was defeated, imprisoned, and killed. A temporary stop-gap, Dawar Bakhsh, son of Khusru, vanished as soon as Shah-Jahan appeared from his distant exile in Sind. The great empress proudly retired into private life, wearing thenceforward the white robe of mourning for her queer, loving husband. She was held in honour, and drew a handsome pension ; but she appeared no more in public, and maintained her rigid seclusion until in 1646 she was laid in her grave close beside the tomb of Jahangir at Lahore.

CHAPTER XIII

SHAH–JAHAN

THE MAGNIFICENT

1628–1658

LIKE his father, Prince Khurram, who ascended the throne as Shah-Jahan in January, 1628, was the son of a Rajput princess, a daughter of the rana of Marwar, and had more Indian than Moghul blood in his veins. From what has been recorded of his previous history, as one 'flattered by some, envied by others, loved by none,' in Sir Thomas Roe's words, one is prepared to find a haughty, reserved man, wrapped in political intrigues, personally indifferent to creeds and scruples, and disposed to favour his mother's race. In every one of these respects Shah-Jahan refutes prophecy. All his former cold severity seems to have melted when once he had made a clean sweep of his rivals, and after his accession the new emperor was the most accessible though the most stately of monarchs. He discontinued the obnoxious ceremonial of prostration before the throne, upon which Jahangir had laid

great stress; and his infailing kindness and benevo-
lence, joined to a gracious publicity and display,
endeared him to the people.   He was the most
popular of all the great Moghuls, though not specially the idol of the Hindus.   There was a tinge
of intolerance in his perfectly orthodox, if not very
ardent, profession of Sunni Mohammedanism, and
this slightly bigoted twist was encouraged by his
ever-beloved wife, Arjumand Banu, known as Mum-
taz-i-Mahall, 'the elect of the palace,' the mother of
his fourteen children, whose exquisite monument,
the Taj at Agra, still witnesses to her husband's devotion.   Good Muslim as he was, Shah-Jahan was a
man of sound judgment and knowledge of the
world, and he was the last king to dream of let-
ting religion over-ride statesmanship.   Many of his
generals were Hindus, and his great minister, Sa'd-
Allah, though converted, was a Hindu by birth.
Jesuit missionaries were still welcomed at Agra,
where their tombstones may still be seen in the
'Padre Santo,' and where, as Bernier records, they
had a large and 'very fair' church, with a 'great
steeple' and bell, which 'might be heard all over
the town' in spite of the Muslim's prejudice against
'the devil's musical instrument.'[1]

The result of all this popularity and good statesmanship — for in his father-in-law Asaf Khan, Mahabat († 1634), and Ali Mardan the emperor had

---

[1] This toleration did not extend to the Portuguese of Hugli, whose
piracy led to their destruction in 1631, save such as were sent
prisoners to Agra, where the church was then partly destroyed in
the temporary excitement of fanaticism.

counsellors as wise and upright even as Sa'd-Allah
— was a reign of extraordinary prosperity. The
French traveller Tavernier writes of the gracious
rule of the emperor that it resembled 'that of a
father over his children,' and testifies to the firm
administration of justice and the universal sense of
security. A Hindu contemporary almost outshines
the Muslim and Christian eulogists in extolling the
equity of the government, the wise and generous
treatment of the cultivators, the probity of the law-
courts, and the honesty of the exchequer personally
audited by this magnificent paragon of monarchs.
There is, no doubt, exaggeration in these panegyrics. Shah-Jahan knew how to tickle the imagin-
ations of his subjects by gorgeous pageants and
profuse expenditure, and he could be good-natured
and generous when it did not interfere with his
personal comfort. But he was too shrewd a man
to pamper the people, and his expensive tastes
demanded so much money that there must have
been severe pressure on the taxpayers, who naturally had no voice in revising the eulogies of contemporary chroniclers.

That such was the case may be gathered from
the observations of Mandelslo, who ranks quite as
high, as an intelligent traveller, as the more famous
Della Valle. He was a native of Mecklenburg, and
was educated as a page at the court of the Duke of
Holstein. When this potentate in 1633 despatched
an embassy to 'the Great Duke of Muscovy and
the King of Persia,' Albert Mandelslo, then only
nineteen, begged to be allowed to accompany the

ambassadors and explore the distant countries to
which they were accredited. He was attached to the
embassy as a 'Gentleman of the Chamber,' and was
even granted leave to pursue his travels further,
when the ambassadors' business was accomplished.
Accordingly when their Excellencies the Sieurs
Crusius and Brugman departed from Ispahan in the
beginning of 1638, Mandelslo pushed on to India by
way of Persepolis, Shiraz, and Gombroon, where he
took sail in an English ship, the 'Swan,' three hundred tons, twenty-four guns, Master Honywood,
bound for Surat, and after nineteen days' voyage
made the port on the 25th of April. Mandelslo's
travels in India — he went on afterwards to China
and Japan — were chiefly limited to the usual stay
at Surat, and a journey through Ahmadabad to
Agra and back by Lahore to Surat. Out of the
eight months of his sojourn in the Moghul empire,
five were spent at Surat, while his stay at Agra was
unexpectedly brought to an end, apparently before
he had been a month at the capital.

Like Della Valle, he was much impressed with the
Dutch and English factories at Surat. 'They have
there their Lodges, their Store-houses, their Presi-
dents, their Merchants, and their Secretaries, and
indeed have made it one of the most eminent Cities
for Traffick of all the East.' This was just thirty
years after Hawkins had vainly attempted to save
one cargo from the clutches of the Moghul governor,
and another from the Portuguese. The new companies had evidently lost no time in strengthening
their position. 'The English particularly have made

it the main place of all their Trading into the Indies,
and have established there a President, to whom the
Secretaries of all the other Factories are oblig'd to
give an accompt. He manages affairs with the assistance of 20 or 24 Merchants and Officers, and
hath under his superintendency the Factory of Agra,
where they have a Secretary accompanied by six
persons; that of Ispahan, where they have a Secretary and seven or eight other Merchants; that of
Mesulipatan, with fifteen; that of Cambay, with
foure; that of Amadabat, with six; that of Brodra
and Broitscheia, with foure; and that of Dabul with
two persons; who are all oblig'd to come once a
year to Suratta, there to give an accompt of their
Administration to the President.'

Mandelslo was treated by both Dutch and English
with the princely hospitality which has ever been a
tradition in India. He was met by a coach drawn
by two white oxen, and heartily welcomed by the
president, who begged him to stay with him five or
six months, and entertained him royally. ' At dinner he kept a great Table of about fifteen or sixteen
dishes of meat, besides the Desert.' The favourite
rendezvous for the English colony was the president's 'great open Gallery,' where his friends enjoyed the sea-breezes of an evening. There was a
fair garden outside the city where they all resorted
on Sundays after sermon, and where on week-days
Mandelslo made a small fortune by winning pistol-
matches, ' shooting at Butts.' Sometimes they made
a night of it over some bottles of sack; but Mandelslo was an exceedingly virtuous young man, and

spoke no English,— two effectual bars to excessive conviviality.

When he went into the interior, the same hospitable reception awaited him, not only at the hands of the European agents, but also of the Mohammedan merchants. Short as his stay was, the assistance of his hosts enabled him to make the most of his opportunities, and his native gift of observation stood him in good stead. A knowledge of Turkish appears to have served him well, as it did Hawkins. As he goes towards Agra we pick up hints which help us to understand the state of the provincial government under Shah-Jahan. In spite of the testimony of other writers, travelling seems to have been anything but safe in Gujarat in 1638. The Rajputs — a kind of 'High-waymen or Tories,' Mandelslo calls them — infested the roads, and our traveller had to journey in company with large caravans, and even then had occasion to fight for his life. He describes the governor of Ahmadabad as a 'judicious, understanding man, but hasty, and so rigorous, that his government inclin'd somewhat to cruelty.' The 'somewhat' appears inadequate, when Mandelslo goes on to describe how, when some dancing girls refused to come and perform at his bidding, this 'hasty' governor instantly had their heads cut off in the presence of a company which included the English and Dutch factors. 'Assure yourselves, Gentlemen,' said he, 'that if I should not take this course, I should not long be Governour of Amadabat.' 'There is no King in Europe,' adds Mandelslo, 'hath so noble a Court as the Governour of Guzaratta, nor any that appears in public with greater magnificence. In his palace he is served as a King. He makes his advantages of all the Levies and Impositions which are made in his Government, so that in a short time he becomes Master of incredible wealth.'

Mandelslo describes Agra in his day as the noblest city of Hindustan, and the one in which the Moghul most delighted ; but it must be remembered that New Delhi was not then built. He says it was as much as a horseman could do to ride round the city in a day. 'Its Streets are fair and spacious, and there are some of them Vaulted, which are above a quarter of a League in length, where the Merchants and Tradesmen have their Shops, distinguished by their Trades and the Merchandizes which are there sold ; every Trade and every Merchant having a particular Street and Quarter assigned him.' There were eighty caravanserais for foreign merchants, ' most of them three Stories high, with very noble Lodgings, Store-houses, Vaults, and Stables belonging to them.' He counted seventy great mosques, and estimates the number of public baths ' or Hot-Houses ' at above 800, the tax on which brought in a considerable revenue to the state. In and outside the city he saw numerous palaces of the rajas and lords, and chiefest of all the imperial palace, fortified with a moat and drawbridge. The treasure there jealously guarded was estimated on credible authority at above fifteen hundred millions of crowns, or over £300,000,000. 'This wealth,' he explains, 'is more and more augmented every day, not so much out of the ordinary Revenue coming in from the great Kingdoms he hath (in regard that as his Ordinary Expence abates not anything of his Treasure; so is it seldome seen that he increases it, by ought remaining at the years end of his Revenue) as by the presents which are made him, and the Escheats falling to him at the death of great Lords and Favourites, who make the Moghul Heir to what they had gotten by his favour; insomuch that the Children have no hope to enjoy ought of their Fathers Estates, either Reall or Personall. For the Moghul's Authority is such, and his Power so absolute, that the Estates of all his Subjects are at his disposai. . . . There is no hereditary Dignity in all his country. That of Rasgi or Raja, which he bestows rather upon the accompt of Merit, than Birth, is Personall, as that of Chan in Persia, and is not deriv'd to Posterity, but by the recommendation of Vertue. Not that it is to be inferr'd hence, that the Moghul does exclude from Charges the Children of such as have done him good service; but he gives them lesser charges by which they may advance themselves to the Chiefest in the Kingdome, if either an extraordinary Vertue or the Princes Favour call them thereto.'

Mandelslo describes the daily levees of the emperor, his appearance in the gallery at sunrise, when the nobility ' salute him with their Patschach Salammet,' at noon, when he comes to see the beasts fight, and at sunset; but it does not appear that he was personally received at court. Agra was a very densely inhabited city at this time, ' of such extent

and so populous, that were there a necessity, there
might be rais'd out of it two hundred thousand men
able to bear Armes. There is no Nation in all the
East but hath some commerce or other at this place;
but most of the inhabitants are Mahumetans, and
all the Merchandizes that are imported into it, or
exported out of it, pay ten in the hundred.' The
muster of the Moghul army has often been a matter
of dispute, but Mandelslo gives a detailed account
of the force commanded by Shah-Jahan in 1630,
which numbered no less than 144,500 horse, besides
elephants, camels, etc. They were armed with bows
and arrows, javelins or pikes, scimetars, and daggers,
with a shield for defence. 'They have no fire Armes
with wheeles, nor yet Fire-locks but their Infantry
are expert enough at the Musquet,' a statement
distinctly contradicted by Bernier, who says the
musketeers were horribly afraid when their guns
went off, and lived in dread of their beards catching
fire. 'They know nothing,' adds Mandelslo, 'of
the distinction of Van-guard, main Battle, and Rear-
guard, and understand neither Front nor File, nor
make any Battalion, but fight confusedly without
any Order. Their greatest strength consists in the
Elephants, which carry on their backs certain Towers
of Wood, wherein there are three or foure Harque-
buses hanging by hooks, and as many men to order
that Artillery. The Elephants serve them for a
Trench, to oppose the first attempt of the Enemy;
but it often comes to pass that the Artificial Fires,
which are made use of to frighten these creatures,
put them into such a disorder, that they doe much

more mischief among those who brought them to the Field, then they do among the Enemies. They have abundance of Artillery, and some considerable great Pieces, and such as whereof it may be said, the invention of them is as ancient as that of ours. They also make Gun-Powder, but it is not fully so good as what is made in Europe. . . . Their Armies do not march about five Cos [ten miles] a day, and when they encamp they take up so great a quantity of ground, that they exceed the compass of our greatest Cities.'

In the *Itinerario* of Father Sebastian Manrique, the Augustinian missionary, published at Rome in 1649, we read that in 1640 the city of Agra stretched for six miles along the Jumna, and had a population of 600,000, excluding strangers, who crowded thither. He mentions the Jesuit mission and church, and afterwards journeying to Lahore, where the emperor was then residing, he describes an interview with the prime minister, Asaf Khan, Nur-Jahan's brother, to whom he was presented by a Portuguese Jesuit, F. da Castro. Asaf Khan dwelt in a splendid palace adorned with pictures, some of which illustrated the life of S. John Baptist. At a banquet at which the emperor himself was present, Father Sebastian was amazed at the sumptuous fare and also at the presence of ladies of rank unveiled. This was in 1641, and Asaf Khan died the same year, leaving an immense fortune, in spite of the quarter of a million sterling that his palace at Lahore cost him. But, as Roe remarked, he, like all the court, was 'greedy of gifts.' Manrique learned from Father da Castro that

THE TAJ-MAHALL AT AGRA.

337

22

the architect of the famous Taj at Agra was Geron-
imo Verroneo, a Venetian, and this accounts for its
difference from other Moghul works. As the learned
topographer and historian, Mr. Keene, has well said,[1]
'As a building and apart from its surroundings it
cannot be pronounced to be an organic whole. No
relation can be discovered among any of the dimen-
sions; the outline of the dome does not express the
inward form of the vault it covers; the disengaged
towers at the four corners have no use or purpose,
either apparent or real. The fenestrations give little
shadow outside, no light within. Yet, masked by
the modern garden, and consecrated by the repose
of the whole scene — glittering, gleaming, distinguished — there is something about the Taj, as
we now see it, which is perhaps unequalled by any
building in the world for that mysterious fascination
which we express by the single short word "charm." '
It has been called 'a dream in marble, designed by
Titans, and finished by jewellers': but Zoffany
flippantly remarked that 'it only needed a glass case.'

The Taj-Mahall was finished in 1648, nearly eighteen years after the death of the queen who lay
meanwhile in a tomb in the garden. Tavernier saw
it building, and says 20,000 workmen were continu-
ously employed. Long before this the other buildings which Shah-Jahan carried out at Agra were
complete. The palaces in the Fort were erected
between 1628 and 1637, the great Mosque in 1644–
50, and the Moti' Masjid or 'Pearl Mosque' was
completed in 1653. But the Taj was to be the

---

[1] H. G. KEENE, *Sketch of the History of Hindustan* (1885), 214.

SHAH-JAHAN'S PALACE AT AGRA.

339

supreme masterpiece dedicated to a supreme love, and there was to be no haste, but yet no rest, about its elaborate and stately growth.

Whatever the glories of Agra — the capital of Babar and Akbar, enlarged and enriched by Shah-Jahan — they were eclipsed by the splendour of the new city which the prince of Moghul builders laid out at Delhi. Agra is full of his noble works, but New Delhi, or Shahjahanabad as he named it and as it is still called, was his creation. It was begun about the time that Mandelslo was in India, and ten years later, in 1648, it was finished, and according to all accounts it must have been the most magnificent royal residence in the world. The learned French physician Bernier,—the pupil of Gassendi and school-fellow of Molière,— who lived at the court for many years in the succeeding reign of Aurangzib, has left a graphic description of the new capital, extracts from which will be found in the next chapter. Fergus-son, the historian of architecture, said of the palace of Shahjahanabad that it was 'the most magnificent in the East—perhaps in the world.' The fort in which it stands is about a mile and a half in circuit, the massive walls rising 60 feet above the river, and higher still on the moated side towards the land. 'Two barbicans, each 110 feet high, guard the main entrance on that side, two smaller gates opening on the side facing the Jumna. Within was a vast series of public and private halls and apartments, with a mosque, bath-house, and gardens; the whole per-meated by a marble channel bringing in the bright and wholesome water of the canal.' The great

mosque, dated 1658, the year of Shah-Jahan's de-
position, 'is raised on a rocky basement, and has
three domes, and two lofty towers each 130 feet
high. Its outside area is 1400 square yards, and the
approach is up a flight of thirty-three steps. Three
sides of the quadrangle are arcades or open cloisters,
the fourth being the sanctum itself, 260 feet long,
with a depth of 90 feet. The hall of worship is
paved with black and white marble, marked out for
899 worshippers.'[1]

In this stately city Shah-Jahan spent his luxurious old age, sometimes leaving it for a summer
villeggiatura in the lovely valleys of Kashmir,
whither he would journey with a set of travelling
tents so numerous and complete that they took
two months to pitch at the successive stages of
the royal route. His coronation anniversaries were
observed with splendid extravagance, and he would
then be weighed according to Moghul custom in
scales against the precious metals; bowls of costly
gems were poured over him, and all these riches,
to the value of a million and a half, were ordered to
be distributed among the people. The emperor
and the court had reached a pitch of luxury that
fostered effeminacy. In his youth and early manhood Prince Khurram had been a brave soldier,
a brilliant general, a prudent counsellor, and a stern
and resolute governor. As he grew old he abandoned all active pursuits, gave himself up more and
more to pleasure, and suffered himself to be managed by his children. His adored wife, the lady of

[1] H. G. KEENE, *l. c.*, 215, 216.

the Taj, had died in 1631 in giving birth to their fourteenth child, and Shah-Jahan, essentially an affectionate 'family man,' whilst denying himself none of the pleasures of the zenana, became engrossed in his devotion to his eldest daughter, the Princess Begum, Jahan-Ara. He was still the benevolent and popular king that he had always been since his accession, but his strength of character was gone; he had become a mere sensual pageant of royalty, given over to ease and the æsthetic delights of the eye and taste. Dryden has drawn the contrast in 'Aureng-Zebe':

> 'O! had he still that character maintain'd
> Of Valour which in blooming Youth he gain'd!
> He promised in his East a glorious Race;
> Now, sunk from his Meridian, sinks apace.
> But as the Sun, when he from Noon declines,
> And with abated heat less fiercely shines,
> Seems to grow milder as he goes away,
> Pleasing himself with the remains of Day:
> So he who in his Youth for Glory strove
> Would recompense his Age with Ease and Love.'

The burden of state interfered with his enjoyment, and he sought to devolve his power upon his four sons, to each of whom he gave the vice-royalty of a distant province, in the hope of stilling their dangerous jealousies. The sceptre was falling from his hand, and he tried to secure peace by breaking it in pieces. It was a fatal policy. The fragments of the sceptre, like the rods of Pharaoh's sorcerers, turned into so many serpents, which strangled the

SHAH-JAHAN.

343

remnant of his power, till the rod of Aurangzib swallowed up the rest, and with them the Peacock Throne itself.

The Deccan was the Dauphiné of the Moghul empire. It was there that Shah-Jahan had mustered his strength to try conclusions with his father; and it was thence that Aurangzib drew his forces in the struggle which ended in his coronation. As the chief warlike events of Jahangir's reign centred round his son's career, so Shah-Jahan's later wars were mainly fought by Aurangzib. History had shown that whoever could rule the Deccan was fit to be master of India. Shah-Jahan had won his spurs in that never tranquil government. It will be remembered that Akbar had annexed Khandesh and a portion of Berar but had not conquered any of the four kingdoms into which the Bahmanid empire of the Deccan had broken up. The Nizam Shahs of Ahmadnagar, the Adil Shahs of Bijapur, the Kutb Shahs of Golkonda, were still powerful, though the Barid Shahs of Bidar were no more. The Nizam Shahs, being nearest to the Moghul frontier, were the most obnoxious, and their able vezir, an Abyssinian named Malik Amber, repeatedly routed the imperial armies, recovered Ahmadnagar of which they had temporary possession, and drove them back to Khandesh. Malik Amber's skilful tactics with light Maratha cavalry, afterwards so successful in the hands of the same people against Aurangzib, perpetually harassed the Moghul troops and wore them out, till it seemed as if the empire of Delhi must once more withdraw north of the dividing mountain range. It was then that Shah-Jahan had shown his mettle. Arriving in the Deccan in 1616, he skilfully detached the king of Bijapur from the support of Amber, and soon brought the vezir to his knees: in a year's campaign Ahmadnagar was recovered and Malik Amber became a tributary vassal. Then followed Shah-Jahan's rebellion, disgrace, and flight, and the Deccan province was intrusted to his brother Parviz, who speedily drank himself to death, leaving the command to the general Khan-Jahan.

Throughout Shah-Jahan's reign the Deccan had been constantly disturbed by wars and rebellions. Khan-Jahan revolted in 1629, was defeated, and killed in Bandelkhand (1631); but his conciliatory policy towards the Deccan kings, to whom he sold Ahmadnagar in order to strengthen his power, had weakened the Moghul position. The campaigns of A'zam, Mahabat, and Asaf Khans did little to restore the lost prestige; but when Shah-Jahan advanced in person in 1635, the king of Bijapur at length found himself outmatched, and in the following year consented to a peace by which he agreed to pay £200,000 to Delhi in annual tribute. The Nizam Shah's dominions were absorbed in the Moghul empire, and his dynasty extinguished. So matters remained for nearly twenty years, until Aurangzib became viceroy of the Deccan in 1655, and proved it once more to be the Dauphiné that led to the steps of the throne. This third son of Shah-Jahan, born in 1618, had already been governor of the Deccan in 1636 immediately after his father's successful campaign against Bijapur; but the youth of seventeen seems to have been more occupied with thoughts of the world to come than with the earth beneath his eyes. In 1643, when only twenty-four, he announced his intention of retiring from the world, and actually took up his abode in the wild regions of the Western Ghats and adopted the rigorous system of self-mortification which distinguished the fakir or mendicant friar of Islam. The novelty of the experiment, however, soon faded away; the fakir grew heartily tired of his retreat; and the prince returned to carry out his notions of asceticism in a sphere where they were more creditable to his self-denial and more operative upon the great world in which he was born to work.

It is true his first campaigns were unsuccessful. Ordered in 1647 to take command of the provinces of Balkh and Badakhshan beyond the Hindu Kush, recently conquered from the Uzbegs by Shah-Jahan's generals, Aurangzib found the position untenable in face of the inveterate hostility of the indomitable hill tribes, and withdrew his forces with heavy loss. Nor were his attempts in 1649 and 1652 to recover Kandahar from the Persians, who had retaken it in 1648, more successful. Aurangzib had again to retreat discomfited, as his elder brother Dara did from a third attempt in 1653. These campaigns in Afghanistan and beyond the Hindu Kush are of no importance in the history of India, except as illustrating the extreme difficulty of holding the mountain provinces from a distant centre; but they were of the greatest service to Aurangzib. They put him in touch with the imperial army, and enabled him to prove his courage and tactics in the eyes of the best soldiers in the land. The generals learnt to appreciate him at his true value, and the men discovered that their prince was as cool and steady a leader as the best officer in India. He had gone over the mountains a reputed devotee, with no military record to give him prestige. He came back an approved general, a prince whose wisdom, coolness, endurance, and resolution had been tested and acclaimed in three arduous campaigns. The wars over the north-west frontier had ended as such wars have often ended since, but they had done for Aurangzib what they did for Stewart and Roberts: they placed their leader in the front rank of Indian generals.

The inevitable destiny of a prince who had displayed such ability was to govern the ever critical province of the Deccan. His arrival in 1655 was the sign for a vigorous 'forward policy.' Not only were the kings of Golkonda and Bijapur in possession of provinces which had once been part of the kingdom of Delhi, but they were Shi'a heretics, whom it was the duty of an orthodox Muslim to chastise. Aurangzib found an invaluable ally in Mir Jumla, a Persian of brilliant military genius, who in many campaigns, as vezir of Golkonda, had shown himself a very scourge of idolatry and persecutor of Hindus. This talented and ambitious officer had fallen out with his king, and now threw

himself upon the protection of the Moghul. Over-
joyed at the pretext Aurangzib marched upon Golkonda (1656), and, but for urgent commands from
his pacific father, would have added that kingdom
then and there to the Moghul empire. Foiled on
the very eve of victory, he sent Mir Jumla to Agra,
where the crafty Persian so worked upon the cupidity of the old emperor, by describing the wealth of
the decrepit southern kingdoms that were ready to
fall like over-ripe fruit into his hands, and by presenting him with an earnest of the treasures to be

GOLD COIN OF SHAH-JAHAN, A.H.1066 (A.D. 1655–6).

amassed in the shape of the famous Koh-i-nur diamond,[1] which after a series of strange adventures
now reposes among the crown jewels of England,
that Shah-Jahan consented to an aggressive policy.
Aurangzib, reinforced by Jumla, accordingly wrested
Bidar from the king óf Bijapur, occupied Kulbarga
and Kaliani, and was on the point of conquering
Bijapur itself, the capital of the Adil Shah, when
his father's alarming illness in 1657 summoned him
to the north. Once more he was baulked on the
very eve of triumph.

[1] See above p. 204.

Shah-Jahan was believed to be dying. There was no law of succession, and each of the four sons prepared to fight for the throne. Shuja' was away to the east, governor of Bengal; Aurangzib was down south in the Deccan; Murad-Bakhsh was in the west, making merry in Gujarat. To Dara was assigned the government of Multan and Kabul; but he had become so necessary to his father that he deputed his functions to others, and himself remained at Delhi attached to the king's person. Each of the princes behaved more like an independent sovereign than a lieutenant of the emperor. They had the command of rich revenues, which they devoted to the formation of large armies in preparation for the struggle which they knew to be inevitable.

Shah Shuja' was first in the field. He at once announced that his father had been poisoned by Dara; proclaimed himself emperor; engraved his name on the coinage of Bengal, and set out to march upon Agra. Almost at the same moment Murad-Bakhsh caused coins to be struck at Ahmadabad and the prayer for the king to be recited in his own name, and displayed his lordly instinct by immediately assaulting the city of Surat and extorting six lacs of rupees from its luckless merchants. Aurangzib, in the Deccan, alone of the four brothers, assumed no royal function. Whatever his designs may have been, for the present he kept them to himself.

Dara lost no time in sending out the imperial armies to chastise Shuja' and Murad-Bakhsh. The former was easily repulsed: Raja Jai Singh surprised him at his camp near Benares, and attacked before sun-rise, while the careless *bon vivant* was yet heavy with wine. After a brief contest the rebels gave way, and the dazed prince, hardly awake, hastily took to flight, abandoning his camp and treasure, artillery and ammunition. Meanwhile Aurangzib had made up his mind to join forces with his younger brother, Murad-Bakhsh, and shortly met him near the Narbada at the head of the Deccan army. Towards the close of April, 1658, the combined forces came upon the royal army, under the Maharaja Jaswant Singh, on the opposite banks of the Narbada. Under a withering storm of arrows and javelins, Murad-Bakhsh charged across the ford, followed by the whole strength of the Deccan, and crashed into the royal forces with an overwhelming shock. Kasim Khan and his Mohammedans fled from the field. The Rajputs fought desperately, till of their 8000 men, only 600 remained. The wounded remnant sadly followed their chief back to his desert fastness in Marwar. There he was received with bitter scorn. His high-mettled wife shut the castle gates in his face, saying that a man so dishonoured should not enter her walls: ' If he could not vanquish, he should die.'

The Moghul capital was in an uproar. Dara, exasperated by the defeat, resolved to wipe out the disgrace, and led a magnificent array to the encounter: the lowest calculation places his army at 100,000 horse, 20,000 foot, and 80 guns, but many were half-hearted in his cause. At the Chambal, Dara found that his brothers, making a circuit, had already crossed the river on the 2nd of June.

The two armies came in sight of each other on the 7th, at Samugarh, afterwards known as Fathabad, ' the place of victory.' For a day or more they remained observing one another. The heat was such as is only known on the plains of India. It was a true Agra summer, and the men were fainting and dying in their heavy armour. Early in the morning, Aurangzib marshalled his men. ' Keeping the command of the centre for himself, he placed Murad-Bakhsh in the left wing, appointed Bahadur Khan to lead the right, and sent forward his own son Mohammad with the advance guard to act with the artillery, which was, as usual, in the van. Dara meanwhile disposed his forces in a similar order. He placed his cannon in front, linked together by iron chains, so that the enemy's cavalry might not break through. Immediately behind the cannon, he ranged a line of light artillery-camels, mounting brass pieces worked on swivels, and fired by the rider. Then came infantry armed with muskets. The mass of the army was composed as usual of cavalry armed with sabres, pikes, and arrows. The last was the favorite weapon of the Moghuls and Persians ; the hand-pike being the special arm of the Rajputs. Khalil-Allah Khan commanded the right, Rustam Khan the left, and Dara himself was with the centre.

' The battle began, as Moghul battles always did, by an artillery engagement ; cannon were fired ; rockets or hand-grenades were thrown to excite a stampede among the enemy's horses and elephants, and then the infantry came into action with their clumsy matchlocks, whilst flights of arrows flew over their heads from the archers behind. Dara's advance guard, under his son Sipihr Shukoh, then came out and drove in Prince Mohammad's squadrons, and this advantage was immediately followed up by bringing the left wing to bear upon Aurangzib's right, which wavered, and seemed on the point of breaking, when reinforcements opportunely came up from the centre. After this the engagement became general. Dara, towering high above his horsemen on a beautiful Ceylon elephant, led his centre against Aurangzib, carried the enemy's guns, after severe loss, and routed the camel corps and infantry. With the shock of horsemen against horsemen the real struggle began. No Moghul prince, as yet, knew the colour of the " white feather," and Dara displayed all the splendid valour of his famous blood. Emptying their quivers upon the Deccan horse, he and his men came to the sword, and fought hand to hand till the enemy began to break and fly.

' It was the critical moment of the fight. The day was going against Aurangzib. The flower of his cavalry was driven back, and he was now standing, with scarcely a thousand men about him, awaiting Dara's onslaught. Never was cool courage put to a severer test ; but Aurangzib's nerve was steel. "*Dili, Yarana*, Take heart, my friends," he cried. " *Khuda-he !* There is a God ! What hope have we in flight ? Know ye not where is our Deccan ? *Khuda-he ! Khuda-he !*" Thereupon he ordered the legs of his elephant to be chained together, to make retreat impossible. The mere order was enough to restore the ebbing courage of the few squadrons that still stood beside him.

'Meanwhile Murad-Bakhsh was hotly engaged with Dara's right, fighting like a lion and reeking with slaughter. Three thousand Uzbegs charged up to his ensanguined elephant, and arrows, spears, and battle-axes rained so thickly that the frightened animal turned to fly. The Moghul courage was again put to the test. The elephant's legs were quickly chained. Then Raja Ram Singh, of the valiant Rantela stock, came riding up with his Rajputs, insolently shouting, "Dost *thou* dispute the throne with Dara Shukoh?" and hurling his spear at the prince, tried to cut his elephant's girths. The Moghul, wounded as he was, and sore beset on all hands, cast his shield over his little son, who sat beside him in the howdah, and shot the raja dead. The fallen Rajputs, in yellow garb, and stained with their war-paint of turmeric, were heaped about the elephant's feet, and "made the ground like a field of saffron."

'The cool courage of the one prince and the fiery valour of the other daunted Dara's division. Aurangzib and Murad-Bakhsh were still perilously hemmed in by raving Rajputs, maddened with *bang*, and furious at the death of their chiefs, but it needed little to turn the balance of fortune either way. It was Dara's unlucky destiny always to turn it against himself. At this crisis he committed the most fatal error that an Indian commander could perpetrate. All the army looked to his tall elephant as to a standard of victory. Yet now, when the day seemed almost his own, he must need dismount.

23

Murad-Bakhsh was still there on his gory elephant, with his howdah stuck as full of arrows as a porcupine with quills, grimly dealing blow for blow and shaft for shaft. Aurangzib towered high above a seething scrimmage of Rajputs. But where was Dara? It was though the sun had vanished in mid-heaven. A blind panic seized upon the all but victorious army, and every man fled for dear life. Once a panic has got hold of an Indian army, no power can save it. In a brief moment the tide had turned, and the all but vanquished became the victors. For a terrible moment Aurangzib had steadily maintained his seat on his besieged elephant, and his reward was the Peacock Throne. A little too soon Dara had dismounted, to be "numbered among the most miserable of princes," a fugitive and a vagabond in the earth. Then, and not till then, did Aurangzib descend from his elephant, and prostrating himself on the bloody field, give thanks to God for this great and glorious victory.'[1]

The victory of Samugarh was the signal for all the world to come and tender their homage to Aurangzib, who remained on the field of his triumph, busily engaged night and day in negotiating with his father's amirs. They required little inducement to come over to the side of the rising man. The Raja Jai Singh, who commanded the army which had successfully repulsed Shuja' in Bengal, gave in his adhesion to the coming man. The Maharaja Jaswant Singh, burying the hatchet, presently followed his

---

[1] LANE-POOLE, *Aurangzib* (Clarendon Press, 1893), 46-50, from which further extracts are subjoined.

example and tendered his fealty to the new power.
Dara had already fled with a few hundred followers,
and his father had sent money and five thousand
horsemen to assist him. Aurangzib now turned his
attention to his most dangerous rival, the still popular Shah-Jahan.

The father tried to induce his son to visit him,
but Aurangzib, suspecting a trap, sent his son Mohammad, who entered the fort of Agra on the
18th of June, overcame the guard, and turned the
palace into a prison. Shah-Jahan never left the castle
during his seven remaining years of life. ' He was
allowed every enjoyment that his sensuous nature
demanded, loaded with presents, and supplied with
such amusements as most entertained him. His
daughter, the Begam Sahib, and all his numerous
women, kept him company. Cooks skilfully min-
istered to his appetite, and dancers and singing
girls enlivened his senile revels. Like many another aged voluptuary, he became wondrously
devout at times, and holy Mullas came and read
the blessed Koran to him. Even Bernier, who
disliked Aurangzib, says that the indulgence and
respect he showed to his captive father were ex-
emplary. He consulted him like an oracle, and
there was nothing he would not give him, except
liberty. The two became partly reconciled, and
the father bestowed his blessing and forgiveness on
the son: but they never met. Shah-Jahan died
at the beginning of 1666 at the age of seventy-six.
The new emperor hastened to Agra to pay respect
to his obsequies, and the body was laid in a tomb

near the beautiful Taj which the late sovereign had set up in memory of his wife.'

The day after Shah-Jahan had been safely locked up, Aurangzib entered Agra, seized Dara's house and treasure (17 lacs of rupees'), and at once pursued his brother. Murad-Bakhsh, who had been enjoying the honours of kingship, accompanied him in all the glory of mock sovereignty and twenty-six lacs of rupees in his money bags. On the road Aurangzib found or made his boorish brother disgracefully drunk, and, protesting that such a violator of the law of Islam could never sit on the throne, threw him into chains (July 5). That night he was secretly conveyed to the state prison in the island fortress of Salimgarh, opposite Delhi, where he was executed three years later.

The successful schemer led the combined forces in the footsteps of Dara, by forced marches, day and night, with his usual unflagging energy, living the life of a common soldier, and sleeping on the bare ground. His stoicism awed his followers ; but Dara's own tendency to political suicide saved his brother trouble. To sum up many months of misfortune, Dara once more braved the army of Aurangzib in the hills near Ajmir, and, after four days' hard fighting, was again put to flight. With his wife and daughter and a few servants he made for Ahmadabad. The servants plundered his baggage and ravished the jewels of the princesses, and, to

---

¹ The rupee at that time was worth 2/3. The lac (*lakh*) is 100,000 rupees (£11,250), and the cror (*karor*) 100 lacs, or 10,000,000 rupees (£1,125,000).

crown his misery, when the fugitive at length
reached the once friendly city, he found its gates
closed against him. His wife died of hardship
and misery, and he deprived himself of his scanty
escort in order to send her body to be honourably
interred at Lahore. At last 'after few welcomes
and many rejections, after bitter bereavement and
weary wanderings, the crown prince and would-be
emperor of India was betrayed into the hands of
his enemy. He was paraded through the streets
of Delhi dressed in the meanest clothes, on a
wretched elephant, covered with filth; and the
tumult which this barbarous humiliation stirred up
among the people nearly amounted to a rebellion.'
'Everywhere,' says Bernier, ' I observed the people
weeping and lamenting the fate of Dara in the
most touching language : men, women, and children
wailing as if some mighty calamity had happened
to themselves.' In face of such alarming sympathy
Aurangzib resolved upon a speedy execution. A
council was held; Dara was found to be an apostate
and the friend of infidels; and on the 15th of Sep-
tember, 1659, he was ordered to death. ' Many
wept over his fate.'

Meanwhile Shuja' was again in arms as viceroy
in Bengal, and was pushing his way up the Ganges
valley : but in vain. He was soon hunted away to
Arakan, conveyed by Portuguese pirates, who at
once robbed and saved him (1660). ' The last
glimpse we get of him is tragical: wounded and
insulted, he fled over the mountains, with but one
woman and three faithful followers — and was heard

of no more.' The last rival was accounted for, but Aurangzib had not waited for this. He had already twice assumed the throne: first hurriedly proclaimed in the garden of Shalimar outside Delhi in the last days of July, 1658, he formally ascended the throne in state on the 26th of May, 1659.

CHAPTER XIV

THE PURITAN EMPEROR

AURANGZIB

1659-1680

AURANGZIB took for his title the Persian word engraved on the sword which his captive father had given him—Alamgir, ' World-compeller ' — and by this title he was known to his subjects and to succeeding generations of Muslims. Before we consider the use he made of his power we must realize something of his character.

' Aurangzib was, first and last, a stern Puritan. Nothing in life—neither throne, nor love, nor ease— weighed for an instant in his mind against his fealty to the principles of Islam. For religion he persecuted the Hindus and destroyed their temples, while he damaged his exchequer by abolishing the time-honoured tax on the religious festivals and fairs of the unbelievers. For religion's sake he waged his unending wars in the Deccan, not so much to stretch wider the boundaries of his great empire, as to bring the lands of the heretical Shi'a within the dominion of orthodox Islam. Religion induced Aurangzib to abjure the pleasures of the senses as completely as if he had indeed become the fakir he had once desired to be. No animal food passed his lips, and his drink was water ; so that, as Tavernier says, he became " thin and meagre, to which the great fasts which he keeps have contributed. During the whole of the duration of the comet [four weeks, in 1665], which appeared very large in India, where I then was, Aurangzib only drank a little water and ate a small quantity of millet bread ; this so much affected his health that he nearly died, for besides this he slept on the ground, with only a tiger skin over him ; and since that time he has never had perfect health." [1]   Following the Prophet's precept that every Muslim should practise a trade, he devoted his leisure to making skull-caps, which were doubtless bought up by the courtiers of Delhi with the same enthusiasm as was shown by the ladies of Moscow for Count Tolstoi's boots. He not only knew the Koran by heart, but copied it twice over in his fine calligraphy, and sent the manuscripts, richly adorned, as gifts to Mekka and Medina. Except the pilgrimage, which he dared not risk lest he should come back to find an occupied throne, he left nothing undone of the whole duty of the Muslim.

'Aurangzib, it must be remembered, might have cast the precepts of Mohammad to the winds and still kept — nay, strengthened — his hold of the sceptre of Hindustan. After the general slaughter

[1] TAVERNIER'S *Travels*, transl. V. BALL (1889), i, 338.

AURANGZIB.

of his rivals, his seat on the Peacock Throne was as secure as ever had been Shah-Jahan's or Jahangir's. They held their power in spite of flagrant violations of the law of Islam ; they abandoned themselves to voluptuous ease, to " Wein, Weib, und Gesang," and still their empire held together ; even Akbar, model of Indian sovereigns, owed much of his success to his open disregard of the Mohammedan religion. The empire had been governed by men of the world, and their government had been good. There was nothing but his own conscience to prevent Aurang-zib from adopting the eclectic philosophy of Akbar, the luxurious profligacy of Jahangir, or the splendid ease of Shah-Jahan. The Hindus would have pre-ferred anything to a Mohammedan bigot. The Rajput princes only wanted to be let alone. The Deccan would never have troubled Hindustan if Hindustan had not invaded it. Probably any other Moghul prince would have followed in the steps of the kings his forefathers, and emulated the indolence and vice of the court in which he had received his earliest impressions.

' Aurangzib did none of these things. For the first time in their history the Moghuls beheld a rigid Muslim in their emperor — a Muslim as sternly re-pressive of himself as of the people around him, a king who was prepared to stake his throne for the sake of the faith. He must have known that com-promise and conciliation formed the easiest and safest policy in an empire composed of hetero-geneous elements of race and religion. He was no youthful enthusiast when he ascended the throne at

Delhi, but a ripe man of forty, deeply experienced in the policies and prejudices of the various sections of his subjects. He must have been fully conscious of the dangerous path he was pursuing, and well aware that to run a-tilt against every Hindu sentiment, to alienate his Persian adherents, the flower of his general staff, by deliberate opposition to their cherished ideas, and to disgust his nobles by suppressing the luxury of a jovial court, was to invite revolution. Yet he chose this course, and adhered to it with unbending resolve through close on fifty years of unchallenged sovereignty. The flame of religious zeal blazed as hotly in his soul when he lay dying among the ruins of his Grand Army of the Deccan, an old man on the verge of ninety, as when, in the same fatal province, but then a youth in the springtime of life, he had thrown off the purple of viceregal state and adopted the mean garb of a mendicant fakir.

'All this he did out of no profound scheme of policy, but from sheer conviction of right. Aurangzib was born with an indomitable resolution. He had early formed his ideal of life, and every spring of his vigorous will was stretched at full tension in the effort to attain it. His was no ordinary courage. That he was physically brave is only to say he was a Moghul prince of the old lion-hearted stock. But he was among the bravest even in their valiant rank. In the crisis of the campaign in Balkh, when the enemy " like locusts and ants " hemmed him in on every side, and steel was clashing all around him, the setting sun heralded the hour of evening prayer :

Aurangzib, unmoved amid the din of battle, dismounted and bowed himself on the bare ground in the complicated ritual of Islam, as composedly as if he had been performing the *rik'a* in the mosque at Agra. The king of the Uzbegs noted the action, and exclaimed, " To fight with such a man is self-destruction ! " ' [1]

We may read Aurangzib's ideal of enlightened kingship in his reply to one of the nobles who remonstrated with him on his incessant application to affairs of state : ' I was sent into the world by Providence,' he said, ' to live and labour, not for myself, but for others ; it is my duty not to think of my own happiness, except so far as it is inseparably connected with the happiness of my people. It is the repose and prosperity of my subjects that it behooves me to consult ; nor are these to be sacrificed to anything besides the demands of justice, the maintenance of the royal authority, and the security of the state. . . . It was not without reason that our great Sa'di emphatically exclaimed, " *Cease to be Kings !   Oh, cease to be Kings !   Or determine that your dominions shall be governed only by yourselves.*" ' [2]   In the same spirit he wrote to Shah-Jahan : ' Almighty God bestows his trusts upon him who discharges the duty of cherishing his subjects and protecting the people. It is manifest and clear to the wise that a wolf is no fit shepherd, neither can a faint-hearted man carry out the great duty of government. Sovereignty is the guardianship of the people, not self-indulgence

[1] LANE-POOLE, *Aurangzib*, 65, ff.
[2] BERNIER, 130, 144.

and profligacy.' And these were not merely fine
sentiments but ruling principles. No act of injustice,
according to the law of Islam, at least after his accession, has been proved against him. Ovington, who
was informed by Aurangzib's least partial critics, the
English merchants at Bombay and Surat, says that
the Great Mogul is 'the main ocean of justice. . . .
He generally determines with exact justice and
equity ; for there is no pleading of peerage or privilege before the emperor, but the meanest man is as
soon heard by Aurangzib as the chief Omrah :
which makes the Omrahs very circumspect of their
actions and punctual in their payments.'[1] A native
chronicler tells us that the emperor was a mild and
painstaking judge, easy of approach and gentle of
manner : and the same character is given him by Dr
Careri, who was with him in the Deccan in 1695. So
mild indeed was his rule that 'throughout the imperial dominions no fear and dread of punishment
remained in the hearts' of the provincial district
officials, and the result was a state of corruption and
misgovernment worse than had ever been known
under the shrewd but kindly eye of Shah-Jahan.[2]

Yet his habit of mind did not lend itself to trust-
ing his officials and ministers overmuch, whether
they were efficient or corrupt. He was no believer
in delegated authority ; and the lessons in treachery
which the history of his dynasty afforded, and in
which he had himself borne a part during the war
of succession, sank deep into a mind naturally prone

[1] OVINGTON, *Voyage to Suratt in the Year 1689* (Lond. 1696), 198.
[2] KHAFI KHAN, in ELLIOT and DOWSON, vii, 246-8.

to suspicion. That he lived in dread of poison is only what many Moghul princes endured: he had of course a taster, and Ovington says that his physician had to 'lead the way, take pill for pill, dose for dose,' that the emperor might see their operation upon the body of the doctor before he ventured himself. His father had done the like before him. Like him Aurangzib was served by a large staff of official reporters, who sent regular letters to keep the Great Moghul informed of all that went on in the most distant as well as the nearest districts. He treated his sons as he treated his nobles; imprisoned his eldest for life, and kept his second son in captivity for six years upon a mere suspicion of disloyalty. He had good reason to know the danger of a son's rebellion, but this general habit of distrust was fatal to his popularity. Good Muslims have often extolled his virtues; but the mass of his courtiers and officers lived in dread of arousing his suspicion, and, while they feared, resented his distrustful scrutiny. Aurangzib was universally respected, but he was never loved.

'Simple of life and ascetic as he was by disposition, Aurangzib could not altogether do away with the pomp and ceremony of a court which had attained the pinnacle of splendour under his magnificent father. In private life it was possible to observe the rigid rules and practise the privations of a saint: but in public the emperor must conform to the precedents set by his royal ancestors from the days of Akbar, and hold his state with all the imposing majesty which had been so dear to Shah-

Jahan. A Great Moghul without gorgeous darbars, dazzling jewels, a glittering assemblage of armed and richly habited courtiers, and all the pageantry of royal state, would have been inconceivable or contemptible to a people who had been accustomed for centuries to worship and delight in the glorious spectacle of august monarch enthroned amid a blaze of splendour.' Among orientals especially the clothes make the king.

'The emperor divided his residence between Delhi and Agra, but Delhi was the chief capital, where most of the state ceremonies took place. Agra had been the metropolis of Akbar, and usually of Jahangir: but its sultry climate interfered with the enjoyment of their luxurious successor, and the court was accordingly removed, at least for a large part of the year, to New Delhi, the "City of Shah-Jahan." The ruins of this splendid capital, its mosques, and the noble remains of its superb palace are familiar to every reader. To see it as it was in its glory, however, we must look through the eyes of Bernier, who saw it when only eleven years had passed since its completion. His description was written at the capital itself in 1663, after he had spent four years of continuous residence there ; so it may be assumed that he knew his Delhi thoroughly.

'The city,' he tells us, 'was built in the form of a crescent on the right bank of the Jumna, which formed its north-eastern boundary, and was crossed by a single bridge of boats. The flat surrounding country was then, as now, richly wooded and cultivated, and the city was famous for its luxuriant gardens. The circuit of the walls was six or seven miles ; but outside the gates were extensive suburbs, where the chief nobles and wealthy merchants had their luxurious houses ; and there also were the decayed and straggling remains of the older city just without the walls of its supplanter. Numberless narrow streets intersected this wide area, and displayed every variety of building, from the thatched mud and bamboo huts of the troopers and camp-followers, and the clay or brick houses of the smaller officials and merchants, to the spacious mansions of the chief nobles, with their courtyards and gardens, fountains and cool matted chambers, open to the four winds, where the afternoon siesta might be enjoyed during the heats. Two main streets, perhaps thirty paces wide and very long and straight, lined with covered arcades of shops, led into the "great royal square" which fronted the fortress or palace of the emperor. This square was the meeting-place of the citizens and the army, and the scene of varied spectacles. Here the Rajput rajas pitched their tents when it was their duty to mount guard; for Rajputs never consented to be cooped up within Moghul walls. Beyond was the fortress, which contained the emperor's palace and *mahall* or seraglio, and commanded a view of the river across the sandy tract where the elephant fights took place and the rajas' troops paraded. The lofty walls were slightly fortified with battlements and towers and surrounded by a moat, and small field pieces were pointed upon the town from

THE JAMI' MASJID OR GREAT MOSQUE AT DELHI.

369

24

the embrasures. The palace within was the most magnificent building of its kind in the East, and the private rooms or *mahall* alone covered more than twice the space of any European palace. Streets opened in every direction, and here and there were seen the merchants' caravanserais and the great workshops where the artisans employed by the emperor and the nobles plied their hereditary crafts of embroidery, silver and gold smithery, gun-making, lacquer-work, painting, turning, and so forth.

'Delhi was famous for its skill in the arts and crafts. It was only under royal or aristocratic patronage that the artist flourished ; elsewhere the artisan was at the mercy of his temporary employer, who paid him as he chose. The Moghul emperors displayed a laudable appreciation of the fine arts, which they employed with lavish hands in the decoration of their palaces. A large number of exquisite miniatures, or paintings on paper designed to illustrate manuscripts or to form royal portrait-albums, have come down to us from the sixteenth and seventeenth centuries. The technique and detail are admirable, and the colouring and lights often aston-ishingly skilful. They include portraits of the emper-ors, princes, and chief nobles, which display unusual power in the delineation of individual countenances ; and there are landscapes which are happily con-ceived and brilliantly executed. There is no doubt that the Jesuit missions at Agra and other cities of Hindustan brought western ideas to bear upon the development of Indian painting. Jahangir, who was by his own account, " very fond of pictures

and an excellent judge of them," is recorded
to have had a picture of the Madonna behind a
curtain, and this picture is represented in a con-

LATTICE IN BATHROOM OF SHAH-JAHAN'S PALACE AT DELHI.

temporary painting which has fortunately been
preserved.[1] Tavernier saw on a gate outside Agra

[1] In the collection of Colonel H. B. Hanna.

a representation of Jahangir's tomb "carved with a great black pall with many torches of white wax, and two Jesuit Fathers at the end," and adds that Shah-Jahan allowed this to remain because "his father and himself had learnt from the Jesuits some principles of mathematics and astrology."[1] The Augustinian Manrique, who came to inspect the Jesuit missions in the time of Shah-Jahan, found, as we have seen, the prime minister Asaf Khan at Lahore in a palace decorated with pictures of Christian saints. In most Moghul portraits, the head of the emperor is surrounded by an aureole or nimbus, and many other features in the schools of painting at Agra and Delhi remind one of contemporary Italian art. The artists were held in high favour at court, and many of their names have been preserved. Their works added notably to the decoration of the splendid and elaborate palaces which are amongst the most durable memorials of the period.'

The scene in the Hall of Audience on any great occasion was almost impressive enough to justify the inscription on the gateway: 'If there be a Heaven upon earth, it is here, it is here.' The emperor's approach was heralded by the shrill piping of the hautboys and clashing of cymbals from the band-gallery over the great gate : —

'The king appeared seated upon his throne at the end of the great hall in the most magnificent attire. His vest was of white and delicately flowered satin, with a silk and gold embroidery of the finest texture. The turban of gold cloth had an aigrette whose base

[1] *Travels*, i., 111.

THE DIWAN-I-AMM AT DELHI.

373

was composed of diamonds of an extraordinary size and value, besides an oriental topaz which may be pronounced unparalleled, exhibiting a lustre like the sun. A necklace of immense pearls suspended from his neck reached to the stomach. The throne was supported by six massy feet, said to be of solid gold, sprinkled over with rubies, emeralds, and diamonds. It was constructed by Shah-Jahan for the purpose of displaying the immense quantity of precious stones accumulated successively in the treasury from the spoils of ancient rajas and Patans, and the annual presents to the monarch which every Omrah is bound to make on certain festivals. At the foot of the throne were assembled all the Omrahs, in splendid apparel, upon a platform surrounded by a silver railing and covered by a spacious canopy of brocade with deep fringes of gold. The pillars of the hall were hung with brocades of a gold ground, and flowered satin canopies were raised over the whole expanse of the extensive apartment, fastened with red silken cords from which were suspended large tassels of silk and gold. The floor was covered entirely with carpets of the richest silk, of immense length and breadth. A tent, called the *aspck*, was pitched outside [in the court], larger than the hall, to which it joined by the top. It spread over half the court, and was completely enclosed by a great balustrade, covered with plates of silver. Its supporters were pillars over-laid with silver, three of which were as thick and as high as the mast of a barque, the others smaller. The outside of this magnificent tent was red, and the inside lined with elegant Masulipatan chintzes, figured expressly for that very purpose with flowers so natural and colours so vivid that the tent seemed to be encompassed with real parterres. As to the arcade galleries round the court, every Omrah had received orders to decorate one of them at his own expense, and there appeared a spirit of emulation who should best acquit himself to the monarch's satisfaction. Consequently all the arcades and galleries were covered from top to bottom with brocade, and the pavement with rich carpets.' [1]

Aurangzib maintained the old Moghul custom on his birthday of being solemnly weighed in a pair of gold scales against precious metals and stones and food, when the nobles one and all came with offerings of jewels and gold, sometimes to the value of £2,000,000. The festivals often ended with the national sport, an elephant-fight. 'Two elephants charged each other over an earth wall, which they soon demolished; their skulls met with a tremendous shock, and tusks and trunks were vigorously plied, till at length one was overcome by the other, when the victor was separated from his prostrate adversary by an explosion of fireworks between them. In the jovial days of Jahangir and Shah-Jahan, the blooming Kenchens or Nautch girls used to play a prominent part in the court festivities, and would keep the jolly emperors awake half the night with their voluptuous dances and agile antics; but Aurangzib was "unco guid" and would as soon tolerate idolatry as a Nautch.'

[1] BERNIER, 270.

'Even on every day occasions, when there were no festivals in progress, the Hall of Audience presented an animated appearance. Not a day passed but the emperor held his levee from the *jharukha* window, whilst the bevy of nobles stood beneath, and the common crowd surged in the court to lay their grievances and suits before the imperial judge. The ordinary levee lasted a couple of hours, and during this time the royal stud was brought from the stables opening out of the court, and passed in review before the emperor, so many each day; and the household elephants, washed and painted black, with two red streaks on their foreheads, came in their embroidered caparisons and silver chains and bells, to be inspected by their master, and at the prick and voice of their riders saluted the emperor with their trunks and trumpeted their *taslim* or homage.'

These gorgeous 'functions' had little interest for Aurangzib. The art of government was his real passion. Of course, with his mixed and jarring population of Hindus, Rajputs, Patans, and Persians, to say nothing of opponents in the Deccan, his first necessity was a standing army. He could indeed rely upon the friendly rajas to take the field with their gallant followers against the Shi'a kingdom in the Deccan, or in Afghanistan, and even against their fellow Rajputs, when the imperial cause happened to coincide with their private feuds. He could trust the Persian officers in a conflict with Patans or Hindus, though never against their Shi'a coreligionists in the Deccan. But he needed a force devoted to himself alone, a body of retainers who looked to him for rank and wealth, and even for the bare means of subsistence. This he found in the species of feudal system which had been inaugurated by Akbar. He endeavoured to bind to his personal interest a body of adventurers, generally of low descent, who derived their power and affluence solely from their sovereign, who 'raised them to dignity or degraded them to obscurity according to his own pleasure and caprice.'

The writings of European travellers are full of reference to these 'Omrahs' (amirs) or 'nobles,' as they call them — though it must not be forgotten that the nobility was purely official and had no necessary connexion with birth or hereditary estates. In Bernier's time there were always twenty-five or thirty of the highest amirs at the court, drawing salaries estimated at the rate of one thousand to twelve thousand horse. The number in the provinces is not stated, but must have been great, besides innumerable petty vassals of less than a thousand horse, of whom there were 'never less than two or three hundred at court.' The troopers who formed the following of the amirs and mansabdars were entitled to the pay of 25 rupees a month for each horse, but did not always get it from their masters. Two horses to a man formed the usual allowance, for a one-horsed trooper was regarded as little better than a one-legged man. The cavalry arm supplied by the amirs and lesser vassals and their retainers formed the chief part of the Moghul standing army, and, including the troops of the

Rajput rajas, who were also in receipt of an imperial subsidy, amounted in effective strength to more than 200,000 in Bernier's time (1659–66), of whom perhaps 40,000 were about the emperor's person. The regular infantry was of small account; the musketeers could only fire decently 'when squatting on the ground, and resting their muskets on a kind of wooden fork which hangs to them,' and were terribly afraid of burning their beards or bursting their guns. There were about 50,000 of this arm about the court, besides a larger number in the provinces; but the hordes of camp-followers, sutlers, grooms, traders and servants, who always hung about the army, and were often absurdly reckoned as part of its effective strength, gave the impression of an infantry force of two or three hundred thousand men. There was also a small park of artillery, consisting partly of heavy guns, and partly of lighter pieces mounted on camels.

The emperor kept the control of the army and nobles in his own hands by this system of grants of land or money in return for military service; and the civil administration was governed on the same principle. The *mansab* and *jagir* system pervaded the whole empire. The govenors of provinces were mansabdars, and received grants of land in lieu of salary for the maintenance of their state and their troops, and were required to pay about a fifth of the revenue to the emperor. All the land in the realm was thus parcelled out among a number of timariots, who were practically absolute in their own districts, and extorted the uttermost farthing from the wretched peasantry who tilled their lands. The only exceptions were the royal demesnes, and these were farmed out to contractors who had all the vices without the distinction of the mansabdars. As it was always the policy of the Moghuls to shift the vassal-lords frequently from one estate to another, in order to prevent their acquiring a permanent local influence and prestige, the same disastrous results ensued as in the precarious appointments of Turkey. Each governor or feudatory sought to extort as much as possible out of his province or

GOLD COIN OF AURANGZIB, STRUCK AT THATTA, A.H. 1072 (A.D. 1661–2).

jagir, in order to have capital in hand when he should be transplanted or deprived, and in the remoter parts of the empire the rapacity of the landholders went on almost unchecked. The peasantry and working classes, and even the better sort of merchants, used every precaution to hide such small prosperity as they might enjoy; they dressed and lived meanly, and suppressed all inclinations towards social ambitions.

Whether we look at the military or the civil side of the system, the Moghul domination in India was even more like an army of occupation than the 'camp' to which the Ottoman Empire has been compared. As Bernier says, ' The Great Moghul is a foreigner in Hindustan : he finds himself in a hostile country, or nearly so ; a country containing hundreds of Gentiles to one Moghul, or even to one Mohammedan.' Hence his large armies; his network of governors and landholders dependent upon him alone for dignity and support ; hence, too, a policy which sacrificed the welfare of the people to the supremacy of an armed minority. Yet it preserved internal peace and secured the authority of the throne, and we read of few disturbances or insurrections in all the half-century of Aurangzib's reign. Such wars as were waged were either unimportant campaigns of aggression outside the normal limits of the empire, or were deliberately provoked by the emperor's intolerance. Mir Jumla's disastrous expedition against Assam was like many other attempts to subdue the north-east frontagers of India. The rains and the guerrilla tactics of the enemy drove the Moghul army to despair, and its gallant leader died on his return in the spring of 1663. The war in Arakan had more lasting effects. That kingdom had long been a standing menace to Bengal, and a cause of loss and dread to the traders at the mouths of the Ganges. Every kind of criminal from Goa or Ceylon, Cochin or Malacca, mostly Portuguese or half-castes, flocked to Chittagong, where the king of Arakan, delighted to welcome any sort of allies against his formidable neighbour the Moghul, permitted them to settle. They soon developed a busy trade in piracy ; 'scoured the neigh-

bouring seas in light galleys, called galleasses, entered the numerous arms and branches of the Ganges,
ravaged the islands of Lower Bengal, and, often
penetrating forty or fifty leagues up the country,
surprised and carried away the entire population of
villages. The marauders made slaves of their unhappy captives, and burnt whatever could not be
removed.'[1] The Portuguese at Hugli abetted these
rascals by purchasing whole cargoes of cheap slaves,
and, as we have seen, were punished by Shah-Jahan,
who took their town and carried the relics of the
population as prisoners to Agra (1631). But though
the Portuguese power no longer availed them, the
pirates went on with their rapine, and carried on
operations with even greater vigour from the island
of Sandip, off Chittagong, where 'the notorious Fra
Joan, an Augustinian monk, reigned as a petty
sovereign during many years, having contrived, God
knows how, to rid himself of the governor of the
island.'

When Shayista Khan, Aurangzib's uncle, came as
governor to Bengal in succession to Mir Jumla, he
judged it high time to put a stop to these exploits.
The pirates submitted to the summons of the new
viceroy (1666), backed by the support of the Dutch,
who were pleased to diminish the failing power of
Portugal. The bulk of the freebooters were settled
under control at a place a few miles below Dhakka,
hence called Firengi-bazar, 'the mart of the Franks,'
where some of their descendants still live. Shayista
then sent an expedition against Arakan and annexed

[1] BERNIER, 174-182.

it, changing the name of Chittagong into Islama-
bad, 'the city of Islam.' He could not foresee that
in suppressing the pirates he was aiding the rise of
that future power whose humble beginnings were
seen in the little factory established by the English
at the Hugli in 1640. Twenty years after the suppression of the Portuguese, Charnock defeated the
local militia, and in 1690 received from Aurangzib a
grant of land at Sutanati, which he forthwith cleared
and fortified. Such was the modest foundation of
Calcutta.

CHAPTER XV

THE RUIN OF AURANGZIB

THE MARATHA WAR

1680–1707

A PROFOUND tranquility, broken by no rebellion of any political importance, reigned
throughout northern India for the first twenty years
of Aurangzib's rule.[1] So far there had been no serious
persecution, no religious disabilities: but there can be
no doubt that Aurangzib was only nursing his zeal for
the faith, until it should be safe to display it against
the unbelievers. Indeed there were signs of the coming storm as early as 1669. In April of that year he
was informed that the Brahmans of Benares and
other Hindu centres were in the habit of teaching
their 'wicked sciences,' not only to their own people,
but to Muslims. This was more than the orthodox
emperor could tolerate; the temple of Vishnu at
Benares was destroyed, and the splendid shrine at
Mathura razed to the ground to make room for a

---

[1] The following pages are abridged from my life of *Aurangzib*, ch.
viii–xii (Clarendon Press, 1893).

magnificent mosque. The idols were brought to Agra and buried under the steps of the mosque, so that good Muslims might have the satisfaction of treading them underfoot. Three years later the fanaticism of the Hindus found vent in an insurrection in Mewat of four or five thousand devotees, who called them-selves Satnamis, which gave the imperial officers no little trouble to subdue. The neighbouring Rajputs and other Hindus began to become infected with the spirit of rebellion, and every day saw fresh addi-tions to the strength of the rioters. The Satnamis fought with the courage of despair and the exalta-tion of martyrs, but the end was not doubtful: thousands were slain; and the revolt was suppressed.

The next step in the policy of persecution was the re-imposition of the hated *jizya*, or poll-tax on un-believers, a few years later. In vain the people wailed and cursed around the palace. Aurangzib had by this time abandoned the salutary custom of appearing at stated hours before his subjects at the levee window: the adulation of the multitude sav-oured of idolatry to his puritanical mind. But seclude himself as he might — and thereby lose the sensitive touch of the populace which had been his father's strength — he could not shut his eyes to the uproar which the new enactment excited. When he went to the mosque, crowds of expostulating and even riotous Hindus blocked his way; and though his elephants forced their path over their bodies, he could not subdue their repugnance to the new tax on religion. His dealings with the Rajput princes kindled these sparks of discontent into a flame. He

endeavoured to get Jaswant Singh's two young
sons sent to Delhi to be educated (and doubtless
made Muslims) under his own supervision. The
Rajputs' loyalty and pride alike forbade such ignominy to their hereditary chiefs; and when they
learned that the ancient law of Mohammad was revived which imposed a tax upon every soul who did
not conform to Islam — a tax which Akbar had disdained, and Shah-Jahan had not dared to think of—
their indignation knew no bounds. They repudiated
the religious tax, and they contrived to spirit away
the infant princes of Marwar out of the emperor's
reach.

It was the first serious rebellion during the reign,
and its provoker little realized the effects which his
fanatical policy would produce. He marched at
once upon Rajputana, where he found two out of
the three leading States, Udaipur (Mewar) and
Jodhpur (Marwar) united against him, and only
Raja Ram Singh of Jaipur (Amber) still loyal to the
empire. The Rajputs kept 25,000 horse, mostly
Rahtors of Jodhpur, in the field, and although frequently driven into their mountains were never
really subdued. At one time they seemed to be
at the point of a decisive victory, and the emperor's
cause appeared lost. Directing operations from Ajmir, he had placed his main body under his fourth
son Akbar, at the same time calling up his elder
sons Mu'azzam and A'zam with their contingents
from their commands in the Deccan and Bengal.
The three princes were busy ravaging the Rajput
country, and Aurangzib was left at Ajmir with hardly

25

a thousand men, when tidings came that Prince Akbar had been seduced by the diplomacy of the Rajput leaders, had gone over with the main army to the enemy, and proclaimed himself emperor of India; nay, more, he was now marching upon his father at the head of 70,000 men. But the prestige, or the diplomacy, of Aurangzib was more than a match for the rebels. The Moghul deserters flocked back to the imperial standard; the Rajput army melted away; and Prince Akbar, with a following of 500 men, fled to the Deccan, whence he eventually sailed for Persia, and never again set foot in the realm of his fathers (1681).

The Rajput snake was scotched, but far from killed. The insults which had been offered to their chiefs and their religion, the ruthless and unnecessary severity of Aurangzib's campaigns in their country, left a sore which never healed. The war went on. The Moghuls ravaged the rich lands of Udaipur, and the Rajputs retaliated by pulling down mosques and insulting the Muslims. The cities were indeed in the hands of Aurangzib, but the mountain defiles were thronged with implacable foes, who lost no opportunity of dealing a blow at the invaders. The rana of Udaipur, the chief sufferer on the Rajput side, succeeded at last in making an honourable peace with the emperor, who was tired of the struggle and anxious to give his whole mind to the affairs of the Deccan. But while the treaty enabled Aurangzib to beat a fairly creditable retreat, it did not appease the indignant Rajputs of the west; even the rana of Udaipur soon rode his elephants through the treaty; and all Rajputana, save Jaipur and the eastern parts, was perpetually in a state of revolt until the end of the reign. *Tantum religio potuit!* But for his tax upon heresy, and his interference with their inborn sense of dignity and honour, Aurangzib might have still kept the Rajputs by his side as priceless allies in the long struggle in which he was now to engage in the Deccan. As it was, he alienated them forever. So long as the great Puritan sat on the throne of Akbar, not a Rajput would stir a finger to save him. Aurangzib had to fight his southern foes with the loss of his right arm.

'Delhi is distant,' says an old Deccan proverb, and many an Indian king has realized its force when grappling with the ineradicable contumacy of his southern province. The Deccan (Dakhin, Dak-han, 'the South') was never intended by nature to have any connexion with Hindustan. The Vindhya and Satpura mountains and the Narbada river form a triple line of natural barricades, which divide the high table-land of Central India from the plains of the Ganges and its tributaries, and should have warned the sovereigns of Delhi that it was wiser to keep to their own country. But the Deccan lands were fertile; their wealth in diamonds and gold was fabulous; and every great ruler of the northern plains has turned his eyes to the mountain barriers and longed to enter the land of promise beyond. They entered, however, at their peril. To conquer the Deccan was risking the loss of Hindustan; for he who invaded the southern people who dwelt between the Ghats was but teaching them the road to the north.

The affairs of the Deccan were no new thing to a prince who had twice been viceroy there, but some years passed before the initial difficulties of settling his kingdom left the new emperor leisure to attend to the southern province. Meanwhile a new power had arisen, a power which sprang from such needy and insignificant beginnings that no one could have foretold its future malignant domination. The Marathas began to make themselves felt.

This notorious Hindu people inhabited the country lying between the Indian Ocean and the river Warda; their northern boundary was the Satpura range, and on the west coast they extended as far south as Goa. Their strength lay in the inaccessible fastnesses of the Western Ghats, which climb precipitously to the great plateau that stretches right across the Deccan to the Bay of Bengal. Between the Ghats and the sea lies the Konkan, where deep valleys and torrent-beds lead from the rocks and forests of the mountain ridge to the fertile plains of the humid tract near the sea, where the torrents merge in sandy creeks among thickets of mangroves. The Ghats and the Konkan were the safe retreats of wild beasts and wiry Marathas.

These people had never made any mark in history before the reign of Shah-Jahan. They were peaceful frugal husbandmen, like the mass of the lower orders of Hindus, and gave no trouble. Their chiefs, or village headmen, were Sudras, of the lowest of the four castes, like their people, though they pretended

to connect themselves with the noble caste of Ksha-
triyas. In the silent times of peace, the Marathas
enjoyed the happiness of the nation that has no
history. War brought out their dormant capacities,
and their daggers soon cut their name deep in the
annals of India. The king of Bijapur was responsible
for educating this hardy race for their career of
rapine. They formed a large proportion of his subjects, and their language, an offshoot of Sanskrit,
became the official script of the revenue department
of his kingdom. Gradually they came to be employed in his army, first in garrison duty, and then
in the light cavalry, a branch of service for which
they displayed extraordinary aptitude. Some of
them rose to offices of importance at Bijapur and
Golkonda. One of these officers, Shahji Bhosla,
once a rebel against Shah-Jahan in the Konkan
(1634) and afterwards governor of Poona and Banga-
lore, was the father of Sivaji, the founder of the
Maratha power.

Sivaji was eight years younger than his great adversary Aurangzib. He was brought up at Poona,
where he was noted for his courage and shrewdness.
He mixed with the wild highlanders of the neighbouring Ghats, and, listening to their native ballads
and tales of adventure, soon fell in love with their
free and reckless mode of life, and learned every
turn and path of the Konkan. He found that the hill
forts were miserably garrisoned by the Bijapur government, and he resolved upon seizing them and in-
augurating an era of brigandage on an heroic scale.
He began by surprising the castle of Torna, some

twenty miles from Poona, and after adding fortress to fortress at the expense of the Bijapur kingdom, without attracting much notice, crowned his iniquity in 1648 by making a convoy of royal treasure 'bail up,' and by occupying the whole of the northern Konkan. Presently his rule extended on the sea coast from Kaliani in the north to the neighbour hood of Portuguese Goa, a distance of over 250 miles; east of the Ghats it reached to Mirich on the Krishna; and its breadth in some parts was as much as 100 miles. It was not a vast dominion, but it supported an army of over 50,000 men, and it had been built up with incredible patience and daring.

He had no anxiety on the score of his eastern neighbour, the King of Bijapur, whose troops he routed and whose lands he plundered at his will; and he now longed for fresh fields of rapine. The Hindus had become his friends, or bought his favour, and offered few occasions for pillage. He therefore turned to the Moghul territory to the north, and pushed his raids almost to the gates of Aurangabad, the 'Throne City.' Several times Aurangzib changed his generals, but still the indomitable Marathas baffled their skill, surprised their quarters, sacked Surat — though Sir George Oxenden beat them off the English factory — and even stopped the ships full of pilgrims for Mekka that were sailing from the port. For a moment indeed there was peace. Serious losses induced Sivaji to make terms and even to appear at Delhi as the emperor's vassal. The sturdy little 'mountain rat' however was out of his element at the splendid court of the Great

THE MIHTAR-I-MAHALL AT BIJAPUR.

391

Moghul, and Aurangzib treated him with undisguised contempt. Seldom was political sagacity more at fault. The rude highlander, who might have been converted into a powerful prop of the empire in the Deccan, was allowed to escape in disguise, affronted and enraged, to resume his old sway in the mountains (1666). Too late the emperor attempted conciliation: the old antagonist had become a personal enemy, and nothing could sooth his resentment. His return to the Deccan was followed by a series of triumphs. Surat was again sacked (1671), and the Maratha swarms spread southerly past Madras to Tanjore, levying blackmail wherever they went. Just as he was meditating still greater aggrandizement, a sudden illness put an end to his extraordinary career in 1680, when he was not quite fifty-three years of age. The date of his death is found in the words *Kafir ba jahannam raft*, 'The Infidel went to Hell.' [1]

'Sivaji always strove to maintain the honour of the people in his territories,' says a Mohammedan historian. 'He persisted in rebellion, plundering caravans, and troubling mankind; but he was absolutely guiltless of baser sins, and was scrupulous of the honour of women and children of the Muslims when they fell into his hands.' Aurangzib himself admitted that his foe was 'a great captain'; and added, 'My armies have been employed against him

---

[1] KHAFI KHAN is proud to be the discoverer of this chronogram. It is, of course, to be interpreted by the numerical values of the consonants: K 20, Alif 1, F 80, R 200, B 2, J 3, H 5, N N 50, 50, R 200, F 80, T 400 = 1091 A. H. (1680).

for nineteen years, and nevertheless his state has always been increasing.'

The great captain was dead, but his spirit lived in the nation he had created. Aurangzib never fully realized the strength of a nation of freebooters or the intolerable weariness of guerrilla warfare, but he at least saw that the time had come to trust no more generals but to take the quarrel into his own hands. At the close of 1681 he arrived at Burhanpur, and took command of the army. The emperor's first step was to endeavour to strike awe into the Marathas by sending his sons to scour the country. The enemy offered no opposition, and left their rugged country to punish the invaders. Prince Mu'azzam accordingly marched through the whole Konkan, and laid it waste, and when he reached the end he found that he had hardly a horse fit to carry him, and that his men were marching afoot, half-starving. The enemy had cut down the grass, so that no fodder could be obtained, and when the Moghuls tried to victual the army by sea, the enemy intercepted the corn-ships. The rocks and forests of the Ghats had been quite as destructive to the cavalry as the spears of the Marathas. Fighting torrents and precipices, and enduring an unhealthy climate and scarcity of food, was an unprofitable business; and the princes were ordered to converge upon Bijapur, whilst Aurangzib pushed forward to Ahmadnagar.

As soon as the enemy's back was turned, Sivaji's son, Sambhaji, swiftly led his active little horsemen behind their flank, and crossing over to Khandesh

burned Burhanpur and set the whole countryside in
a blaze. Before the Moghuls could get at them,
they were safe again in their fastnesses in the Ghats.
The stroke is typical of Maratha warfare. They
never risked an engagement in the open field unless
numbers made victory sure. When the heavy
Moghul cavalry attacked them, these hardy little
warriors, mounted on wiry steeds as inured to fatigue
as themselves and splendidly broken in for their
tactics, would instantly scatter in all directions, and
observe the enemy from a neighbouring hill or wood,
ready to cut off solitary horsemen, or surprise small
parties in ambush ; and then, if the pursuers gave up
the useless chase, in a moment the Marathas were
upon them, hanging on their flanks, dispatching
stragglers, and firing at close quarters into the unwieldy mass. To fight such people was to do battle
with the air or to strike blows upon water. The
Moghul might hold as much ground as his camp and
cities covered, but the rest of the Deccan was in the
hands of the Marathas.

Aurangzib's plan seems to have been, first, to cut
off the Marathas' funds by exterminating the kingdoms of Golkonda and Bijapur, which paid blackmail
to the brigands ; and then to ferret the 'mountain
rats' out of their holes. The first part of his pro-
gramme was the less difficult. The old Deccan
kingdoms were in no condition to offer serious resistance to Aurangzib's Grand Army. They might
have been annexed long before, but for the selfish
indolence of the Moghul generals. The Bijapuris
indeed resorted to their usual tactics : laid waste

THE GREAT MOSQUE OF BIJAPUR.

all the country round the capital till the Moghul army was half famished, and then hovered about its flanks and harassed its movements with a pertinacity worthy of Sivaji himself. In August, 1685, however, Aurangzib in person took command of the siege Under his searching eye the work of intrenching and mining round the six miles of ramparts went on heartily. A close blockade was established, and at last after more than a year's labour Bijapur was starved out in November, 1686. The old capital of the Adil Shahs, once full of splendid palaces, became the home of the owl and jackal. It stands yet, a melancholy, silent ruin. Its beautiful mosques still raise their minarets above the stone walls, which are even now so inviolate that one might fancy one gazed upon a living city. Within, all is solitude and desolation. The 'Visiapur' which astounded so many travellers by its wealth and magnificence, was trampled under the foot of the puritan emperor, and fell to rise no more.

Golkonda soon felt the loss of its protecting sister. It had always pushed forward its neighbour as a buffer to deaden the shock of the Moghul assaults. It had secretly subsidized Bijapur to enable it to defend itself against the Moghuls, and at the same time bribed the imperial officers to attack Bijapur rather than itself. In spite of its ingenuity, Golkonda had been forced to bow the knee before Aurangzib in 1656, and had been growing more and more demoralized in the quarter of a century which had rolled by uneasily since then. Prince Mo'azzam besieged the capital in a half-hearted way in 1685,

and then to his father's disgust consented to a treaty
of peace. Nevertheless Aurangzib resolved to make
an end of the Kutb Shah dynasty. Under cover of
a pilgrimage to a holy shrine, he marched to Kulbarga, half-way to Golkonda. His hostile intentions
were unmistakable. The wretched king, Abu-l-
Hasan, knew that his fall was at hand. In vain he
sent submissive messages to the emperor and laid
his humble protestations of obedience at his feet:
Aurangzib was relentless, and seeing that there was
no hope of mercy the king of Golkonda prepared to
die like a soldier. He cast off his sloth and luxury
of life, and set about ordering his army and making
ready for the siege of his citadel.

In January, 1687, the enemy took ground at gun-
shot range, and the leaguer began. Abu-l-Hasan
had forty or fifty thousand horse outside the walls,
which continually harassed the engineers, and the
garrison plied their cannon and rockets with deadly
effect upon the trenches. The defence was heroic ;
frequent and furious were the sallies ; the fortress
was well found in ammunition and provisions, and a
ceaseless fire was kept up night and day from the
gates and ramparts. At last the lines were pushed
up to the fosse, and Aurangzib himself sewed the
first sack that was to be filled with earth and thrown
into the ditch. Heavy guns were mounted on earth-
works to keep back the defenders, and an attempt
was made to scale the walls by night. Some of the
besiegers had already gained the ramparts, when a
dog gave the alarm, and the garrison speedily dispatched the climbers and threw down the ladders.

Meanwhile famine was reducing the Moghul army to extremities. The friends of Golkonda, and especially the Marathas of 'that hell-dog' Sambhaji, laid the country waste; the season was dry, and there was a terrible scarcity of rice, grain, and fodder. Plague broke out in the camp, and many of the soldiers, worn out with hunger and misery, deserted to the enemy. When the rain came at last, it fell in torrents for three days, and washed away much of the entrenchments: upon which the besieged sallied out in force and killed many of the Moghuls, and took prisoners. The occasion seemed favourable for overtures of peace. Abu-l-Hasan showed his prisoners the heaps of corn and treasure in the fort, and offered to pay an indemnity, and to supply the besieging army with grain, if the siege were raised. Aurangzib s answer was full of his old proud inflexible resolve: 'Abu-l-Hasan must come to me with clasped hands, or he shall come bound: I will then consider what mercy I can show him.' Forthwith he ordered 50,000 fresh sacks from Berar to fill the moat.

Where courage and perseverance failed, treason succeeded. Mines and assaults had been vainly tried against the heroic defenders of Golkonda: money and promises at last won the day. Many of the nobles of the city had from time to time gone over to the besiegers, and at length a bribe admitted the enemy. The Moghuls poured into the fortress and raised a shout of triumph. The only faithful amir, Abd-ar-Razzak, heard it, and leaping on a bare-backed horse, followed by a dozen retainers, galloped to the gate, through which the enemy were rushing. Covered with blood and reeling in his saddle, he fought his way out, and they found him next day lying senseless under a cocoa-nut tree, with more than seventy wounds.[1]

Meanwhile the king had heard the shouts and groans, and knew that his hour was come. He went into the harim and tried to comfort the women, and then asking their pardon for his faults he bade them farewell, and taking his seat in the audience chamber waited calmly for his unbidden guests. He would not suffer his dinner hour to be postponed for such a trifle as the Moghul conquest. When the officers of Aurangzib appeared, he saluted them as became a king, and spoke to them in choice Persian. He then called for his horse and rode with them to Prince A'zam, who presented him to Aurangzib. The Great Moghul treated him with grave courtesy, as king to king, for the gallantry of his defence of Golkonda atoned for his many sins of the past. Then he was sent a prisoner to Daulatabad, where his ally of Bijapur was already a captive, and both

---

[1] He was the hero of the siege. Aurangzib said that had Abu-l-Hasan possessed but one more servant as loyal as this, the contest might have gone on much longer. He sent a European and a Hindu surgeon to attend to the wounded man, and rejoiced when after sixteen days he at last opened his eyes. He showered favours upon the hero's sons, but nothing could shake the loyalty of the father. Lying on his sick bed, he said that ' no man who had eaten salt of Abu-l-Hasan could enter the service of Aurangzib.' Among the universal self-seeking of the Moghul Court such faithfulness was rare indeed, and no one honoured it more sincerely than the emperor who had never been disloyal to his standard of duty.

their dynasties disappear from history. Aurangzib appropriated some seven millions sterling from the royal property of Golkonda.

With the conquest of Golkonda and Bijapur, Aurangzib considered himself master of the Deccan. Yet the direct result of this destruction of the only powers that made for order and some sort of settled government in the peninsula was to strengthen the hands of the Marathas. The majority of the vanquished armies naturally joined them and adopted

GOLD COIN OF AURANGZIB, STRUCK AT BIJAPUR,
A.H. 1099 (A.D. 1687–8).

the calling of the road. The local officials set themselves up as petty sovereigns, and gave the brigands support as the party most likely to promote a golden age of plunder. Thus the bulk of the population of the two dissolved states went to swell the power of Sambhaji and his highlanders, and the disastrous results of this revolution in Deccan politics were felt for more than a century.

At first indeed Aurangzib's armies seemed to carry all before them, and the work of taking possession of the whole territory of the vanished kingdoms even as far south as Mysore, was swiftly accomplished. Sivaji's brother was hemmed in at Tanjore,

and the Marathas were everywhere driven away to
their mountain forts. To crown these successes, Sambhaji was captured by some enterprising Moghuls
at a moment of careless self-indulgence. Brought
before Aurangzib, he displayed his talents for vituperation and blasphemy to such a degree that he
was put to death with circumstances of exceptional
barbarity (1689). The brigands were awed for a
while by the commanding personality and irresistible force of the Great Moghul. He had accomplished
a military occupation not merely of the Deccan, but
of the whole peninsula, save the extreme point
south of Trichinopoly and the marginal possessions
of the Portuguese and other foreigners. Military
occupation, however, was not enough; he would
make the southern provinces an integral part of his
settled empire, as finally and organically a member
of it as the Panjab or Bengal. With this aim he
stayed on and on, till hope and will, unquenchable
in life, were stilled in death. The exasperating
struggle lasted seventeen years after the execution
of Sambhaji and the capture of his chief stronghold:
and at the end success was as far off as ever.

The explanation of this colossal failure is to be
found partly in the contrast between the characters
of the invaders and the defenders. Had the Moghuls been the same hardy warriors that Babar led
from the valleys of the Hindu Kush, or had the
Rajputs been the loyal protagonists who had so
often courted destruction in their devoted service
of earlier emperors, the Marathas would have been
allowed but a short shrift. But Aurangzib had

26

alienated the Rajputs for ever, and they would not risk their lives for him in exterminating a people who were after all Hindus, however inferior to themselves in caste and dignity. As for the Moghuls, three or four generations of court-life had ruined their ancient manliness. Babar would have scorned to command such officers as surrounded Aurangzib in his gigantic camp at Bairampur. Instead of hardy swordsmen, they had become padded dandies. They were adorned for a procession, when they should have been in rough campaigning outfit. Their camp was as splendid and luxurious as if they were on guard at the palace of Delhi. The very rank and file grumbled if their tents were not furnished as comfortably as in quarters at Agra, and their requirements attracted an immense crowd of camp followers, twenty times as numerous as the effective strength. So vast a host was like a plague of locusts in the country: it devoured everything; and though at times it was richly provisioned, at others the Marathas cut off communications with the base of supplies in the north, and a famine speedily ensued.

The Marathas, on the other hand, cared nothing for luxuries: a cake of millet sufficed them for a meal, with perhaps an onion for 'point.' They defended a fort to the last, and then defended another fort. They were pursued from place to place, but were never daunted, and they filled up the intervals of sieges by harassing the Moghul armies, stopping convoys of supplies, and laying the country waste in the path of the enemy. There was no bringing them

to a decisive engagement. It was one long series of
petty victories followed by larger losses. Nothing
was gained that was worth the labour; the Marathas
became increasingly objects of dread to the demoralized Moghul army; and the country, exasperated
by the sufferings of a prolonged occupation by an
alien and licentious soldiery, became more and more
devoted to the cause of the intrepid bandits, which
they identified as their own.

The marvellous thing about this wearisome campaign of twenty years is the way in which the brave
old emperor endured its many hardships and disap-
pointments. It was he who planned every campaign, issued all the general orders, selected the
points for attack and the lines of entrenchment, and
controlled every movement of his various divisions
in the Deccan. He conducted many of the sieges
in person, and when a mine exploded among the
besiegers at Sattara, in 1699, and general despondency fell on the army, the octogenarian mounted his
horse and rode to the scene of disaster ' as if in
search of death.' He piled the bodies of the dead
into a human ravelin, and was with difficulty prevented from leading the assault himself. He was
still the man who had chained his elephant at the
battle of Samugarh forty years before. Nor was
his energy confined to the overwhelming anxieties of
the war. His orders extended to affairs in Afghanistan and disturbances at Agra; he even thought
of retaking Kandahar. Not an officer, not a government clerk, was appointed without his knowledge, and the conduct of the whole official staff

was vigilantly scrutinized with the aid of an army of spies.

We are fortunate in possessing a portrait[1] of Aurangzib, as he appeared in the midst of his Deccan campaigns. On Monday the 21st of March, 1695, Dr. Gemelli Careri was admitted to an audience of the emperor in his quarters, called 'Gulalbar,' at the camp of Galgala. He saw an old man with a white beard, trimmed round, contrasting vividly with his olive skin; 'he was of low stature, with a large nose; slender and stooping with age.' Sitting upon rich carpets, and leaning against gold-embroidered cushions, he received the Neopolitan courteously, asked his business in the camp, and being told of Careri's travels in Turkey, made inquiries about the war then raging between the Sultan and the princes of Hungary. The doctor saw him again at the public audience in a great tent pitched within a court enclosed by screens of painted calico. The Moghul appeared leaning on a crutched staff, preceded by several nobles. He was simply dressed in a white robe tied under the right arm with a silk sash from which his dagger hung. On his head was a white turban bound with a gold web, 'on which an emeraud of a vast bigness appear'd amidst four little ones. His shoes were after the Moorish fashion, and his legs naked without hose.' He took his seat upon a square gilt throne raised two steps above the daïs, inclosed with silver banisters; three brocaded pillows formed the sides and back, and in front was a little

[1] GEMELLI CARERI, *Voyage Round the World*, Churchill Coll., iv 222, 223.

silver footstool. Over his head a servant held a
green umbrella to keep off the sun, whilst two others
whisked the flies away with long white horsetails.
'When he was seated they gave him his scimitar and
buckler, which he laid down on his left side within
the throne. Then he made a sign with his hand for
those that had business to draw near; who being
come up, two secretaries, standing, took their peti-
tions, which they delivered to the king, telling him
the contents. I admir'd to see him indorse them
with his own hand, without spectacles, and by his
cheerful smiling countenance seemed to be pleased
with the employment.'

It is a striking picture of the vigorous old age of
one who allowed no faculty of his active mind to
rust, no spring of his spare frame to relax. But behind that serene mask lay a gloomy, lonely soul.
It was the tragical fate of the Moghul emperor to
live and die alone. Solitary state was the heritage
of his rank, and his natural bent of mind widened
the breach that severed him from those around him.
The fate of Shah-Jahan preyed upon his mind. He
was wont to remind his sons that he was not one to
be treated as he had used his own father. His
eldest son had paid the penalty of his brief and
flighty treason by a life-long captivity; and Aurangzib had early impressed the lesson upon the second
brother. 'The art of reigning,' he told Mu'azzam,
'is so delicate, that a king must be jealous of his
own shadow. Be wise, or a fate like your brother's
will befall you also.' Mu'azzam had been docility
personified, but his father's restless suspicion was

aroused more than once, and he endured a rigorous captivity for seven years (1687–94). On his release, another brother, A'zam, became in turn the object of jealousy, and it is said that he never received a letter from his father without turning pale. One son after another was tried and found wanting. Towards the close of his life the jealous father was drawn closer to his youngest son, Kam-Bakhsh, whose mother, Udaipuri Bai, was the only woman for whom the emperor entertained anything approaching to passionate love.[1] The young prince was suspected of trafficking the imperial honour with the Marathas, and placed under temporary arrest, but his father forgave or acquitted him, and his last letters breathe a tone of tender affection.

The end of the lonely unloved life was approaching. Failure stamped every effort of the final years. The emperor's long absence had given the rein to disorders in the north; the Rajputs were in open rebellion, the Jats had risen about Agra, and the Sikhs began to make their name notorious in Multan. The Deccan was a desert, where the path of the Marathas was traced by pillaged towns, ravaged fields, and smoking villages. The Moghul army was enfeebled and demoralized; 'those infernal foot-

---

[1] Aurangzib's wives played but a small part in his life. According to Manucci the chief wife was a Rajput princess, and became the mother of Mohammad and Mu'azzam, besides a daughter. A Persian lady was the mother of A'zam and Akbar and two daughters. The nationality of the third, by whom the emperor had one daughter, is not recorded. Udaipuri, the mother of Kam-Bakhsh, was a Christian from Georgia, and had been purchased by Dara, on whose execution she passed to the harim of Aurangzib.

soldiers' were croaking like rooks in an invaded rookery, clamouring for their arrears of pay. The finances were in hopeless confusion, and Aurangzib refused to be pestered about them. The Marathas became so bold that they plundered on the skirts of the Grand Army and openly scoffed at the emperor, and no man dared leave the Moghul lines without a strong escort. There was even a talk of making terms with the insolent bandits.

At last the emperor led the dejected remnant of his once powerful army, in confusion and alarm, pursued by skirmishing bodies of exultant Marathas, back to Ahmadnagar, whence, more than twenty years before, he had set out full of sanguine hope and at the head of a splendid and invincible host. His long privations had at length told upon his health, and when he entered the city he said that his journeys were over. Even when convinced that the end was near, his invincible suspicions still mastered his natural affections. He kept all his sons away, lest they should do even as he had done to his own father. Alone he had lived, and alone he made ready to die. He had all the puritan's sense of sin and unworthiness, and his morbid creed inspired a terrible dread of death. He poured out his troubled heart to his sons in letters which show the love which all his suspicion could not uproot.

'Peace be with you and yours,' he wrote to Prince A'zam, 'I am grown very old and weak, and my limbs are feeble. Many were around me when I was born, but now I am going alone. I know not why I am or wherefore I came into the world. I bewail the moments which I have spent forgetful of God's worship. I have not done well by the country or its people. My years have gone by profitless. God has been in my heart, yet my darkened eyes have not recognized his light. Life is transient, and the lost moment never comes back. There is no hope for me in the future. The fever is gone: but only skin and dried flesh are mine. . . . The army is confounded and without heart or help, even as I am: apart from God, with no rest for the heart. They know not whether they have a king or not. Nothing brought I into this world, but I carry away with me the burthen of my sins. I know not what punishment be in store for me to suffer. Though my trust is in the mercy and goodness of God, I deplore my sins. When I have lost hope in myself, how can I hope in others? Come what will, I have launched my bark upon the waters. . . . Farewell! Farewell! Farewell!'

To his favourite Kam-Bakhsh he wrote:—' Soul of my soul. . . . Now I am going alone. I grieve for your helplessness. But what is the use? Every torment I have inflicted, every sin I have committed, every wrong I have done, I carry the consequence with me. Strange that I came with nothing into the world, and now go away with this stupendous caravan of sin! . . . Wherever I look I see only God. . . . I have greatly sinned, and I know not what torment awaits me. . . . Let not Muslims be slain and reproach fall upon my useless head. I commit you and your sons to God's care, and bid you farewell. I am sorely troubled. Your

sick mother, Udaipuri, would fain die with me. . . .
Peace!'

On Friday, the 4th of March, 1707, in the fiftieth
year of his reign, and the eighty-ninth of his life, after
performing the morning prayers and repeating the
creed, the emperor Aurangzib gave up the ghost. In
accordance with his command, 'Carry this creature
of dust to the nearest burial-place, and lay him in the
earth with no useless coffin,' he was buried in all
simplicity near Daulatabad beside the tombs of
Muslim saints.

'Every plan that he formed came to little good ;
every enterprise failed : ' such is the comment of the
Mohammedan historian on the career of the sovereign
whom he justly extols for his 'devotion, austerity,
and justice,' and his 'incomparable courage, long-
suffering, and judgment.' Aurangzib's life had
been a vast failure, indeed, but he had failed
grandly. His glory is that he could not force his
soul, that he dared not desert the colours of his
faith. The great Puritan of India was of such stuff
as wins the martyr's crown.

CHAPTER XVI

THE FALL OF THE MOGHUL EMPIRE

THE HINDU REVIVAL

1707–1765

AURANGZIB was the last of the Great Moghuls, in all save the name. He had been by far the most powerful of the line; he had ruled wider territories and commanded vaster armies than Akbar; and he had governed his teeming populations with an absolute despotism in which no other man had a voice. What Akbar has achieved by broad-minded statesmanship, and Shah-Jahan by imposing majesty and panoplied array, Aurangzib had accomplished by the exercise of an iron will and indomitable personal labour. Through the greater part of his long reign no sovereign was ever more abjectly feared and obeyed; none certainly showed a more marvellous grasp of administration. Then at the last the effects of too close repression, of over-government and centralization, were discovered. The tedious war in the Deccan exhausted his armies and destroyed his prestige, and no sooner was the dominating mind

410

stilled in death than all the forces that he had sternly controlled, all the warring elements that struggled for emancipation from the grinding yoke, broke out in irrepressible tumult. Even before the end of his reign Hindustan was in confusion, and the signs of coming dissolution had appeared. As some imperial corpse, preserved for ages in its dread seclusion, crowned and armed and still majestic, yet falls to dust at the mere breath of heaven, so fell the empire of the Moghul when the great name that guarded it was no more. It was as though some splendid palace, reared with infinite skill with all the costliest stones and precious metals of the earth, had attained its perfect beauty only to collapse in undistinguishable ruin when the insidious roots of the creeper[1] sapped the foundations.

Even had Aurangzib left a successor of his own mental and moral stature, it may be doubted whether the process of disintegration could have been stayed. The disease was too far advanced for even the most heroic surgery. To increase the confusion the Great Moghul had made no nomination to the throne he was vacating, and as usual all the sons claimed the sceptre. The contest was brief: Prince A'zam was slain in battle near Agra, Kam-bakhsh died of his wounds after a defeat near Haidarabad, and the first-born Mu'azzam ascended the throne with the title of Bahadur Shah. He found himself face to face with such difficulties as had not been known since the

---

[1] The *ficus religiosa*. The simile is Mr. H. G. KEENE'S, whose *Fall of the Moghul Empire* (1887), is one of the best and most interesting books on the history of India in the eighteenth century.

days of Humayun. It was not merely the Marathas that had to be dealt with : the Rajput rajas were in revolt ; the Sikhs were rising in the Panjab, and the Jats near Agra; and the English had ventured on bold reprisals, which were to lead to far-reaching consequences in another half-century.

Nor was it only among non-Muslim peoples that the spirit of insurrection was alive. These no doubt had been excited by the religious intolerance of the late emperor; but the Muslims themselves were scarcely in better order. The fatal system of re-warding services or conciliating jealousies by large grants of territory had produced a kind of baronage fully as dangerous and subversive of central author-ity as any corresponding class in feudal Europe. The provincial mansabdars had become petty kings, and were far more interested in coercing their neighbours than in supporting their emperor against his many foes. Nor could Bahadur rely upon his troops as Babar and Akbar had trusted them. The toleration of Akbar's policy, the luxurious splendour of Shah-Jahan's court, had bred both indifference and effeminacy in what had once been an army of hardy mountaineers. India had proved the Capua, of Babar's veterans, and the enervating climate had relaxed their thews and softened their training whilst drink had become the curse not only of the imperial house, many of whom died of it, but also of the nobles and the whole court. ' The heroic soldiers of the early empire and their not less heroic wives had given place to a vicious and delicate breed of grandees. The ancestors of Aurangzib, who swooped down on India from the north, were ruddy men in boots : the courtiers among whom Aurangzib grew up were pale persons in petticoats. Babar, the founder of the empire, had swum every river which he met with during thirty years campaigning ; the luxurious nobles around the youthful Aurangzib wore skirts made of innumerable folds of the finest white muslin, and went to war in palankins.'[1] Nothing but the old emperor's steel hand and high example could have made these men join in his campaigns ; but even so, twenty years of doubtful warfare had exhausted what courage there was, and his successor inherited a thoroughly dispirited army.

With such materials as he had, and against such odds, Bahadur must be credited with both courage and prudence. He showed no rancour against the chiefs who had sided with his brothers in the brief war of succession, but gladly welcomed them to his councils. His great object was to settle affairs in the Deccan so as to be free to deal with the many troubles in Hindustan. Fortunately there was a split among the Marathas, and two claimants to the chief command, one of whom, the rightful heir, was a captive in the Moghul camp. This Sahu was released by Bahadur, who recognized his title on conditions of peace. Leaving the Marathas to arrange their own differences, the emperor went north and made terms with the insurgent Rajputs, practically restoring them to the position they had held in Akbar's reign. The terms might have been less favour-

[1] Sir W. W. HUNTER, *Nineteenth Century*, May, 1887.

able if Bahadur's anxieties had not been concentrated on a new danger.

The Sikhs, who had begun about two centuries before as a purely religious sect of theists, had been driven by Muslim persecution to form themselves into a military organization, with distinctive uniform, customs, and ceremonies; and by the close of the seventeenth century they had developed into a fierce and fanatical soldiery, burning to avenge the atrocities suffered by their leader, Guru Govind, at the hands of the Muslims. The general confusion at the time of Aurangzib's death gave them their opportunity. From their retreats on the upper Sutlej, they raided the eastern Panjab, butchering their enemies, men, women, and children, and destroying the mosques. A second raid, as far as Lahore and even Delhi, brought Bahadur into the field. He drove them to the hills, but without materially shaking their power; and then unfortunately he died (1712). Short as his reign had been, it must be remembered that he was the son of a very old man, and was himself nearly seventy. Had he been in the prime of life there might possibly have been a different story to tell.

After the usual struggle for the throne and ensuing massacre of kindred, his son Jahandar succeeded —utterly incapable and incurably vicious; in less than a year he was murdered, and his nephew, Farrukhsiyar, a despicable poltroon, suffered the like fate six years later (1719), when, after a couple of youths had been tried for a few months, Mohammad Shah received the title of emperor which he retained for twenty-eight years. It was but a title, however, for the power and the glory had departed from the house of Babar, and Mohammad was only able to preserve some semblance of authority by intrigue and combination with the various governors and adventurers who now partitioned the distracted empire. By such means he contrived to rid himself of the dictatorship of the Barha Sayyids, two brothers who for some years had usurped the supreme control of affairs in the time of their wretched tool Farrukhsiyar. But there were other forces which he could not master.

Among these the Sikhs were no longer to be reckoned, for they had been put down in the time of the Sayyids with remorseless brutality, and for many years this valiant people was scarcely heard of. The Marathas, on the other hand, were increasing in power every year. Their only rival in the Deccan was Chin Kulich Khan, better known as Asaf Jah, the founder of the dynasty of the Nizams of Haidarabad which subsists to this day; and Asaf Jah found it expedient to make terms with the enemy and submit to their system of levying the *chauth*, a kind of Danegeld by means of which the Marathas systematically extended their influence with less trouble than if they had immediately insisted on territorial cessions. By the skilful policy of Balaji, and his even abler son Baji Rao, the earliest of the Peshwas,— the real leaders, who stood towards the hereditary Maratha raja much as the Shogan did to the Mikado before the Japanese revolution, — this system of blackmail was enlarged till it was accepted not only in the Deccan but in Gujarat (1731), Malwa, and even as far north as Bandelkhand. By this time some famous names — Pilaji Gaikwar, Holkar, and Sindhia — begin to appear among the officers of the peshwa, and save for old Asaf Jah, who was now the leading man in India, there was no corresponding ability on the Moghul side. Even this veteran, when the Marathas, by way of demonstration, advanced up to the very gates of Delhi, could muster only 34,000 men to oppose them. The result was the cession of the whole of the territories between the Narbada and the Chambal to the successful peshwa (1738).

Whilst the wolves of the Deccan were steadily working up from the south, a new catastrophe from the north befell the vestiges of the Moghul empire. In the midst of the pressing difficulties that surrounded them neither the emperors nor their ministers had been able to pay much attention to what was going on in Afghanistan. Kabul and Ghazni still belonged to the empire of Delhi, as they had done since the time of Babar, but Kandahar, which had been in the possession of the Shahs of Persia since 1648, had been seized by the Ghilzai Afghans, who had carried their successes to the point of seating their chief upon the Persian throne (1722). Their brief triumph was reversed in 1729 by the famous soldier Nadir Shah, who not only gained possession of Persia, but recovered Kandahar (1738) and immediately completed his conquest by seizing Kabul and Ghazni. The Moghuls — it is an instructive precedent — relied on the mountain tribes, whom they had formerly subsidized, to prevent the invaders from penetrating the passes into India ; but the subsidy had lapsed during the recent troubles, and the Afghans offered no obstacles to the Persians. In November, 1738, Nadir crossed the Indus, and after a partial engagement with the Moghul forces, who were half disposed to side with the invaders, the conqueror received the surrender of the emperor in person in February, 1739. The Persians entered Delhi with Mohammad Shah as their captive guest, and in revenge for a murderous onslaught of the populace, the capital was given over to fire, carnage, and rapine. The imperial treasures, including the famous jewelled Peacock Throne, valued by Tavernier at £6,000,000, were seized and transported to Persia, the inhabitants were squeezed to the last mohr, and torture was employed to extort payment. 'Sleep and rest forsook the city. In every chamber and house was heard the cry of affliction. It was before a general massacre, but now the murder of individuals.' The awful visitation of Timur was repeated and even outdone. At last, after two months of colossal pillage, Nadir returned to his own country, carrying with him spoils to the value of eight or nine millions in money alone, besides an immense treasure of gold and silver plate, jewels, rich stuffs, and a crowd of skilled artisans, with herds of elephants, horses, and camels.[1]

This invasion of India from the north, unexpected as it was after a cessation of all such inroads during

[1] See ELPHINSTONE (1866 ed.), 716-720, and the *Siyar-el-Mutakhirin*.

27

two centuries of Moghul power, was too successful
not to invite repetition, and upon the assassination
of Nadir in 1747, Ahmad Shah, the chief of the
Abdali tribe of Afghans, after founding a powerful
kingdom at Kandahar, soon found his way into the
Panjab. This first attempt was strenuously resisted
(1748); the battle of Sirhind saw the Afghans driven
back by Indian troops as they were never driven
again; but Ahmad Shah did not abandon his design. The empire of Delhi was at its weakest; the
old nizam was dead, and the factions at court were
internecine. The new emperor, also named Ahmad,
who succeeded Mohammad in 1748, was so sorely
beset by the Rohillas that he, or rather his vezir
Safdar Jang, nawab or viceroy of Oudh,—the first
to combine the offices of nawab-vezir,— was reduced
to the necessity of calling in the Marathas to his aid.
Holkar and Sindhia enabled the vezir to bring the
Rohillas to submission, but the Deccan wolves in-
demnified themselves liberally for their help, by
levying their *chauth* throughout the conquered districts. Even Bengal had been forced to submit to
their blackmail, and the Marathas were now in a
position to dictate terms at Delhi. Indeed, the empire of Aurangzib had lost the power of resistance.
Not a province of all the wide dominion that still nominally owned the Moghul's sway was really under his
control, except the upper Doab and a few districts
about the Sutlej. The Panjab was in the hands of
the Afghans, Safdar Jang was practically sovereign
at Oudh and Allahabad, Aliverdi Khan held Bengal.
Afghans and Rohillas did as they pleased in the

middle Doab and Rohilkhand, Gujarat and Malwa were Maratha provinces, and the Deccan, even the part held by the second nizam was wholly beyond the mastery of Delhi.

Meanwhile Ahmad Shah still hovered over the Panjab, which was tamely ceded to him in the hope of checking worse demands; but a treacherous attack on his governor at Lahore roused him to a fresh invasion, and in 1756 Delhi experienced all the horrors of a sack over again. On his retiring in the following year, the old intrigues and jealousies revived; the Marathas were again called in, and this time the peshwa's brother actually occupied the capital, where a new puppet-emperor Alamgir II, who had succeeded the debauched Ahmad in 1754, was helpless between the rival interests of the vezir Ghazi-ad-din and the Afghan chief of Rohillas, Najib-ad-daula. The Marathas now made themselves masters of the Panjab and felt that they were within sight of the conquest of the whole of Hindustan. They were in the zenith of their power. Their domestic differences had been accommodated, and a general combination of all their forces was arranged. They were no longer the ill-disciplined band of marauders that had baffled Aurangzib by their guerrilla tactics : besides such predatory hordes, they had well-ordered cavalry and infantry and a better artillery train than the Moghuls themselves. Full of their strength and ambition they raised the cry of Hindustan for the Hindus.

It had become a religious war, centred round the phantom of the Moghul empire. On the one hand

was the Mohammedan Afghan, Ahmad Shah, eager
to recover the Panjab and to take vengeance on the
new power that had robbed him. On the other was
the Moghul vezir of Oudh, Shuja'-ad-daula, son of
Safdar Jang, supported by the forces of the eastern
provinces. Between lay the prostrate capital, over-
awed by the host of the Hindu Marathas. There
was not even a Moghul emperor to hold the balance,
for the harmless figure-head, Alamgir, had been
murdered by the vezir in 1759, and the heir, Shah-
Alam, had fled to the protection of the British in
Bengal in dread of sharing the same fate. Among
all the bold adventurers who played the king in
India at this time, none was more remarkable than
Ghazi-ad-din, the youthful grandnephew of Asaf
Jah, who dominated the political situation from 1752
to 1759 by sheer audacity and brilliant recklessness.
The murder of the emperor, however, was a stroke
that overreached itself, and when the Afghan Shah
moved down upon the capital, the unscrupulous
young assassin fled for his life. Ahmad Shah found
the throne empty, and proceeded to take steps for
the maintenance of the Mohammedan power in India
as master of the situation.

The decisive moment came on January 6, 1761.
The Marathas were intrenched at Panipat with a
force of 70,000 cavalry and 15,000 infantry, nine
thousand of whom were thoroughly disciplined under a Mohammedan who had served in the French
army in India under Bussy. The commander-in-
chief was the peshwa's cousin Sadasheo Bhao, and
Holkar and Sindhia were with him. The Afghans

and Moghuls numbered about 53,000 horse, Afghan, Persian, and Indian, and less than 40,000 infantry, partly Rohillas under Najib; but their field pieces were very inferior to the Marathas' guns. Too weak to attack, the Muslim army intrenched itself over against the Hindus, and for two months the opposing forces that were contending for the crown of India watched each other narrowly. Famine soon began to make itself felt, but Ahmad Shah refused to force an action. He knew that the Deccan wolves were suffering even more than his Pathans. They were even opening negotiations for peace with the nawab-vezir, but the Afghan king, strongly urged by Najib, refused all compromise.

At last the Bhao declared that ' the cup is now full to the brim and cannot hold another drop '; the time for negotiation was past, and the starved Hindus, smeared with turmeric, threw themselves upon the Afghan army. For a time it looked as if Hinduism had triumphed. The Rohillas suffered tremendously; the vezir could hardly hold his ground; the Muslims were skulking or flying. Ahmad Shah, who was watching the battle from his red tent, saw that the time had come to order up his reserves. He rallied the fugitives, cut down all who would not return to the fight, and sent his mailed reserve, 10,000 strong, to support the vezir and charge upon the enemy in close order. The effect of this heavy charge at the close of an exhausting battle was supreme. The Marathas gave way, the Bhao was killed, Holkar and Sindhia left the field, an awful butchery followed. Once more the plain of Panipat had witnessed a decisive battle in the history of India.

The Marathas never recovered from the blow, though they had still a prominent part to play in the annals of Hindustan. For the present the scene of action was transferred from Delhi to Bengal and Bihar, where the new emperor, Shah-Alam, was involved in the complicated difficulties that had sprung up between the Nawab-vezir and the British. There, however, the history of Mohammedan India closes, and the history of British India begins. The victory of Panipat swept away the Marathas only to make a clear path for the English. Less than four years afterwards the battle of Buxar (Baksar) on October 23, 1764, disposed of the power of the Nawab, and the next day Shah-Alam came into the British camp. The treaty then signed made the Nawab-vezir a vassal of Calcutta, and the Moghul emperor a pensioner of the East India Company. Such was the political tragedy of the famous House of Timur.

The dynasty of Babar ended in nothingness, like all its many predecessors. The Mohammedan ascendancy in Hindustan, rising from Mahmud's raids, spreading under the vigorous rule of a few of the Slave Kings and their great successor Ala-ad-din, and attaining its widest scope and severest aspect under Aurangzib, only to fall rapidly to its decline in the weak hands of his descendants, left few traces of its long domination. A new vernacular, compounded of the languages of the Shah Nama and the Ramayana; a multitude of exquisite monuments of the Muslim faith, inspired by analogies in far western lands of Islam, but modified and, if one may say so, sensualized by the grosser architecture of India; a few provinces still owning Mohammedan rulers; a large Muslim minority content to dwell among 'infidels' and to obey the behests of the Christians from the distant islands of the West — such are the chief legacies of Islam to India. Nine centuries of association have produced no sensible fusion between the Muslim and the Hindu, any more than two centuries of intercourse have blended either with the dominant English. There are those who believe that the contact of Western energy with Eastern thought, the infusion of European literature in the subtle Indian mind, and the reaction of the ancient philosophies of the Brahman schools upon the imagination of the West, may end in generating a new force in the world,— another great religion, who knows? — an Indian nation combining the profound speculations of the East with the progressive activities of Europe. Prophecy is no part of the historian's duty; but if any forecast may be deduced from the long period of alien rule surveyed in the preceding pages, it is not favourable to any hopes of such consummation. The conquerors of India have come in hordes again and again, but they have scarcely touched the soul of the people. The Indian is still, in general, what he always was, in spite of them all; and however forcible the new and unprecedented influences now at work upon an instructed minority, one can with difficulty imagine any serious change in the rooted character and time-honoured instincts of the

vast mass of the people: nor is it at all certain that
such change would be for the better.

> The East bowed low before the blast
>   In patient, deep disdain;
> She let the legions thunder past,
>   And plunged in thought again.

MOḤAMMEDAN DYNASTIES

425

426   MOHAMMEDAN DYNASTIES

A. H.   A. D.
558   Ghiyās-ad-dīn ibn Sām........................... 1163
569   Mu'izz-ad-dīn MOHAMMAD GHŌRĪ at Ghaznī....... 1174
570 ff Conquers Hindūstān.............................. 1175ff
599–602 Succeeds Ghiyās-ad-dīn at Ghōr 1201–1206

TREE OF THE SLAVE KINGS OF DELHI

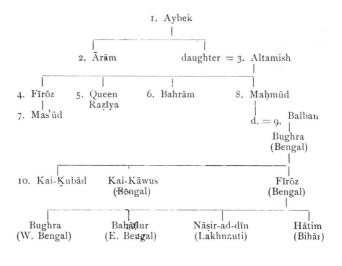

1. Aybek

2. Ārām   daughter = 3. Altamish

4. Fīrōz   5. Queen   6. Bahrām   8. Mahmūd
| Razīya |
7. Mas'ūd   d. = 9. Balban
                                         |
                                      Bughra
                                      (Bengal)
                                         |
10. Kai-Kubād   Kai-Kāwus   Fīrōz
                 (Bengal)   (Bengal)
                                         |
Bughra   Bahādur   Nāsir-ad-dīn   Hātim
(W. Bengal)   (E. Bengal) (Lakhnauti)   (Bihār)

KINGS OF DELHI

I.—SLAVE KINGS

[1] For several pretenders and ephemeral or local sovereigns of this line see Lane-Poole, *The Mohammedan Dynasties*, 328.

TREE OF THE MOGHUL EMPERORS

1. Bābar
   - 2. Humāyūn
   - Kamrān
   - 'Askarī
   - Hindal

2. Humāyūn
   - 3. Akbar
   - *Hakīm (Kābul)

3. Akbar
   - 4. Jahāngīr
   - Dāniyāl
   - Murād

4. Jahāngīr
   - Khusrū
   - Parvīz
   - 5. Shāh-Jahān
   - Jahāndār
   - *Shahriyār

5. Shāh-Jahān
   - *Dāwar Bakhsh
   - Dārā
   - *Shujā'
   - 6. Aurangzīb
   - *Murād-Bakhsh

6. Aurangzīb
   - Mohammad
   - *A'zam
   - 7. Bahādur
   - Akbar
   - *Kām-Bakhsh

7. Bahādur
   - Rafī'-ash-Shān
   - 8. Jahāndār
   - Khujista Akhtar
   - *Nikusiyar
   - Muhyī-as-Sunna

8. Jahāndār

Rafī'-ash-Shān
   - 'Azīm-ash-Shān
   - *Rafī'-ad-daula
   - *Rafī'-ad-darajāt
   - *Ibrāhīm
   - *Shāh-Jahān

9. Farrukhsiyar

12. 'Ālamgīr II
10. Mohammad
11. Ahmad

13. Shāh-'Alam
14. Akbar II
*Bidar-Bakht

15. Bahādur

* The princes marked with an asterisk were proclaimed emperors either as temporary stopgaps or rivals to the reigning emperor, but cannot be said to have reigned.

429

430　MOHAMMEDAN DYNASTIES

KINGS OF THE EAST (JAUNPŪR)

432   *MOHAMMEDAN DYNASTIES*

KINGS OF MALWA

I.—GHŌRĪS

KINGS OF GUJARĀT

BAHMANI KINGS OF THE DECCAN

28

INDEX